HINDU DEITIES IN THAI ART

ŚATA-PITAKA SERIES

INDO-ASIAN LITERATURES
Volume 387

Reproduced in original scripts and languages
Translated, annotated and critically evaluated by
specialists of the East and the West

Founded by
Prof. RAGHU VIRA *M.A., Ph.D., D.Litt., et Phil.*
Continued by
LOKESH CHANDRA

आचार्य–रघुवीर–समुपक्रान्तं

जम्बुद्वीप–राष्ट्राणां
(भारत–नेपाल–गान्धार–शूलिक–तुरुष्क–पारस–ताजक–भोट–चीन–मोंगोल–मञ्जु–
उदयवर्ष–सिंहल–सुवर्णभू–श्याम–कम्बुज–चम्पा–द्वीपान्तरादीनां)

एकैकेषां समस्रोतसां संस्कृति–साहित्य–समुच्चय–
सरितां सागरभूतं

शतपिटकम्

HINDU DEITIES IN THAI ART

GAURI DEVI

INTERNATIONAL ACADEMY OF INDIAN CULTURE
and ADITYA PRAKASHAN, NEW DELHI

First published: 1996

ISBN 81-86471-10-3

Published by Pradeep Kumar Goel for Aditya Prakashan, F-14/65, Model Town II, Delhi–110 009 and printed at D.K. Fine Art Press (Pvt.) Ltd., A-6, Nimri Commercial Centre, Ashok Vihar Phase IV, Delhi–110 052.

CONTENTS

INTRODUCTION

Poet Rabindranath Tagore wrote after his visit to Thailand:

To bathe in the living stream that flows in thy heart,
Whose water descends from the snowy height of a sacred time,
On which arose, from the deep of my country's being,
The sun of Love and Righteousness.

Thailand is the wealth of the heart, the ore of our deep meaning's mine, a hymn to culture, a visual Vande Mataram.

The city of Bangkok has a unique skyline of the spires of temples: like Kumbhakonam in south India which prides in having a kumbha or śikhara at every corner (koṇa). If we ascend the roof of any highrise building in Bangkok, the Divine of the monastic spires surrounds the eyes. My clouded heart sees grace of dream in this heaven thinking. We have yet to see such a splendour of the Divine in the skyline of Delhi.

The kings of Thailand get the designation Rāma on coronation. The present King is Rāma IX. His name is Bhūmipāla Atulyateja भूमिपाल अतुल्यतेज "The King of Unequalled Majesty". Lord Buddha was a scion of the Ikṣvāku dynasty of Sūryavaṁśa kṣatriyas. The coronation ceremonies are performed by Śaiva brāhmaṇas. They also officiate at other royal ceremonies, to which Buddhism provides no counterpart. The Hindu rituals of the Thai court cloak the king with full majesty of divinity and recall the Devarāja rites of earlier periods. They have manuscripts of Devarūpa which depict Hindu gods. The throne in the throne room of the Grand Palace was constructed by Rāma V, King Chulalongkorn चूडालंकार. It is cast in bronze, with worshipping figures and garuḍas. Behind it is a large and brilliant Triśūla, an insignia of the power and authority of the King of Thailand (plate 1).

The Rāmāyaṇa is painted in Thai monasteries. It is illustrated as bas-reliefs at Wat Po, a temple that stands on a tongue of land guarded by two canals. It is the nucleus from which modern Bangkok grew. Here repose the ashes of the first king of the ruling Chakri dynasty. If Thailand has an *omphalos*, it is here. And it is consecrated by the Ramakien, which is the Thai pronunciation of Rāmakīrti. Painting, dance-drama and sculpture are dominated by the Ramakien. In the timeless continuum of Thai perspective, both Rāma of Ayodhya and the historical Ram Khamheng (Rāma the Valiant) of Sukhothai reign supreme. They are the deeper furnishings of the Thai mind. Wat Po enshrines the relics of the king who wrote himself into a relationship with Rāma. The people bring him their flowers to this day.

There are three versions of the Rāmāyaṇa in Thai. They are written in ornate verse (kāvya) either to be read or sung in dramatic performances. All of them have the honour of originating from royal pens of three Thai Kings. The Thai versions agree in the main with Vālmīki, but exotic episodes were introduced in them, some of which can be traced back to the Tamil version of the Rāmāyaṇa.

The Thai Ramakien ends with a banquet in the holy palace atop Mount Krailat (Kailāsa). Phra Isuan (Īśvara) is the host to Phra Ram and Nang Seeda (Sītā). The couple reaffirm their marriage vows. While the heavens sang and the earth danced, the couple was borne back to Ayudhya aboard the diamond chariot of Phra In (Indra).

Khon is a mask performance depicting the scenes from the Rāmāyaṇa. Each character may be recognized by his colour, such as Rāma in deep green, Lakṣmaṇa in gold, Hanumān in white, and Sugrīva in red. The performance is accompanied by music played on instruments modelled after those of ancient India. They are:

Oboe playing the melody (suṣira) सुषिर
Drum with one face (atata) अतत
Drum with two skins connected by means of straps (vitata) वितत
Two-faced drum with skins fastened with nails (ativitata) अतिवितत
Gong working the cadence (ghana) घन

The Thai alphabet is of Indian origin. In A.D. 1283, Ram Khamheng, the great king of the Sukhothai dynasty instituted the present Thai alphabet. Though modelled on the Indian, through the medium of the Khmer or Cambodian characters, the Thai alphabet differs from the Indian and the Cambodian sources in essential points.

Thai is full of Sanskrit words: विद्याकार for academic, उत्साहकर्म for industry, क्षेत्रकर्म for agriculture, स्थानी station, रथयन्त्र motor car, दूरलेख telegram. The Thai pronunciation is very different, e.g. Nakon Pathom for नगर प्रथम the first city where Buddhism or Hinduism landed. Kṣatriya in Sanskrit denotes the warrior class but in Thai it has become *kasat* and means king only. The in-flight journal of the Thai Airways is Sawadee स्वस्ति, which is the usual greeting in Thailand. It is more classical than our modern greeting *namaste* नमस्ते.

Dvāravatī was a flourishing kingdom in the early seventh century. Fine sculptures with a strong influence of Gupta art have been found from ruined sanctuaries. Sanskrit inscriptions of the eighth century stem from southern Thailand.

Buddhism flourished in Thailand as early as the first century A.D. Archaeological finds of images and inscribed terra cotta at Phra Pathom belong to this period. Around the middle of the 13th century Thais drove out the Cambodians who had dominated since the ninth century. The Thai King Śrī Sūryavaṁśa Rāma Mahādhārmika-rājādhirāja introduced Theravāda Buddhism, adopted the life of a monk, and spread Theravāda all over the country.

Few Hindu image have survived in Thailand. The earliest of them is a limestone image of Viṣṇu from Chaiya, considered to have been sculpted on the spot (Boisselier

1975:71, pl.40). It derives from a south Indian tradition and stands at the source of a long iconographical development. It is four-armed, 27 inches in height, holds a conch-shell on the hip in the front left hand, and a club (*gadā*) in the back right hand, and the front right hand may be in abhaya mudrā. He wears a tall mitre and heavy ear-rings (*kuṇḍala*) hang from the ears. O'Connor (1972:39) would like to trace back this image to the 5th or 6th century AD.

The second statue is the impressive image from Takuapā, over six feet high. It is a standing Viṣṇu with four arms, bare chest, plain dhoti secured at the waist by a knot, and he wears the ceremonial mitre (*kirīṭamukuṭa*). O'Connor (1972:48) considers it a product of a peninsular workshop between 650 and 800. Takuapā played a pivotal role in trade between Western Asia, India and China.

The Viṣṇu found at Dong Si Maha Phot (Śrī Mahābodhi) in Prachinburi province is a stone image , 156 cm in height. It is dated to the seventh century. His two upper hands are lost. The lower right holds a symbolic ball of earth and the left hand rests on a club. The ball of earth symbolises the kingdom and as such it must have been a royal image. He wears a mitre (*kirīṭamukuṭa*), ear-rings and sarong (Krairiksh 1979: 94-95). Dong Si Maha Phot remained an art centre for Hindu images as late as the eleventh century, inspired by the Śrīvijaya tradition.

The stone image of Viṣṇu found at Śrīvijaya Hill, Surāṣṭradhānī (O'Connor 1972: 42 fig.18) was produced in the 7-8th century.

A seventh-century stone statue Kṛṣṇa(?) has been found at Si Teb, Petchabun province, 98cm high. He stands in tribhaṅga or triflexion posture. He wears the kirīṭa-mukuṭa of Viṣṇu, and a short Khmer type loin-cloth without frontal pleats (Krairiksh 1979:118-119). The probable position of the left arm suggests that he is Kṛṣṇa lifting Mount Govardhana, similar to his posture in Cambodian art.

A 170cm limestone image of Viṣṇu comes from Dong Si Maha Phot (Prachinburi). It belongs to the 8-9th century Śrīvijaya school. He wears a mitre, a long dhoti and is similar to sculptures found in Cambodia (Boisselier 1975: pl.65 descr. p.228).

Mukhaliṅga of the 8-9th century Śrīvijaya style comes from Nong Wai, Chaiya district, Surāṣṭradhānī province (Bowie 1972: 48-49). Diskul (1980: 27) dates the image to the 6-7th century which cannot be ruled out because it evokes evident influence of the Gupta style.

A ninth century stone image of Viṣṇu 209cm high was discovered at Sri Deb, Petchabun (Bejrapurna) province. All the four arms are broken, the head dress is cylindrical, and the neck seems to be unfinished (Bowrie 1972:58-59). Several other Hindu statues have come to light from this site.

A unique statue of Ardhanārīśvara, an androgynous form of Śiva, was discovered at Ubon Ratchathani. Its headdress and bracelets have no parallel in South East Asia (Boisselier 1975:112 pl.76) but point to India.

Satingpra in Songkhla province has yielded a bronze figure of standing Śiva and his dhoti is draped with a tiger skin. It resembles statues found in central Java. From the same site comes Śiva as Bhaṭāra Guru (Agastya) with a pot-belly. A statue of four-faced Brahmā of unknown provenance is of the Śrīvijaya period. Seven of the eight arms are broken. Its date can be between the ninth and tenth centuries (Diskul 1980:35 pl.37-39).

Waves of Śaivism reached southern Thailand between the eighth and twelfth centuries. Saiva brahmanas could have come from Cambodia (Wales 1931:19) to conduct royal ceremonies. The images of Viṣṇu and Śiva found in Thailand seem to stem from court rituals. The first Tai king of Thailand is Ram Khamheng who succeeded his father Indrāditya in 1273. He established dominion over most of modern Thailand and even Pegu acknowledged him as overlord. He is the national hero, inspite of the fact that his father rebelled against the Khmer and founded the Tai state of Sukhothai (Sukhodaya). His father has been immortalised under the name of Phra Ruang. Ram Khamheng's stele of 1292 gives the clue to a complete break with Khmer iconography of the Buddha: the Khmer style disappears and a totally different conception of Śākyamuni emerges. The Sukhothai kings took over the Hindu court ceremonial of Cambodia and recruited Vaiṣṇava brāhmaṇas thence (Wales 1931:19). A bronze image of Viṣṇu clad in a long unusual drape comes from the 13th century. It can be a representation of Vāmana-avatāra, in which incarnation Viṣṇu conquered the three worlds as a dwarf brāhmaṇa (Boisselier 1975:124 fig.87). It can refer to the glorious exploits of Ram Khamheng who made extensive conquests.

Three Hindu images in Cola style have been found in south Thailand, which may pertain to the 10th or 11th century. Viṣṇu and Baṭuka Bhairava have been discovered at Wieng Sa in the Na Sarn district of Suratthani province. Sūrya comes from Chaiya in the same province (Diskul 1980:24).

An early 13th century bronze image of Viśvakarman from Ayudhya is shown kneeling in the 'Javanese manner'. Krairiksh (1979:146) says that he is the most representative of the Bayon style, in particular his diadem. He is the most eminent of artisans who fashioned the celestial chariots of the deities (Mahābhārata, Bowie 1960: 190 no.69). He wears a yajñopavīta thread (Boisselier 1975:125 fig.88 has the clearest photograph). He can be connected with the Thai ceremonies of royal consecration. The Thai Book of Palace Law entitled *Kaṭa Maṇḍirapāla* gives a detailed account of the Indrābhiṣeka ceremony. On the sixth day "they take one hundred figures of Śiva, Viṣṇu, Indra and Viśvakarmā, and bear utensils for following the custom of entering to offer a blessing" (Wales 1931:123). When Rāmādhipati II brought the northern part of modern Thailand under Ayudhya, and considered himself an emperor, he performed the Indrābhiṣeka ceremony in 1510 (ibid.122).

A bronze image of Viṣṇu (8.8 cm) of the 13-14th century is in the Khmer style. His dress is of Bayon and post-Bayon style. He rode on the shoulders of Garuḍa who is now missing. His legs are bent in the posture of combat (Bowie 1927:77 fig.39).

King Luthai began his rule as the Viceroy of Si Satchanalai around 1340. He conquered Sukhothai about 1347 and ruled over the two sister cities as Mahādharmarāja I. Inscription IV says that "Luthai ruled supreme in the land of Sukhothai, successor to his father and his grandfather (Ram Khamheng)". He established a royal monastery at a site distinguished by a mango grove, planted by his grandfather. He sanctified this Mango Grove Monastery by religious images. It had two edifices: the Si Thon mondop for an image of the Buddha (now lost) and Devālaya-mahākṣetra for two statues of Śiva and Viṣṇu now kept in the National Museum at Bangkok. The two bronzes are tall and magnificent, dressed in royal attire and decked with ornaments. Inscription IV refers to their installation in the temple. The Kings of Sukhothai had brāhmaṇa advisors and priests who performed royal ceremonies (Bowie 1960: 96). Śiva is 149.5cm and Umā is 146cm. The attributes in both hands are lost. His yajñopavīta is a nāga/serpent. The sarong is held fast by a cloth belt. The third eye on the forehead, crescent moon and the letter OM decorate the jaṭāmukuṭa. It is the finest Hindu image of the Sukhothai period. The graceful figure of Umā follows the canons of śilpaśāstra: no bones, muscles or veins are seen. It personifies anatomical symphony in undulating curves and embodies the classic grace of Thai feminity (Krairiksh 1979:170-173). The distinctive drapery of Umā relates to the costumes of Simhalese dancers in the 14th and 15th centuries. The Sukhothai kings were departing from Khmer models, as these statues were symbols of Thai independence. A bronze image of Harihara of the Sukhothai period (154cm) is from the same atelier as the statues of Śiva and Umā. Its garments and adornments too are influenced by the costumes of Simhalese dancers in the Gampola period (1341-1415, Boisselier 1975:137 fig.98). Another eight-armed Harihara in Sukhothai style is a 120 cm high bronze statue (Diskul 1970: fig.61). They figured in royal cults and so are lavishly adorned, wear diadems, and are masterpieces of sculpture.

A bronze image of Gaṇeśa, 16 cm high, from the Ayudhya period, pertaining to the 14-15th century (Boisselier 1975:212 fig.157).

The Sukhothai style of icons continued in the early 16th century. From this period stems a 113 cm bronze torso of Lakṣmī from the Śiva shrine San Phra Isuan at Kamphaeng Phet. She must have been cast as the companion figure to the Four-armed Viṣṇu in the Kamphaeng Phet Museum. They were originally consecrated in the San Phra Isuan shrine. A standing Śiva image dated AD 1510 was discovered from the same shrine

(Krairiksh 1979:206). A 280 cm (9ft 2 in) high imposing bronze executed by a master artist of the Sukhothai school is inspired by a Khmer model. It breathes an aura of power and authority (Boisselier 1975: 17 fig.134). All the three images must have been cast for a royal consecration ceremony.

The role of brāhmaṇas has been crucial in royal rituals. The first independent kingdom of Thailand was founded at Sukhothai in 1237. King Ram Khamheng (1276-1317) recruited Śaiva brāhmaṇas from Cambodia. In the Ayudhya period (1350-1762), the second great Thai kingdom, Śaiva brāhmaṇas were recruited from the Peninsula. When the Burmese destroyed the old capital in 1767, the brāhmaṇas fled to Nagara Sri Dharmaraja (Ligor). They were recalled to Bangkok on its foundation in 1782 to conduct court ceremonies. Today there are Vaiṣṇava (Brāhmaṇa Bṛdhipaśa) and Śaiva (Brāhmaṇa Bidhī) brāhmaṇas in Bangkok. They have three temples to Nārāyaṇa (Viṣṇu) in the north, Īśvara (Śiva) in the south, with a temple to Gaṇeśa in the middle. The Śiva temple is the larger one. Images of Harihara have been shifted from the temple to the National Museum. They are in the Cola style and date from the tenth century. The High Priest of Śiva (Brah Mahā Rāja Grū) presides over all Hindu ceremonies at the Royal Court. The High Priest of Viṣṇu takes part in the coronation ceremonies only from among the brāhmaṇas: he has no separate identity (Wales 1931:72). For the ceremony of the octagonal throne of fig-wood (udumbara), the King appears in a gold-embroidered tunic and dhoti, preceded by sixteen brāhmaṇas with images, drums and conches (ib.77).

The tonsure ceremony survives in Thailand, alongwith three other saṁskāras: shaving the first hair of the new-born, naming the child and taking a child to water to learn swimming. In the tonsure, the prince proceeds to the Kailāsa mountain for reception by Śiva. The King, dressed in full regalia, wearing the great crown of victory, holding the sword of victory, impersonates Śiva, to receive the young prince (for details see Wales 1931:130-132).

The swinging festival was one of the important state ceremonies which was practised in the earlier capitals of Sukhodaya and Ayudhya, and in chief cities of the realm in ancient times. The swing stands at Nagara Sri Dharmaraja. It is in honour of god Śiva who visits this world once a year and stays here for ten days. The King nominates a noble to impersonate Śiva, who has unlimited powers over the state and is temporary king or temporary god (both king and god are deva in Thai, ib.238-239). When Śiva leaves this world, Viṣṇu arrives. When Śiva leaves, the procession of Nareśvara, of brāhmaṇas, goes to the Grand Palace and the King presents three images of Śiva, Umā and Gaṇeśa to them (ib.251).

The ceremony of Viṣṇu's sleep was celebrated in the eighth month of āṣāḍha since ancient times. The King lay down on a dais in the centre of a pond in the royal temple grounds. The pond represents the sea, the dais the serpent Śeṣa, and the King is Viṣṇu. The King imitates the god for the good of the kingdom.

The festival of Śivarātri was celebrated since ancient times but was discontinued after the fall of Ayudhya. It was revived by King Rāma IV who ruled from 1851 to 1868. It is a purely Śaiva ceremony.

The Hindu images of Śiva, Umā, Gaṇeśa, Viṣṇu, Kṛṣṇa, Harihara, Brahmā, Indra, Viśvakarmā were used in royal rites and emanate from court ceremonies. King Rāma III (ruled 1824-51) promoted the renewal of Buddhist art and established canons of iconography. He created forty attitudes illustrating the forty most important events in Buddha's life. The representation of Buddha's disciples and ascetics (ṛṣis) became more important in the art of the Bangkok period than in that of Ayudhya. King Rāma III commissioned metallic images of eighty ṛṣis in an alloy of zinc and tin at the Wat Po monastery. They represented yoga postures which were medically beneficial. The King wanted to assemble all traditional knowledge of Thailand and present a visual encyclopaedia at the monastery (Boisselier 1975:186). He had Hindu iconography collected in *Tāmrā Devarūpa*, which were written on black *khoi* paper in white or yellow colour (Boisselier 1976:233). During the reign of King Rāma V (ruled 1868-1910) the iconographical texts were disseminated in manuscripts, and bronzes of the Hindu deities inspired by them were cast in numbers. One of the bronzes is illustrated in Boisselier (1975: 188 fig.143) who is Bṛhaspati on his usual mount, the deer, as one of the nine planets (navagraha).

In this book we reproduce three albums of Tāmrā Devarūpa, illustrating Hindu deities in their several forms known to the Thai brāhmaṇas. Album I has 90 figures (nos.1-90), album II has 69 (nos.91-159) and the third album has 114 (nos.160-273). All of them begin with the mukhaliṅga, termed Svāyambhuva-nātha in the Thai captions. The name Svāyambhuva-natha recalls Kambu Svāyambhuva. Thc Kambuja kings trace their descent from him. Jayavarman II liberated Cambodia from Javanese vassalage and is said to have founded Angkor or Nagara, that is an ordered state. He revived the old tradition of the Sūryavaṁśa of King Kambu, as against Bhavavarman and his successors who allude to Kauṇḍinya and Somā as their ancestors like the kings of Funan (Majumdar 1944: 85). The primacy of Svāyambhuva may indicate that the Thai tradition is as ancient as the Angkor period.

ŚIVA

The iconography of Śiva in the three albums can be summarised as follows:

(1) Svāyambhuva-nātha, mukhaliṅga with three visible faces. I.1, II.91, III.160, Sarma 1.

(2) Four-armed Parameśvara subdues Apasmāra-puruṣa the symbol of ignorance. Dancing. I.2, II.113, III.186, Sarma 4a.

(3) Four-armed Parameśvara subdues Andhaka. I.3, II.136, III.187, Sarma 19b.
(4) Īśvara and Umā on Nandin on their way to Kailāsa. I.4, II.131, III.180, 188, Sarma 8.
(5) Īśvara and Umā on the gold-fish Notopterus chitala. I.5, III.189, Sarma 13a.
(6) Mahājaya on the gold-fish. II.158, III.170, Sarma 13b.
(7) Īśvara and Umā on a crocodile. I.6, III.190, Sarma 14.
(8) Parameśvara, right hand in the mudrā of teaching, left: book. Represents the aspect of Bhaṭāra Guru. I.7, III.191, Sarma 18b.
(9) Four-armed Śiva, seated. R.h. discus, l.h. lasso (pāśa), two original hands in mudrā. Sarma 28a.
(10) Four-armed Īśvara, with bow and arrow, sword and shield, and wearing a garland of crania. I.52, III.234, Sarma 30.
(11) Parameśvara carrying bow and quiver.
Rāma's attributes have been assigned to Śiva. The Thai Kings of the Chakri dynasty are designated as Rāma, while their coronation is Śaiva. This may have led to the assimilation of Śiva and Rāma. III.223, Sarma 41a.
(12) Four-armed Īśvara on Himavān. R.h. ḍamaru, l.h. antelope, two main hands free. I.67, III.249, Sarma 44.
(13) Īśvara on elephant, r.h. rosary, l.h. elephant tusk. I.70, III.253.
(14) Īśvara entwined by a serpent. I.71, III.254.
(15) Īśvara vanquishes Mahiṣāsura (?). I.72, III.255, cf. Sarma 45.
(16) Four-armed Īśvara slays Tripura asura. Tripurāntaka. I.73, III.256, cf. Sarma 28b (the illustration differs).
(17) Eight-armed Īśvara seated on Kumbha yakṣa armed with sword and shield. R.h. trident, sabre, kris sword, mudrā, l.h. ḍamaru, shield, severed head, mudrā. I.50, II.102, III.232, Sarma 46.
(18) Four-armed Śiva. R.h. trident, abhaya, l.h. lasso, varada. I.62, III.244.
(19) Twenty-armed Īśvara annihilating — asura. I.81, III.264.
(20) Parameśvara Cakrapāṇi II.115.
(21) Īśvara vanquishing Andhaka. III.246. cf.(3).

GAṆEŚA

(22) Eight-armed Vighneśvara, three faces, standing. I.28, II.99, Sarma 7a.
(23) Eight-armed Vighneśvara, three faces, sitting. I.29, III.211.
(24) Eight-armed Vighneśvara, one face. II.98, Sarma 7b.
(25) Four-armed Mahāvighneśvara on a tortoise. I.24, II.101, III.206, Sarma 10a.
(26) Four-armed Mahāvighneśvara on his rat. I.23, II.100, III.184, Sarma 10b.

(27) Four-armed Mahāvighneśvara with an awl(?) and noose. I.22, II.92, III.183, Sarma 11a.
(28) Devakarma, I.26, II.95, III.208, Sarma 11b.
(29) Devakarma, I.27, II.97, III.185, Sarma 12a.
(30) Six-armed Kauñjarānaneśvara, with three visible heads. I.50, II.94, III.228, Sarma 12b.
(31) Four-armed Mahāvighneśvara, with left foot on rat. I.25, II.93, III.207.
(32) Mahāvighneśvara, II.96.
(33) Śivaputra, I.51, III.229.

SKANDA

(34) Twelve-armed Skandakumāra on a peacock. I.48, II.159, III.230, Sarma 39.
(35) Twelve-armed Skandakumāra on a peacock, Sarma 25.

NĀRĀYAṆA

(36) Four-armed Nārāyaṇa going to Vaikuṇṭha, borne on his garuḍa who is devouring a serpent. I.8, II.132, III.192, Sarma 4b.
(37) Four-armed Nārāyaṇa going to Kailāsa on a lion. I.10, II.133, III.194, Sarma 9.
(38) Four-armed Nārāyaṇa seated. I.18, II.125, III.202, Sarma 18a.
(39) Two-armed Nārāyaṇa vanquishes with the cakra. III.142.
(40) Four-armed Nārāyaṇa in a dancing posture. I.65, III.247.
(41) Four-armed Nārāyaṇa meditating on a nāga. I.11, II.139, III.195, Sarma 15b.
(42) Four-armed Nārāyaṇa playing the flute. Represents Kṛṣṇa. I.14, II.123, III.198, Sarma 21a.
(43) Four-armed Nārāyaṇa subduing a nāga. Represents Kṛṣṇa on Kāliya. I.9, III.193, Sarma 15a.
(44) Six-armed Nārāyaṇa with a rope to subdue Ekadanta. I.12, II.116, III.196, Sarma 19a.
(45) Six-armed Nārāyaṇa subdues the elephant. I.75, III.258.
(46) Four-armed Nārāyaṇī (female) tames Nandukkha (?). II.129, Sarma 21b.
(47) Four-armed Nārāyaṇa going to tame Nandukkha (?). Sarma 21c.
(48) Eight-armed Devakarma Nārāyaṇī, with three visible faces. I.19, II.119, III.203, Sarma 32b.
(49) Six-armed Nārāyaṇa tames Nandukkha (?). I.45, III.225, Sarma 32a.
(50) Four-armed Nārāyaṇa becomes a danceuse to entice Brahmā. I.64.
(51) Four-armed Nārāyaṇa dancing. II.122, Sarma 20a, 22a.
(52) Two-armed Nārāyaṇa going to the city Citramalā. I.16, II.135, III.200, Sarma 20b.

(53) Four-armed Nārāyaṇa standing upright. I.15, II.124, III.199, Sarma 22b
(54) Lakṣmī, I.40, II.127, III.220, Sarma 23a.
(55) Maheśvarī. I.41, II.128, III.221, Sarma 23b.
(56) Umā bhagavatī. I.42, II.126, III.222, Sarma 23c.
(57) Umā subdues a crocodile. I.13, III.197.
(58) Elephants offering their tongues to Umā. I.17, III.201.
(59) Nārāyaṇa flanked by Lakṣmī and Maheśvarī. II.90, III.273.
(60) Four-armed Nārāyaṇa lying on the nāga, accompanied by Brahmā and Śrīdevī. I.21, II.118, III.205, Sarma 16.
(61) Nārāyaṇa on a lion, flanked by Bhūdevī and Śrīdevī. I.38, II.181, Sarma 24.
(62) Four-armed Nārāyaṇa meditating afloat on the ocean, accompanied by Bhūdevī and Śrīdevī. I.20, II.134, III.204, Sarma 17.
(63) Four-armed Nārāyaṇa dormant on Śeṣa-nāga, with a lotus emerging from the navel. I.74, III.257.
(64) Four-armed Viṣṇu. I.68, II.112, III.251, Sarma 27b.
(65) Eight-armed Nārāyaṇa vanquishes Mahiṣ-āsura. I.66, III.248, Sarma 45.

THE TEN INCARNATIONS OF VIṢṆU (DAŚĀVATĀRA)

(66) Matysāvatāra to vanquish the group of Śaṅkhāsura. I.53, III.235, Sarma 42a.
(67) Kacchapāvatāra to vanquish the Maccha asura. I.54, III.236, Sarma 42c.
(68) Śvetavarāha to vanquish the Hiraṇya asura. I.55, III.237, Sarma 41b.
(69) Siṁhāvatāra tearing the Hiraṇya yakṣa. I.56, III.238, Sarma 31.
(70) Kubjāvatāra. I.57, III.239, Sarma 38b.
(71) Paraśurām-āvatāra. I.58, III.240, Sarma 41c.
(72) Rāmāvatāra. I.59, III.241, Sarma 38a.
(73) Kṛṣṇāvatāra who vanquished Bāṇāsura in the legend of Aniruddha. I.60, III.242, Sarma 38c.
(74) Buddhāvatāra who is destined to regain the Śivaliṅga carried away by Tripura asura. I.61, II.243, Sarma 28b.
(75) Daśamāvatāra. I.63, II.245, Sarma 40.

BRAHMĀ

(76) Sixteen-armed eight-faced Śraddhāsiddha(?). I.34, II.114, III.216, Sarma 6a.
(77) Ten-armed four-faced Śraddhāsiddha(?). I.35, II.117, III.217, Sarma 6b.
(78) Twenty-armed eight-faced Śraddhādeva. I.37, II.108, III.219, Sarma 34a.
(79) Twentyfour-armed eight-faced Śraddhādeva. I.36, II.107, III.218, Sarma 34b.
(80) Four-faced Brahmanātha. III.213, Sarma 26a.

(81) Four-armed four-faced Brahmanātha. I.31, II.130, III.213, Sarma 27a.
(82) Four-armed four-faced Brahmā Dhātā. I.69, II.111, III.252, Sarma 26b.
(83) Eight-armed four-faced Brahmā Dhātā. I.30, II.103, III.212, Sarma 37b.
(84) Fourteen-armed four-faced Brahmā-maheśvara. I.33, III.215, Sarma 36a.
(85) Fourteen-armed Brahmā-maheśvara. II.106 (four-faced), Sarma 36b (one-faced).
(86) Eight-armed four-faced Sahāṁpati Brahmā. I.32, II.105, III.214, Sarma 37a.

NAVAGRAHA/NINE PLANETS

(87) Āditya/Sun on a lion, red colour. II.149, III.171.
(88) Candra/Moon on a horse, white colour. II.150, III.172.
(89) Aṅgāra on a buffalo, pink colour. II.151, III.173.
(90) Budha on an elephant, green colour. II.152, III.174.
(91) Bṛhaspati on a deer, brown colour. II.153, III.175.
(92) Śukra on a buffalo, yellow colour. II.154, III.176.
(93) Śani on a tiger, black colour. II.155, III.177.
(94) Rāhu on a yakṣa, violet colour. II.156, III.178.
(95) Ketu on a nāga, red colour. II.157, III.179.

DIKPĀLAS/DEITIES OF THE DIRECTIONS

(96)	Indra on Airāvata. II.140, III.163, Sarma 35.	(East)
(97)	Agni on a peacock. II.147, III.164 (rhino).	(SE)
(98)	Yama on an owl. II.141, III.165.	(South)
(99)	? II.142.	(SW)
(100)	Varuṇa on a nāga. II.146, III.167.	(West)
(101)	Vāyu on a galloping horse. II.144, III.169.	(NW)
(102)	Nārāyaṇa on garuḍa. II.145, III.166.	(North: Kubera)
—	Īśāna	(NE)
(103)	Brahmā on a haṁsa/goose. II.148, III.182.	(Zenith)
—	Pṛthivī	(Nadir)
(104)	Candra/Moon on a horse. II.143, III.168.	

The eight dikpālas are: Indra (E), Agni (SE), Yama (S), Nirṛti (SW), Varuna (W), Vāyu (NW), Vaiśravana (N), Īśāna (NE).
Brahmā (zenith), Pṛthivī (nadir), Sūrya/Sun, Candra/Moon.

DIVERSE DEITIES

(105) Karmasiddhi-deva. I.44, II.109, III.224, 225, Sarma 33. Deity of success in work.
(106) Four-armed Pañcaśikha playing vīṇā. I.49, II.104, III.231, Sarma 43.

(107) Uthenurāja (?) playing vīṇā, surrounded by elephants. I.83, III.266.
(108) Maharṣi playing vīṇā and elephants listening. I.82, III.265.
(109) Nang Devī. I.78, III.261.
(110) Four-armed Konchai (?). I.79, III.262.
(111) Mahāmeṣa (?). I.80, III.263.
(112) Viśvakarmā. I.85, III.268.
(113) Guru of horses. I.84, III.267.
(114) Trainer of elephants. I.86, III.269.
(115) Goddess with a rope to control elephants. I.87, III.270.
(116) Trainer of elephants. I.88, III.271.
(117) Trainer of elephants. I.89, III.272.
(118) God of ploughing. II.138.
(119) Six-finger deity. I.39, II.120, III.209.
(120) Drahriṅ (?). I.76, Sarma 29.
(121) The monkey-king Jāmbavant. I.51, III.233, Sarma 42b.

SAGES/ṚṢI

(122) Aśman ṛṣi. Sarma 5b.
(123) Baladeva. I.77, III.260, Sarma 3a.
(124) Ṛṣi with a fan. I.48, 49, II.162, III.227.
(125) Drupada ṛṣi. Sarma 5a.
(126) Nārada. Sarma 2a.
(127) Deva Paśusakha. I.46, II.121, III.226, Sarma 3b.
(128) Ṛṣyaśṛṅga ṛṣi. II.110, Sarma 5c.
(129) Kalaikoṭṭu ṛṣi. I.47, II.137, III.161, Sarma 2b.

SANSKRIT AND TAMIL TEXTS

In 1962 Prof. Raghuvira was invited for the birthday celebrations of His Majesty King Bhumibol Adulyadej on 5 December. On the sixth of December three Śaiva brāhmaṇas went to the royal court, circumambulated His Majesty, and performed the rites of *arati.* They were led by Vamadeva-muni. Vamadeva-muni passed the elementary school from Thailand. The course lasts for twelve years (6-17 years). He studied commerce at the Waseda University, Tokyo for four years after completing two years of Japanese (19-24 years). He joined the Śiva temple in 1959 and took up reading and writing Tamil from the older brāhmaṇas, an hour every day. He got up early at 6.00 in the morning, bathed, and recited mantras before taking breakfast. People do not come for worship, but invite him occasionally to their homes when they purchase new land, build a new house, or cut the first hair (culakata=cūḍākarma). He is also invited to bless new couples by sprinkling holy water on the bride and bridegroom. As they bow down and receive drops of holy water, Muni puts *mongkon* on the head of the pair. Guests gathered for the occasion take a few drops. The ceremony is very short: a mere five minutes. The rich give ten to three hundred bahts, while the poor give nothing. He also invests brāhmaṇas with the sacred thread of yajñopavīta, but not the public. The second of the three brāhmaṇas who had gone to bless His Majesty had learnt Tamil, and joined the Śiva temple at the age of seventeen years. He performed the rituals as handed down by tradition, without understanding Tamil or Sanskrit. Hindus from India do not come to this temple. The future of the Śiva temple and brāhmaṇa priests depends on the King and the Government. The brāhmaṇas are Buddhists by religion. The Government pays them a salary of 450 bahts per month, besides the requisites for worship. They conduct three major ceremonies: the saṁkrānti festival in April, the first-furrow to commence ploughing in spring, and the coronation day (chatramaṅgala) on the fifth of May.

The precints of the Śiva temple in Bangkok are located in the Ban Din Saw street and are 180 years old. They go back to the founding of Bangkok by King Rama I. It has three temples to Śiva and Brahmā, Gaṇeśa and Viṣṇu. The main images are of bronze. Four delapidated images of Gaṇeśa can be seen behind his central bronze image. In the Viṣṇu temple, the bronze image of Viṣṇu is flanked by Lakṣmī and Maheśvarī, on whose sides are brass icons of Haṁsa. In front of the image of Viṣṇu is a swing, on which Haṁsa is swung during the rites. Haṁsa signifies Viṣṇu in the Śāṇḍilya-saṁhitā 1.4.45-52 (bhaktikāṇḍa) and the Thai manuscripts have a Haṁsa-pūjā-vidhi.

Haṁsa	Lakṣmī	VIṢṆU swing	Maheśvarī	Haṁsa

Till the reign of Rāma V there were two ancient brāhmaṇa families called Gurukula and Raśmibrāhmaṇa-kula (Ransi). The first family came to an end in the period of Rama V. From the second family only Sivacala is a priest. His brothers have become professionals: a brother is a trader, and the youngest is a defence officer. This family had come from Ramnagar, Varanasi. Now they have no contact with India. There are thirteen other male members in the family who do not perform priestly functions. They come together at marriages and other family rituals. They bear the sacred thread of yajñopavīta.

Prof. Raghuvira met eight brāhmaṇas at the temple on 8 December 1962. All of them were wearing the yajñopavīta. Their names are: Pra Rajakru (rājaguru) Vamadevamuni (40 years), Pra Kru Asadachariya (83), Pra Kru Sivachariya (83), Pra Kru Satanandamuni (72: Śatānandamuni), Brahmana Sang Klincharung (-), Brahmana Yoi Komalayetin (54), Brahmana Khab Nakavetin (50), Aied Ratana brahmana (43). They showed eight Sanskrit-Tamil manuscripts to Prof. Raghuvira. They were written with chalk on black paper, in a careful script. They are long concertina books about 4x14 inches, and sometimes with interlinear notings in the Thai script. The eight concertina manuscripts have been reproduced at the end of this work as central to rites of the Hindu deities illustrated in the three pantheons.

LITERATURE CITED

Boisselier 1975

Jean Boisselier, *The Heritage of Thai Sculpture*, Tokyo (Weatherhill).

Boisselier 1976

Jean Boisselier, *Malerei in Thailand*, Stuttgart (Verlag W. Kohlhammer).

Bowie 1960

Theodore Bowie (ed.), *The Arts of Thailand*, Bloomington (Indiana University Press).

Bowie 1972

Theodore Bowie (ed.), *The Sculpture of Thailand*, New York (The Asia Society, Inc.).

Diskul 1970

M.C. Subhadradis Diskul, *Art in Thailand*: a brief history, Bangkok (Silpakorn University).

Diskul 1980

M.C. Subhadradis Diskul, *The Art of Śrīvijaya*, Oxford University Press, UNESCO.

Filliozat 1965

Jean Filliozat, Kailāsaparamparā, in *Felicitation Volumes of Southeast-Asian Studies presented to His Highness Prince Dhaninivat*, Bangkok (The Siam Society).

Krairiksh 1979

Piriya Krairiksh, *The Sacred Image (Sculptures from Thailand)*, Köln (Museum für Ostasiatische Kunst der Stadt Köln).

Majumdar 1944

R.C. Majumdar, *Kambuja-deśa*, University of Madras.

May 1954

Reginald le May, *The Culture of South-East Asia*, London (George Allen and Unwin).

O'Connor 1972

Stanley J. O'Connor, Jr., *Hindu Gods of Peninsular Siam*, Ascona (Artibus Asiae).

Sarma 1972

Neelakanta Sarma, *Textes Sanskrits et Tamouls de Thailande*, Pondichéry (Institut Français d'Indologie).

Sarma 1973

Neelakanta Sarma, Un album thailandais d'iconographie indienne, *Arts Asiatiques* 26(1973). 157-190.

Wales 1931

H.G. Quaritch Wales, *Siamese State Ceremonies*, London (Bernard Quaritch, Ltd.).

LIST OF ILLUSTRATIONS

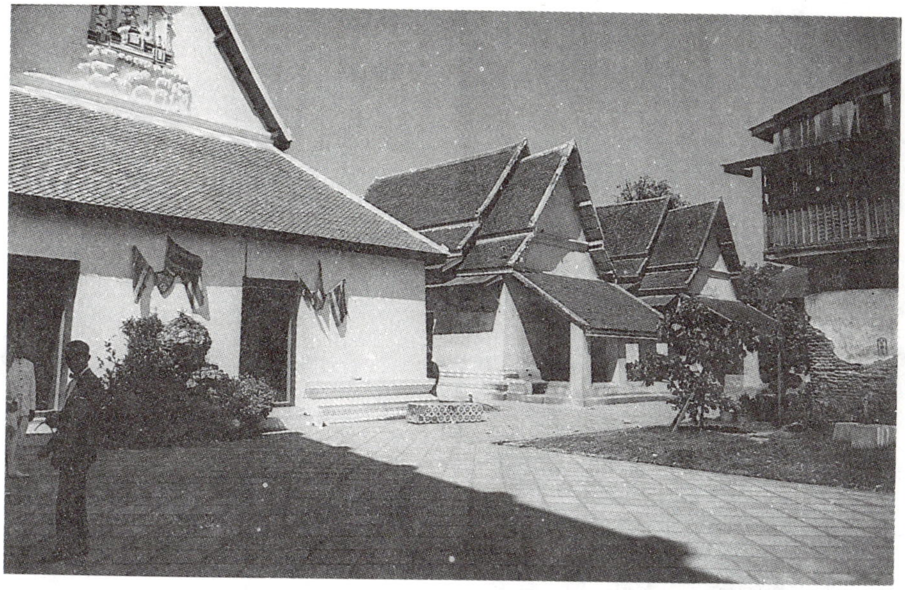

1. General view of the Brahmana Temple at Bangkok.

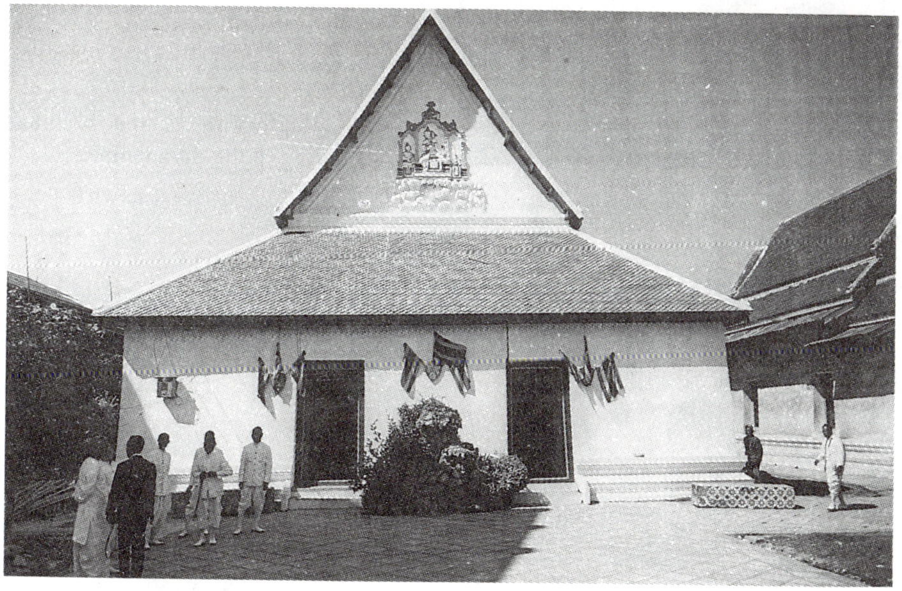

2. Śiva temple.

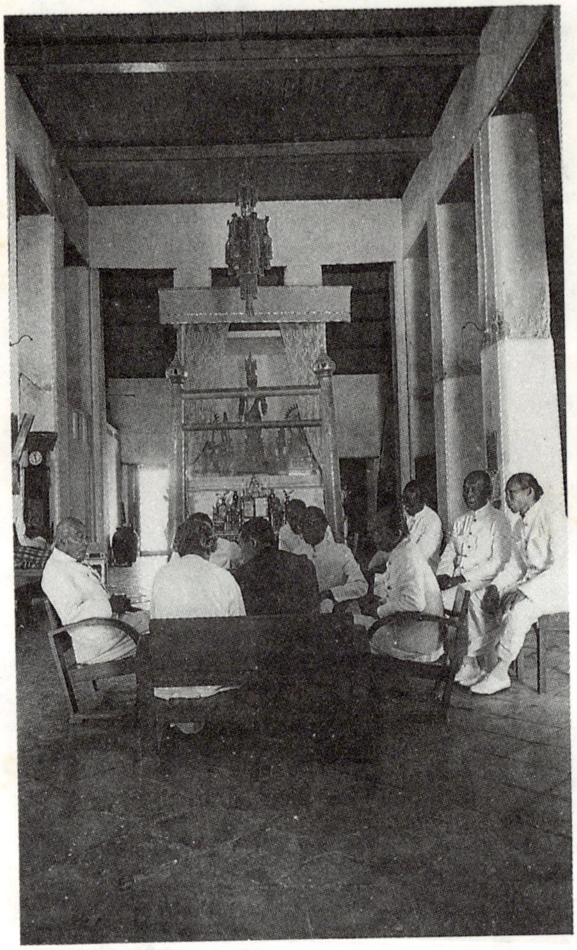

3. Prof. RaghuVira in the brahmana gathering in the Śiva temple.

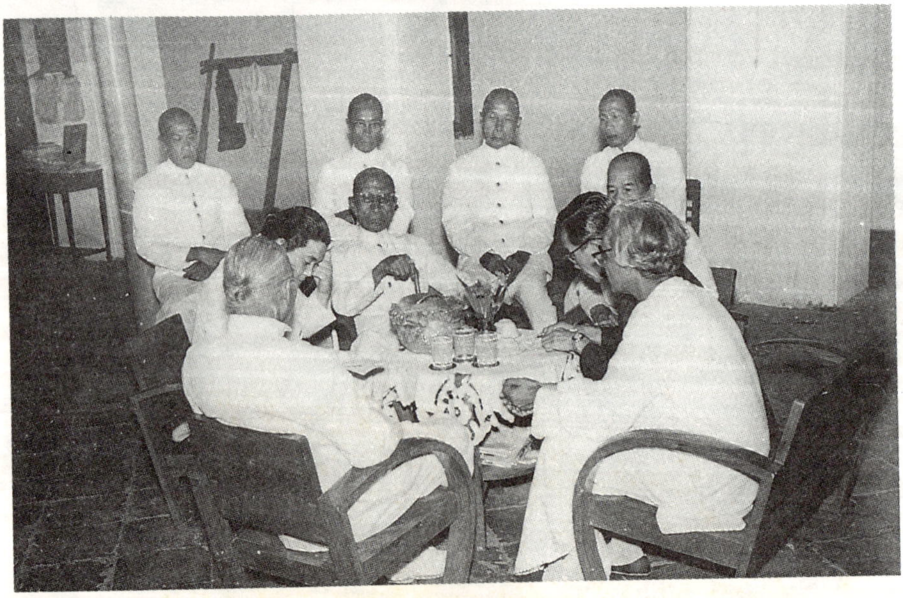

4. Prof. RaghuVira in conference with the eight Thai brahmanas.

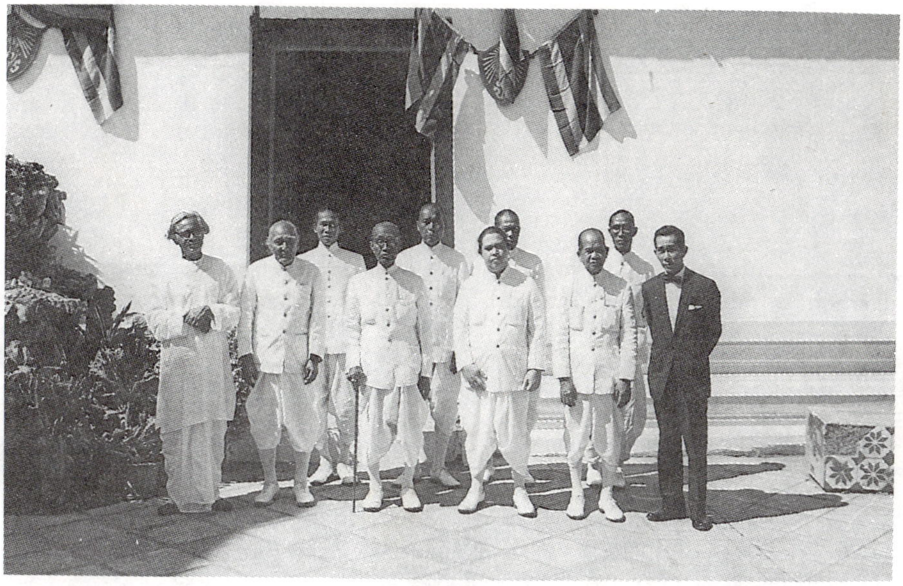

5. Prof. RaghuVira and the brahmanas.

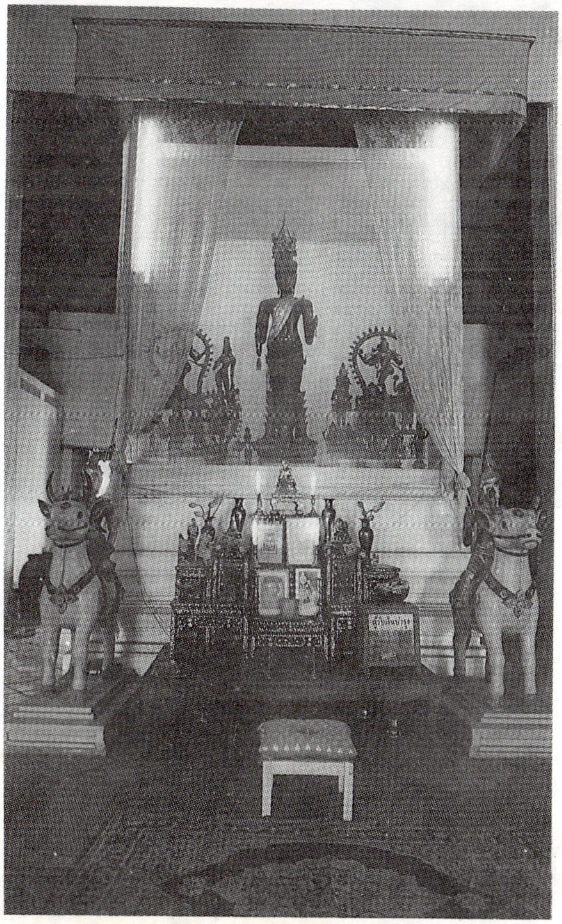

6. The altar and shrine of the Śiva temple.

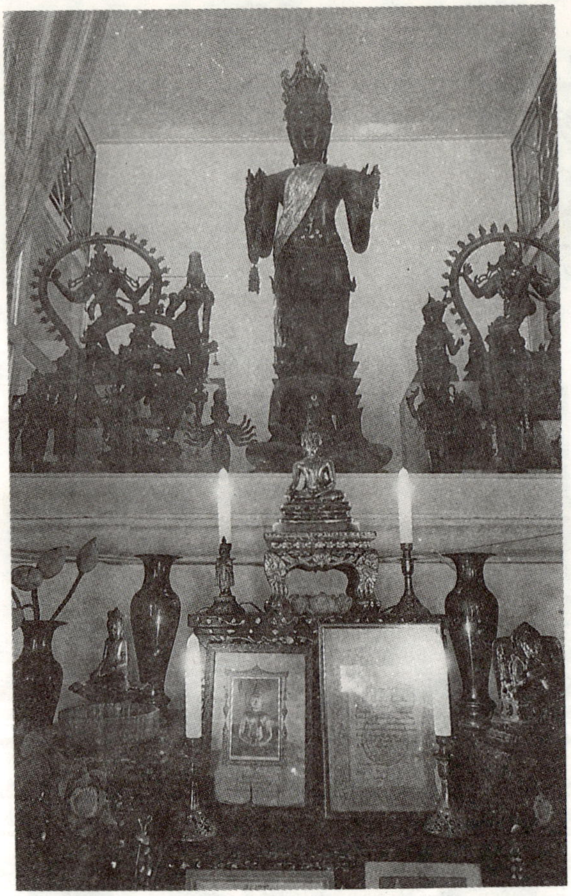

7. Close up of the shrine of Siva.

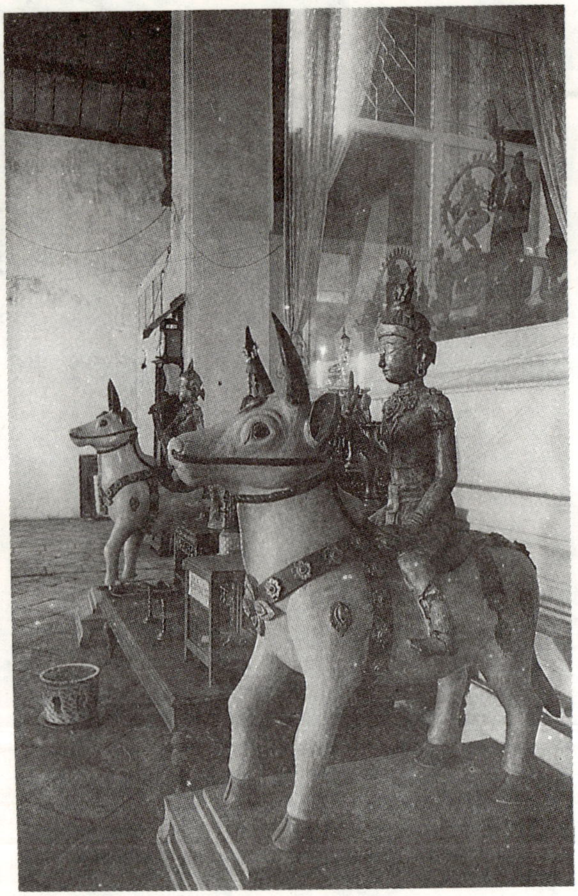

8. The two Nandin bulls in the Siva temple.

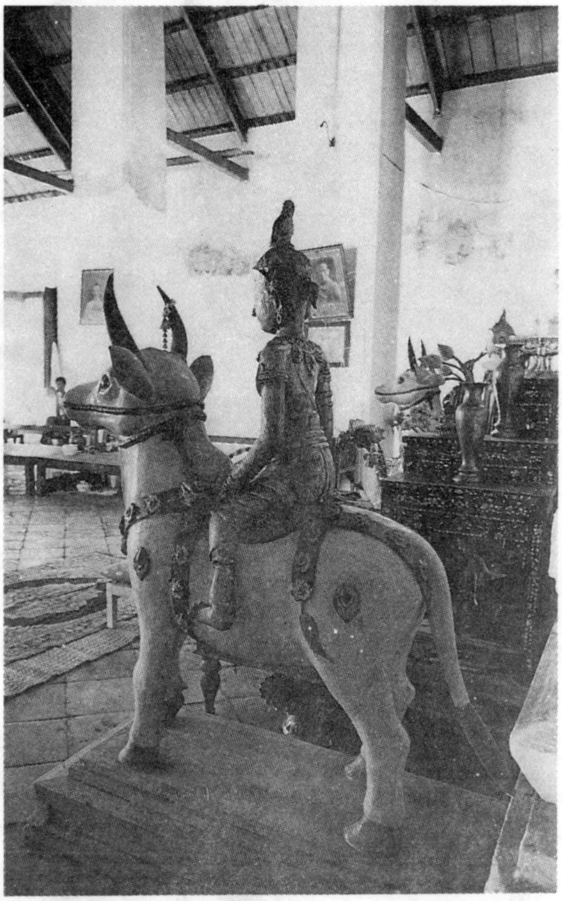

9. Close up of no.8.

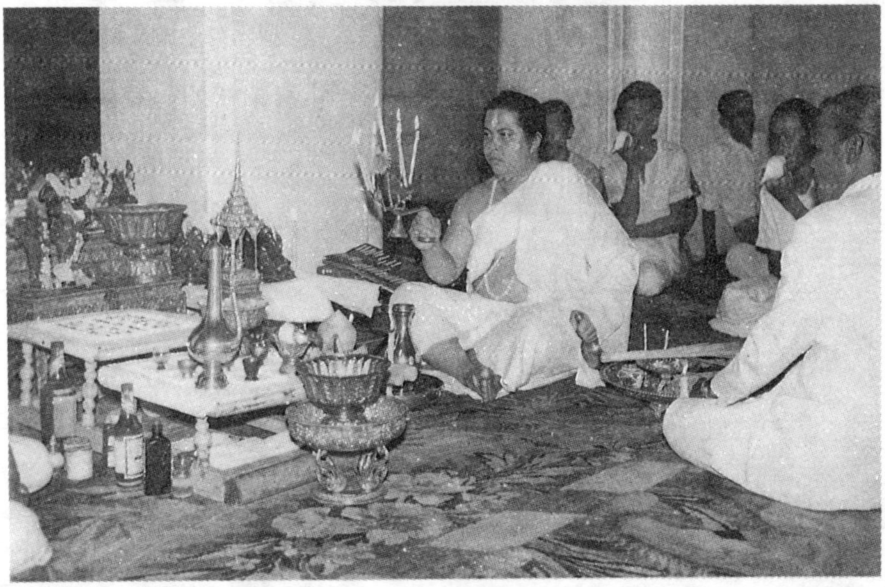

10. Vamadevamuni performing Śaiva worship.

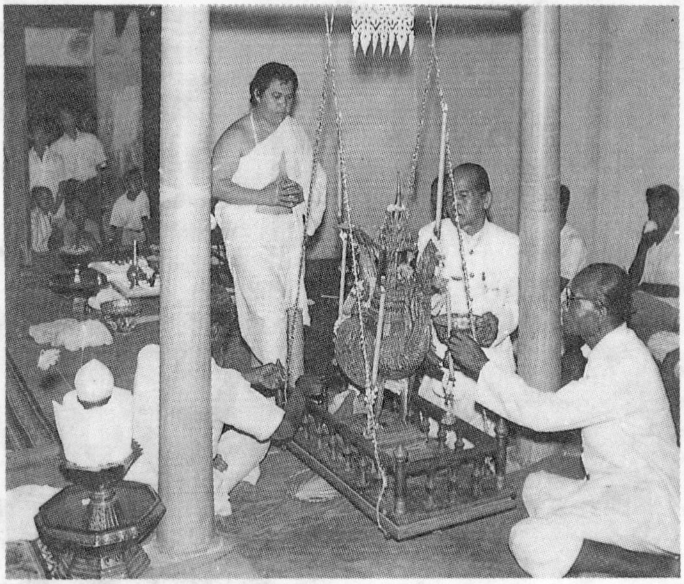

11. Rocking the Haṁsa.

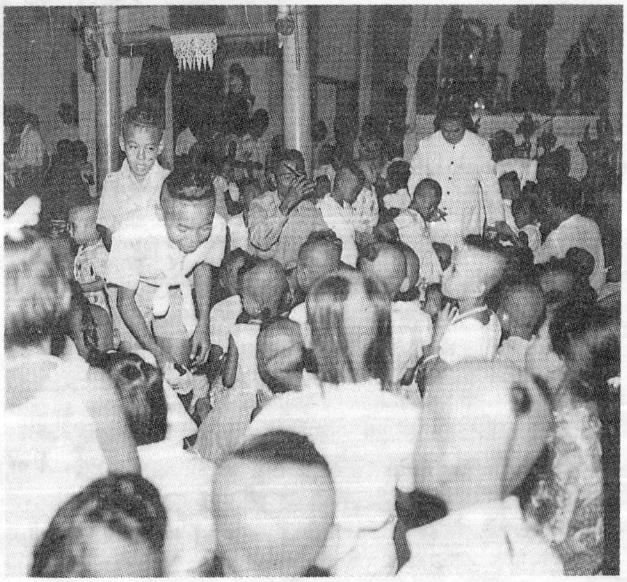

12. Tonsure ceremony of children.

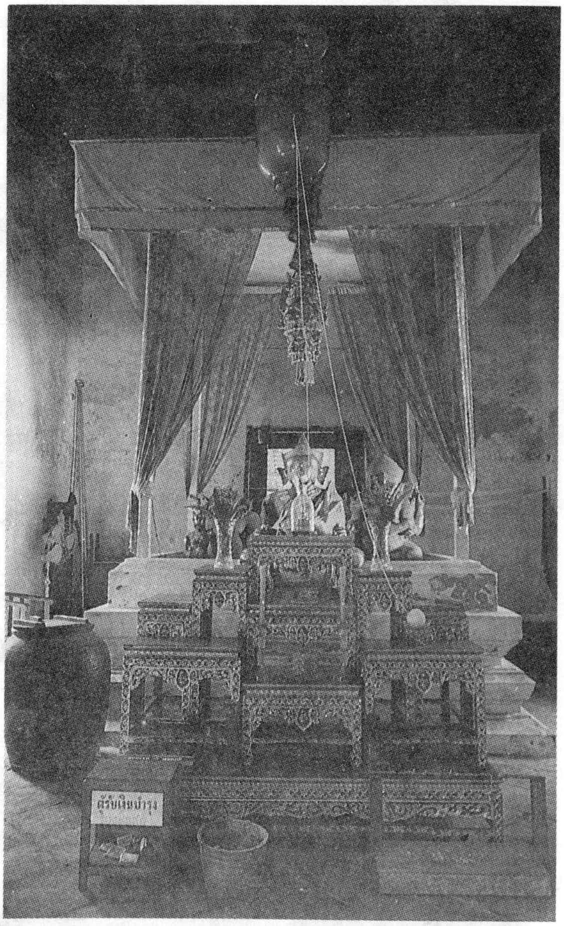

13. Altar of the Gaṇeśa temple.

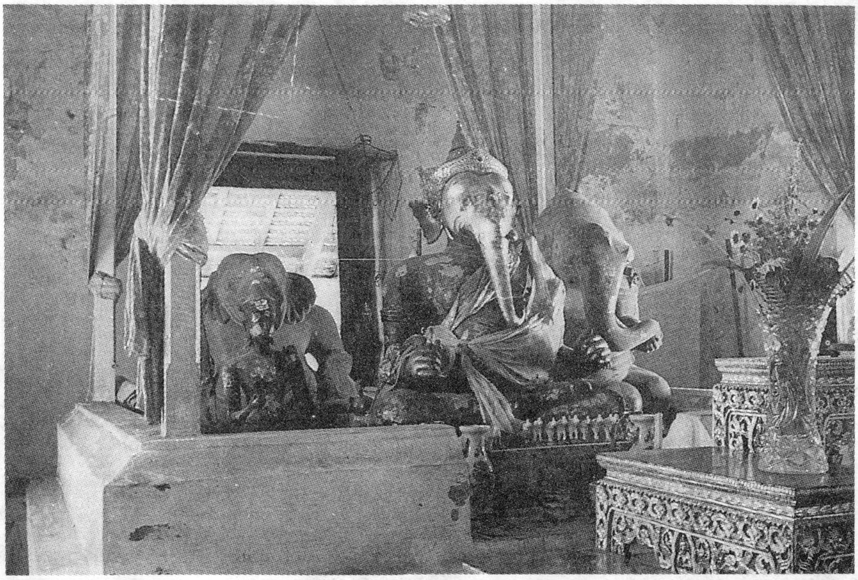

14. Statue of Gaṇeśa.

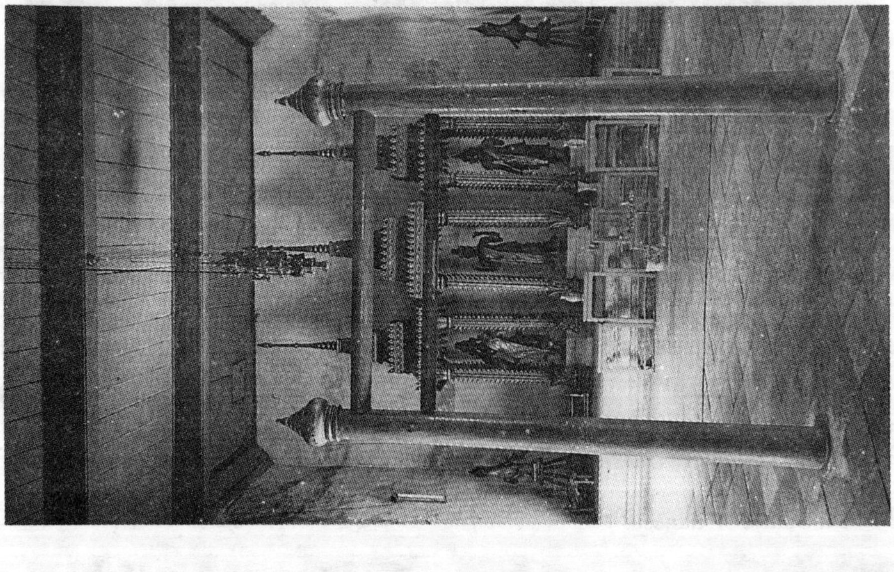

15. The statues of Viṣṇu, Lakṣmī and Maheśvarī in the Viṣṇu temple.

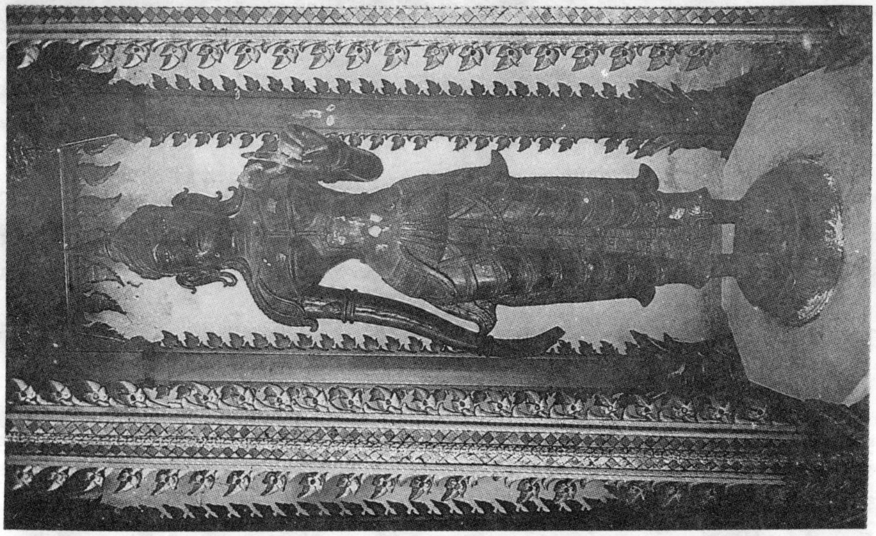

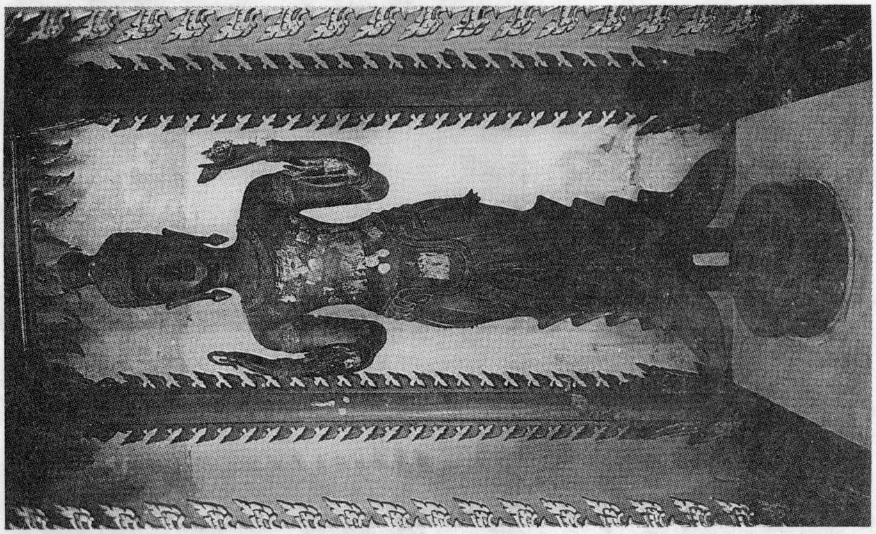

16,17. Lakṣmī and Maheśvarī.

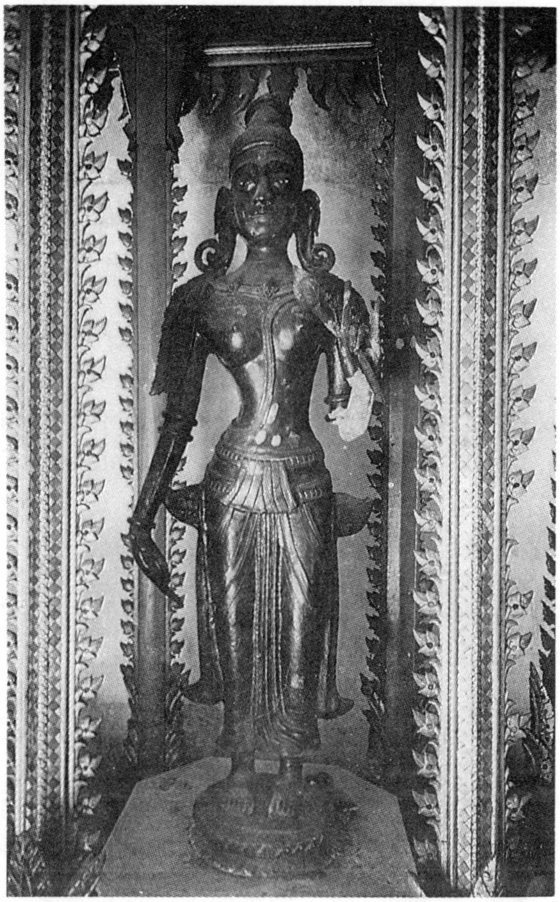

18. Viṣṇu.

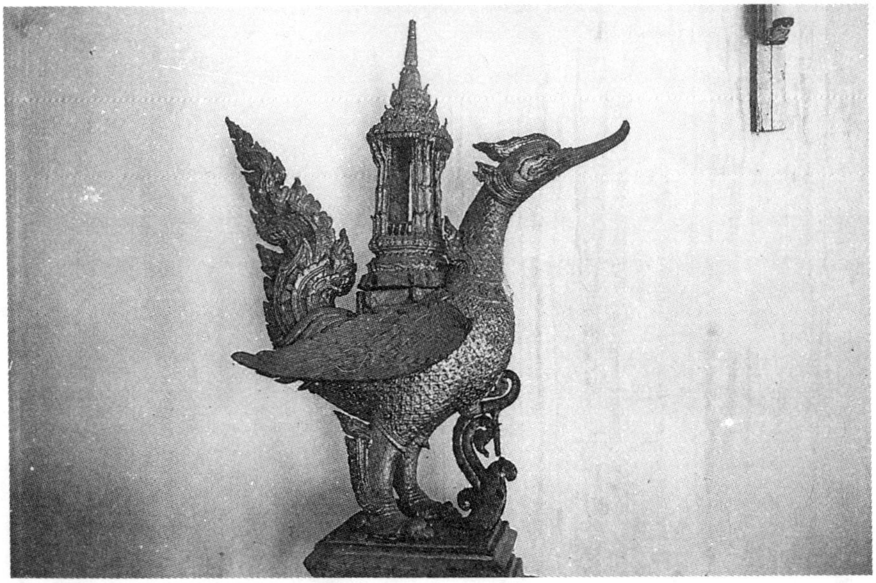

19. Haṁsa in the Viṣṇu temple.

1. Svāyambhuvanātha, represented as Mukhaliṅga.
   See 91, 160, Sarma no.1 rūP nī[2] gōēa aṅg', braḥ symbhūvaḥnād || ‹‹this image is the body of Braḥ Sayambhūvanād››.

2. Parameśvara tramples over Apasmārapuruṣa. Nṛttamūrti of Śiva. MuyalakaN (Tamil) represents inconscience and is termed Apasmāra-puruṣa in Sanskrit. See 113, Sarma no.4a braḥ praḥmeśvr heyīyp mūlāgaḥnī || ‹‹B. Parameśvara tramples Mūlāga››.

3. Parameśvara tramples over Andhaka. Śiva is dancing over a person. Four arms. Right hand: trident, left hand: disc, two main hands in mudrā.
   See 136, 187, Sarma 19b braḥ iśvr heyiyp ăṅgukaḥ brhm | ‹‹B. Īśvara tramples Aṅguka.›› Aṅguka for Antaka (t and g can be confused in Thai script. Tamil AntakaN = Andhaka, a daitya son of Kaśyapa and Diti killed by Śiva, Harivaṁśa 2.86).

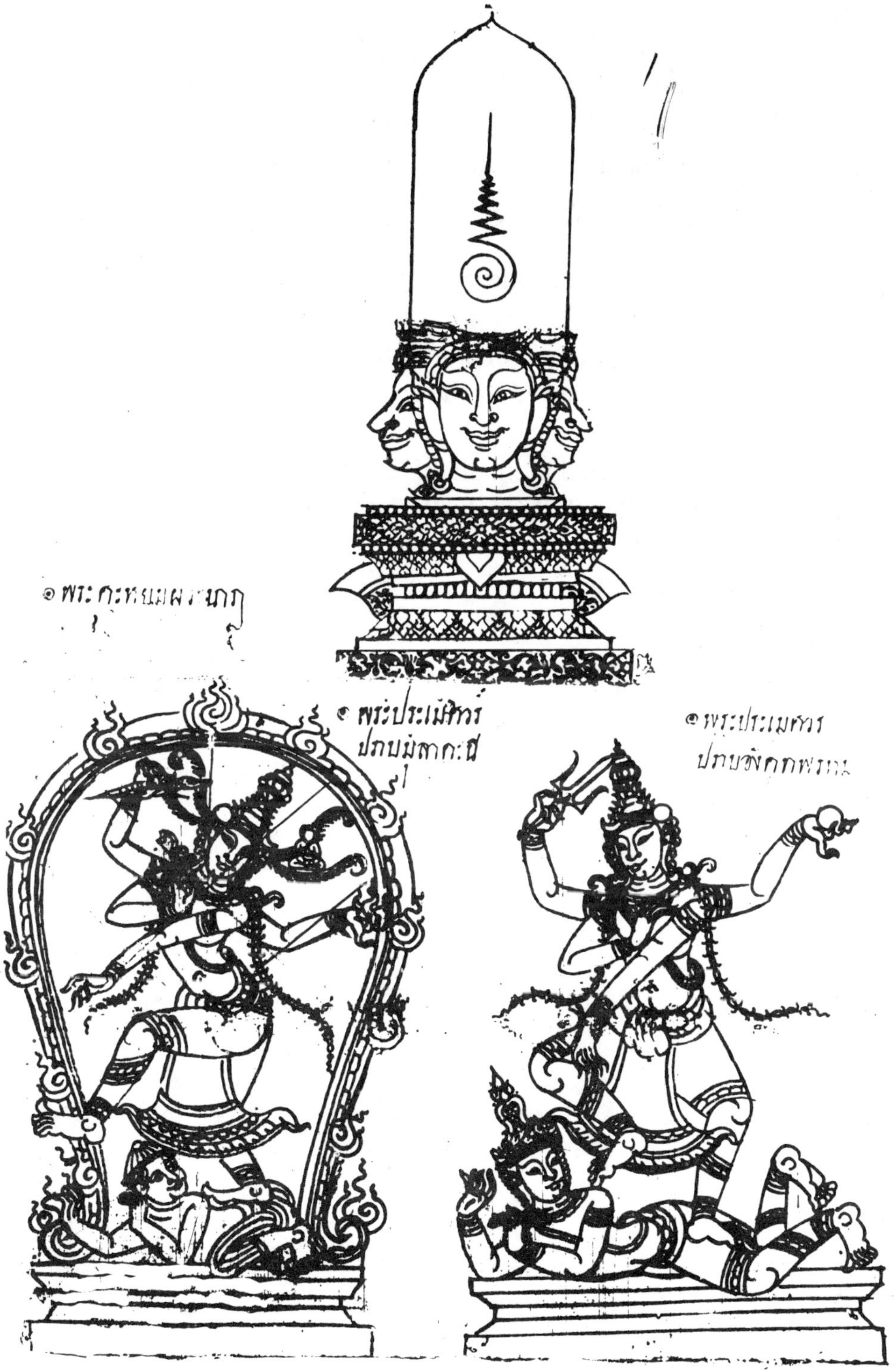

4. Umā-Maheśvara going to Kailāsa on bull Nandin.
   See 131, 180, 188, Sarma 8 braḥ iśvr setc' Paï kairlāś || ‹‹B. Īśvara going to Kailāsa››.

5. Umā-Maheśvara on gold-fish Notopterus chitala. Īśvara has a trident in the r.h. and ear of corn in the l.h. Umā has an ear of corn.
   See 189, Sarma 13a braḥ iśvr drṅ Plākrāy daṅ | ‹‹B. Īśvara carried by the gold-fish Notopterus chitala››.

6. Umā-Maheśvara on a crocodile. Śiva has a trident in the right hand and Umā a lotus bud.
   See 190, Sarma 14 braḥ isvr braḥ umāvaḥtī drṅ craḥkhe[2] | ‹‹B. Īśvara and B. Umā (Umābhagavatī) carried by the crocodile››.

7. Parameśvara. Right hand in mudrā of teaching, left has a book.
   See 191, Sarma 18b braḥ Prśvr | ‹‹B. Parameśvara››.

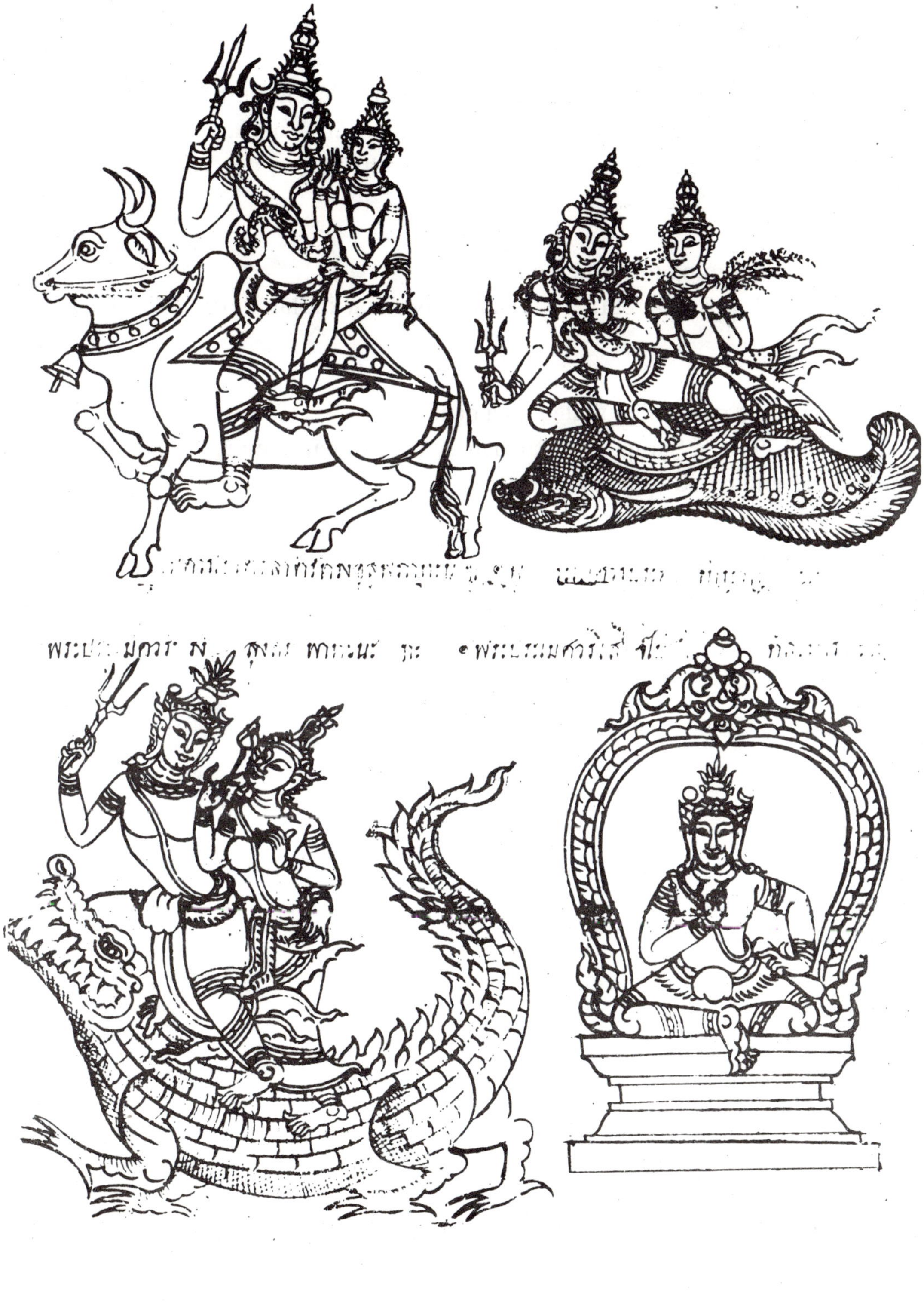

8. Nārāyaṇa going to Vaikuṇṭha. Nārāyaṇa borne by Garuḍa who holds a serpent.
See 132, 192, Sarma 4b braḥ nrāyn' sete Paï gijpănbT ‖ ‹‹B. Nārāyaṇa going to G. =Vaikuṇṭha››.

9. Nārāyaṇa carried by a nāgarāja. Four-armed Viṣṇu on nāga, with a disc and conch in the right hands. Kṛṣṇa slaying the Kāliya nāga.
See 193, Sarma 15a braḥ naḥrāyn' drṅ braḥyā nāg | ‹‹B. Nārāyaṇa carried by the King of Nāgas››.

10. Nārāyaṇa going to Kailāsa on a lion.
See 118, 133, 194, Sarma 9 braḥ naḥrāyn' Paï kaïllāś ‖ ‹‹B. Nārāyaṇa going to Kailāsa››.

11. Nārāyaṇa meditating seated on a nāga.
See 139, 195, Sarma 15b braḥ naḥrāy cāṃ śil păn lăn nāg | ‹‹ Nārāyaṇa meditates enthroned on a nāga››.

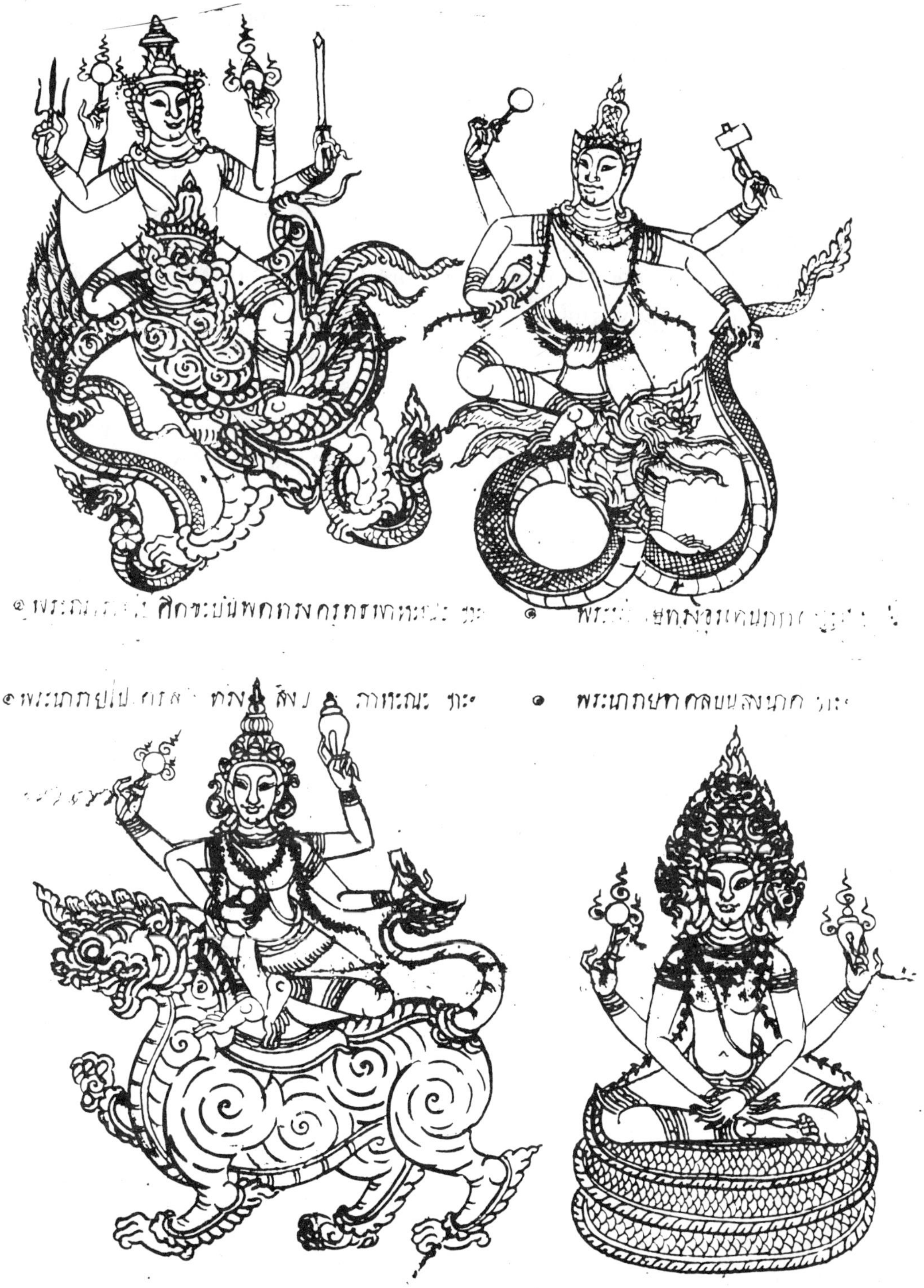

12. Nārāyaṇa with a rope to subdue Ekadanta. Dancing, Six arms. R.h. fire, parasols, stūpa (?) like object, l.h. conch, — , noose (pāśa).
    See 116, Sarma 19a braḥ nrāyn' drṅ j ak pāj Prāp ekdănd' | ‹‹B. Nārāyaṇa with a rope to subdue Ekadanta››.

13. Umā subdues a crocodile.
    cf. Sarma no.14.

14. Nārāyaṇa playing the flute.
    See 123, 198, Sarma 21a braḥ nrāyn' drṅ khuly[1] | ‹‹B. Nārāyaṇa playing the flute.›› Tamil kuLāy 'flute.'

15. Nārāyaṇa standing in upright position (cāṁ sthān). R.h. conch, lotus, l.h. disc, baton.
    See 124, 199, Sarma 22b braḥ nrāyn' cāṃ sthān yīn | ‹‹B. Nārāyaṇa in upright position››.

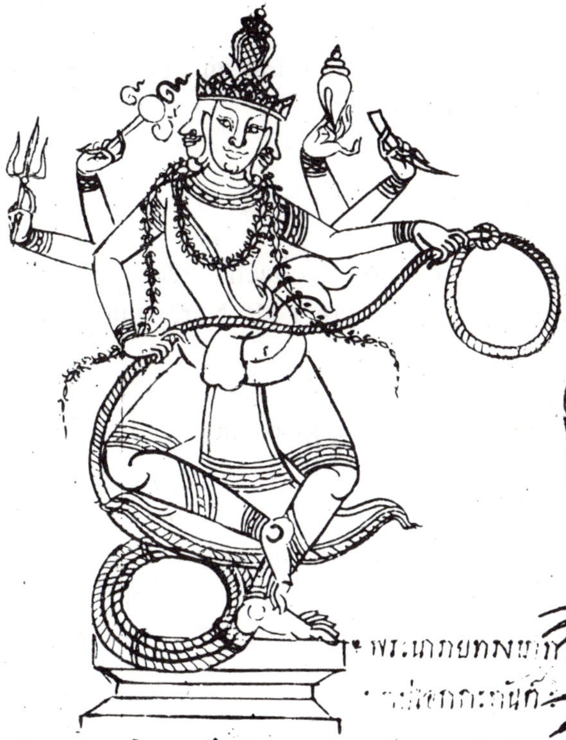

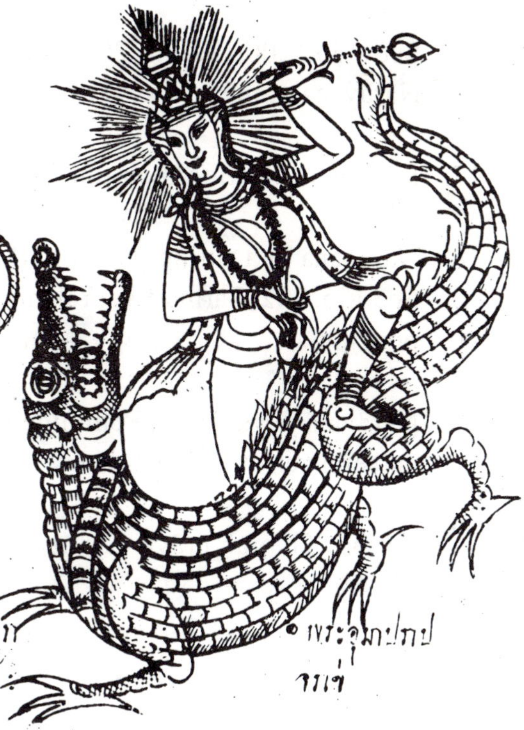

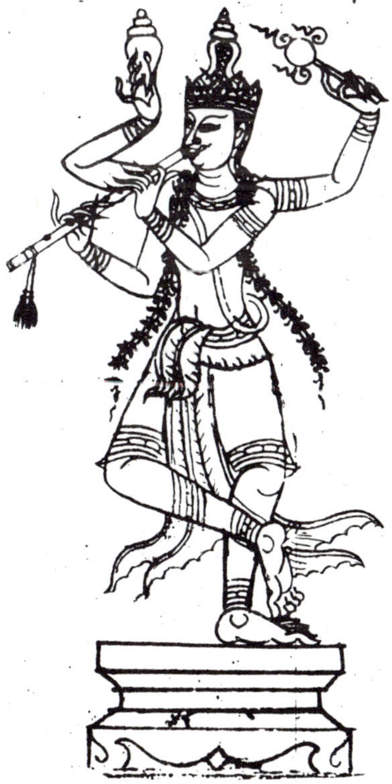

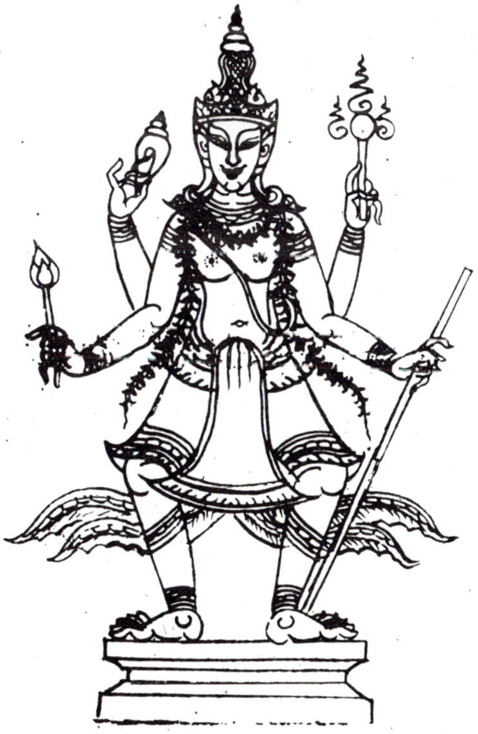

16. Nārāyaṇa going to the city of Citramalā (?). Performs a step of dance. R.h. baton, l.h. ball.
See 135, 200, Sarma 20b braḥ nrāyn' setc[2] Paï miey aṅ ciTrmlāṃ I ‹‹B. Nārāyaṇa going to the city of Citramalā (?)››.

17. Elephants offering their tongues to Umā.

18. Nārāyaṇa in a sitting position. R.h. disc, baton, l.h. conch, trident.
See 125, 202, Sarma 18a braḥ nrāyn' cāṃ sthān nāṅ I ‹‹B. Nārāyaṇa in a sitting position››.

19. Nārāyaṇī devakarma. Feminine figure seated on a pedestal, three visible faces and eight arms. R.h. bow in two hands, conch, mudrā, l.h. noose, trident, arrow, disc.
Sarma 32b braḥ nrāyn devkrrm' I ‹‹B. Nārāyaṇa devakarma››.

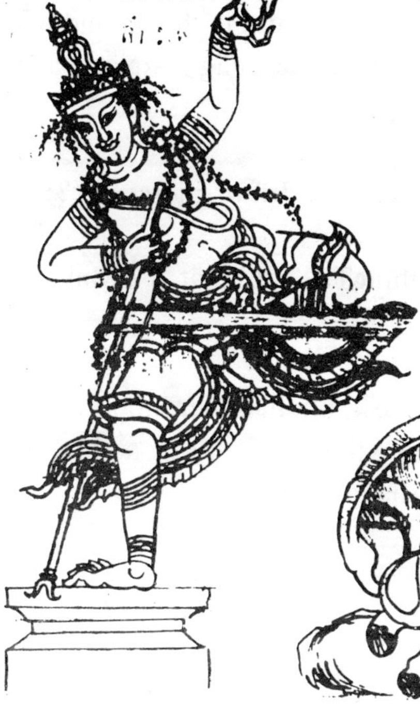

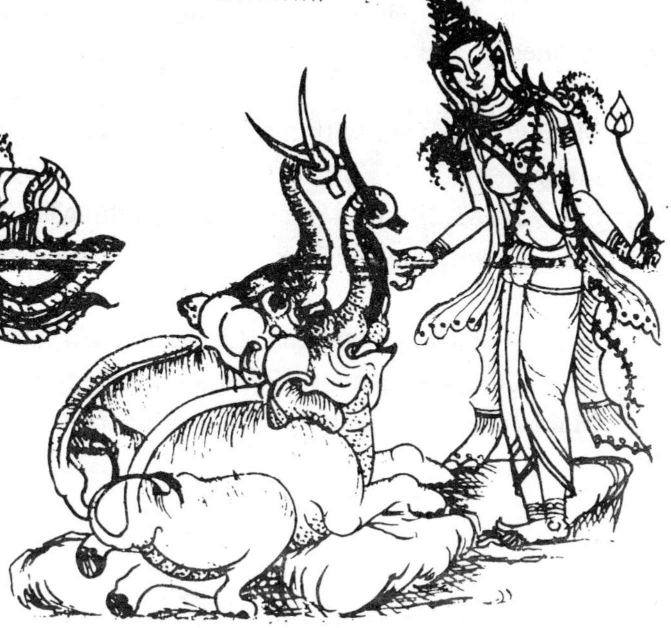

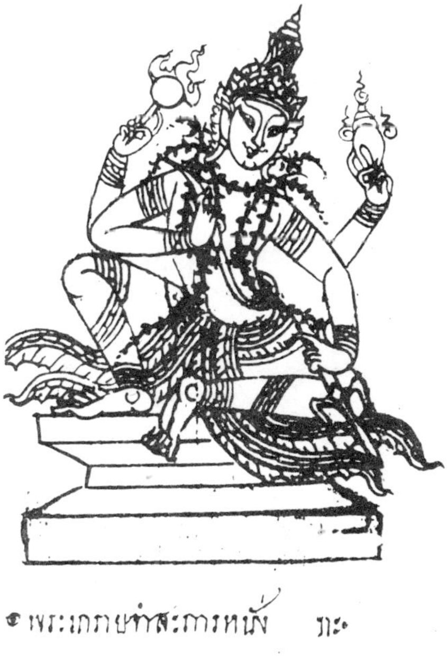

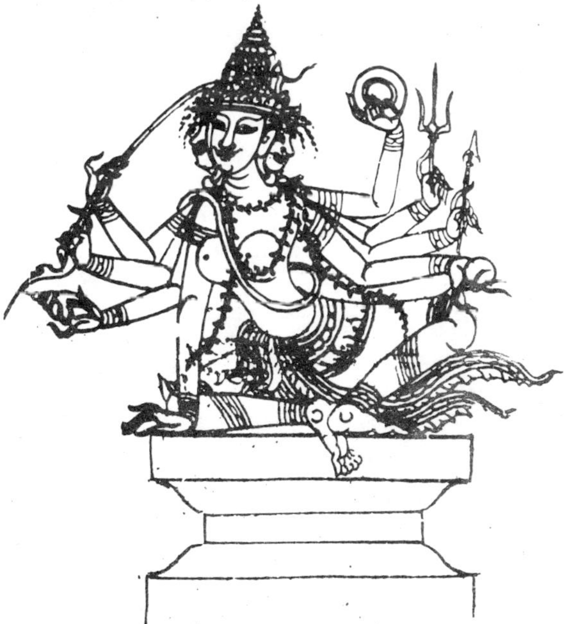

๑ พระเกกยทำสะการหนั้ง ๅะ ๑ พระนากยปกบนนกกหนั้ง

20. Nārāyaṇa meditating lying on the ocean, accompanied by Bhūdevī and Śrīdevī. See 134, 204, Sarma 17. braḥ nrāyn' păndhm sindhu nāï kraḥśeīyr smud I ‹‹B. Nārāyaṇa meditates lying on the ocean››.

21. Nārāyaṇa lying on a lion, with Brahmā adoring him in the air and with Śrīdevī. See 118, 205, Sarma 16 braḥ nrāy păndm pănlăṅ nāg I ‹‹Nārāyaṇa lying enthroned on the nāga››.

22. Mahāvighneśvara with a rope. R.h. hook, mudrā of piercing (?), l.h. noose, mudrā.
See 92, 183, Sarma 11a braḥ mhāvikghīneTr' Tăt hmāt II ‹‹Mahāvighneśvara piercing with an awl (?)››.

23. Mahāvighneśvara on a rat. R.h. hook, tusk, l.h. hammer, noose.
See 100, 184, Sarma 10b braḥ mhā vikghineŤr Prāp asrbhăṅghī II ‹‹B. Mahāvighneśvara subjugating asura Bhaṅgin (?)››.

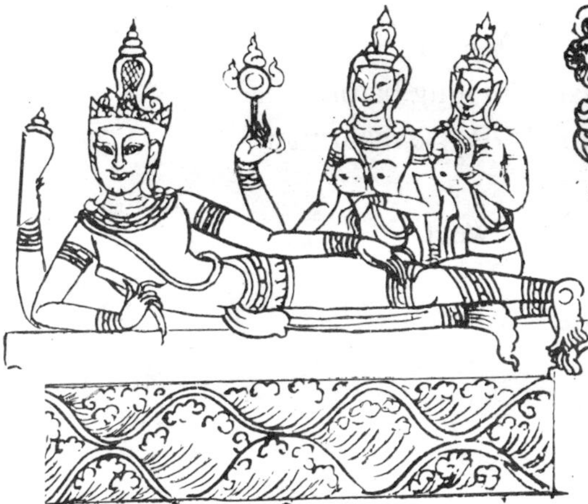

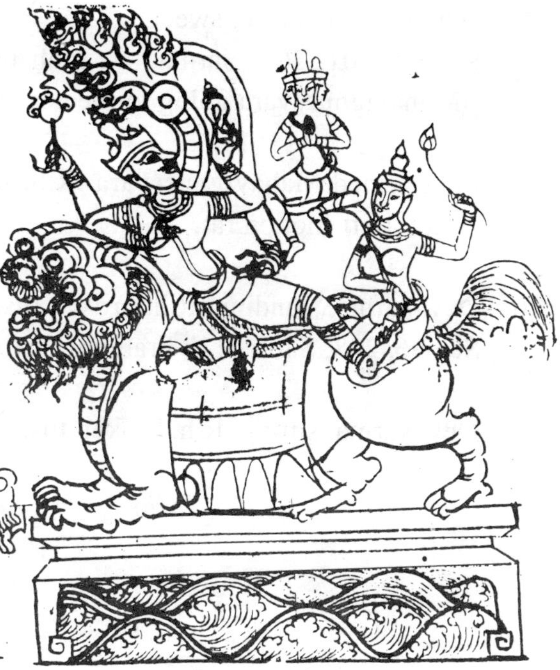

๑ พระเกภยบันทมสินในะทะคิลสะมุทร ๑ะะ

๑ พระนารายบันทมบนหลังนาค ะกะ๓

๑ พระมหาวิกฆเนศร์คงบาท ระ๓

๑ พระมหาวิกฆเนศรเปปกษสุระพงฆิกผมุลิกะกะนุะนะ๕

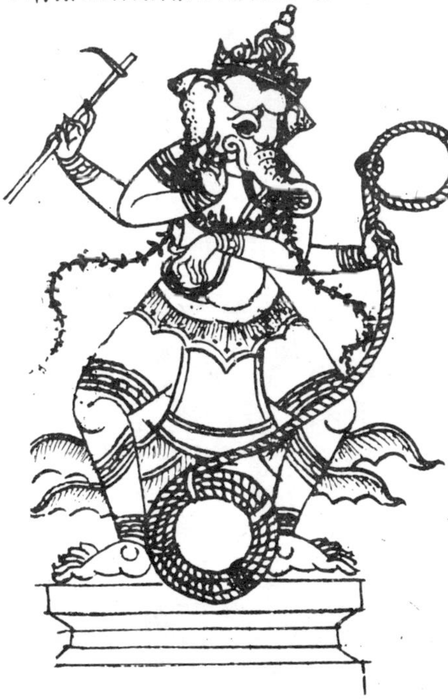

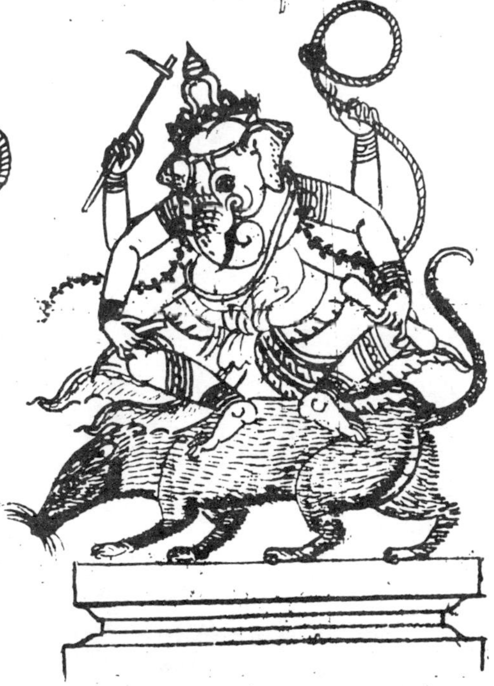

๑ พระมหาวิกฆเนศรไปกระเสียนสะมุท กะ

พระวิกฆเนศร์ ะกะการะนะ

24. Four-armed Mahāvighneśvara going to the ocean on a tortoise. R.h. hook, broken tusk, l.h. noose, sweet.
See 93, 101, 206, Sarma 10a braḥ maḥhāvikghīneTr Paï kraḥśeiyr smud ‖ ‹‹Mahāvighneśvara going to the ocean››.

25. Four-armed Mahāvighneśvara. R.h. hammer, broken tusk, l.h. flaming disk, sweet. Left foot on rat.

26. Devakarma, standing. R.h. broken tusk, l.h. long baton.
See 96, 208, Sarma 11b braḥ devkarm' ‖ ‹‹B. Devakarman››

27. Devakarma, sitting. R.h. broken tusk, l.h. sweet.

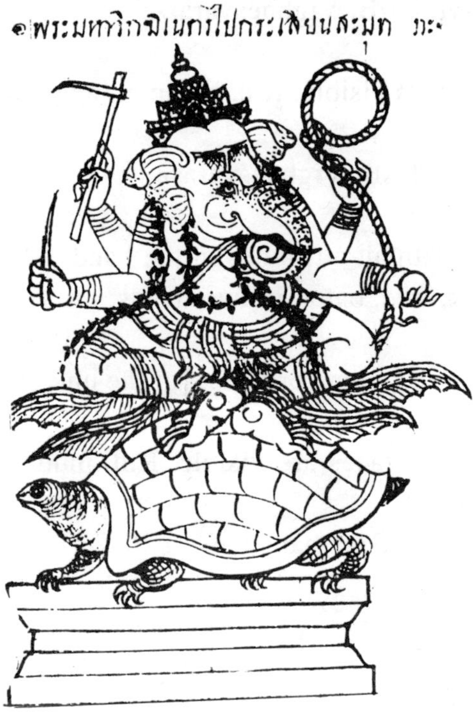
๏ พระมหาวิกฆเนศไปกระเสียนสะมุท ทะ

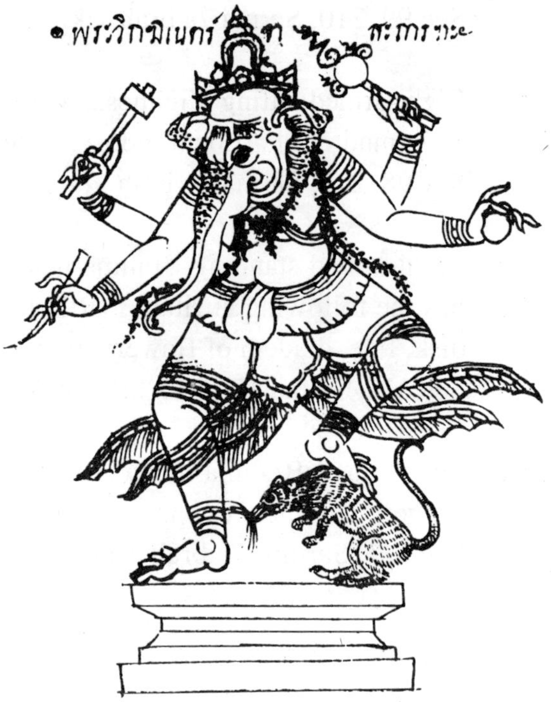
๏ พระวิกฆเนศ

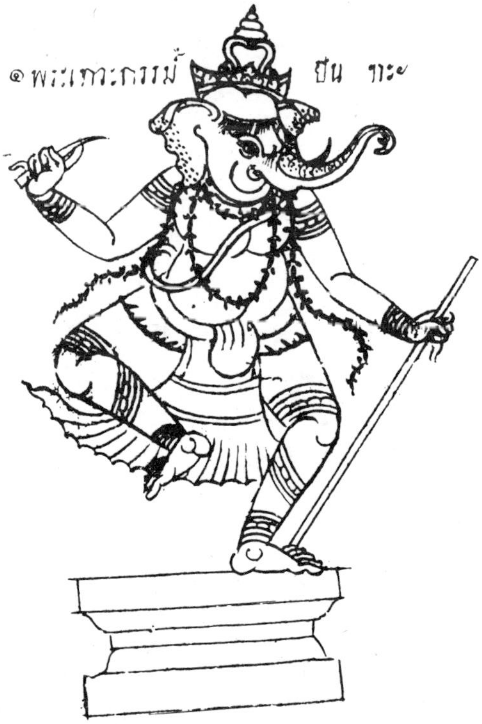
๏ พระเกาะกรรม ยืน ทะ

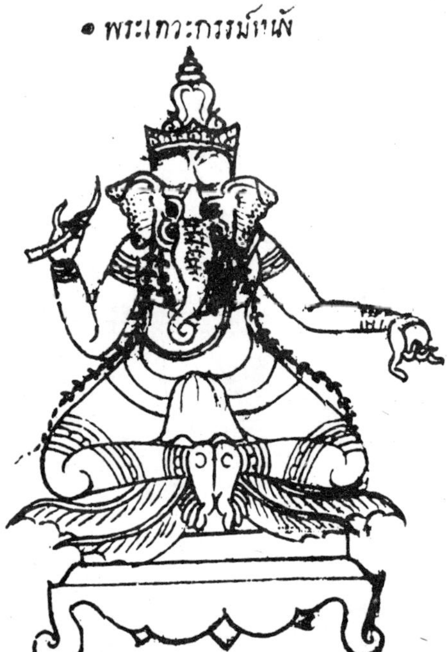
๏ พระเกาะกรรมหนัง

28. Eight-armed standing Vighneśa. Three heads visible. R.h. elephant-hook, axe, knocker, broken tusk, l.h. hammer, trident, flaming disk, conch.
See 99, 210, Sarma 7a braḥ vikghineśvr ‖ ‹‹B. Vighneśvara››.

29. Eight-armed sitting Vighneśa. Three heads visible. R.h. hammer, axe, broken tusk, mudrā, l.h. trident, noose, conch, —.
See 98, 211, Sarma 7b braḥ vigghinīśvr ‖ ‹‹B. Vighneśvara››.

30. Eight-armed standing Brahmā Dhātā (without attributes in the hands). Sarma has the following attributes: R.h. book, free, baton in two hands, l.h. flaming disk, free, diadem of flowers, free.
See 212, Sarma 37b braḥ brhm dhātā | ‹‹Brahman ordainer [of the universe]››.

31. Four-armed Brahma-nātha, sitting. Three faces are visible. R.h. mudrā, l.h. flowering branch, two hands in mudrā.
See 111, Sarma 27a braḥ brhm nārth | ‹‹B. Brahmanātha››.

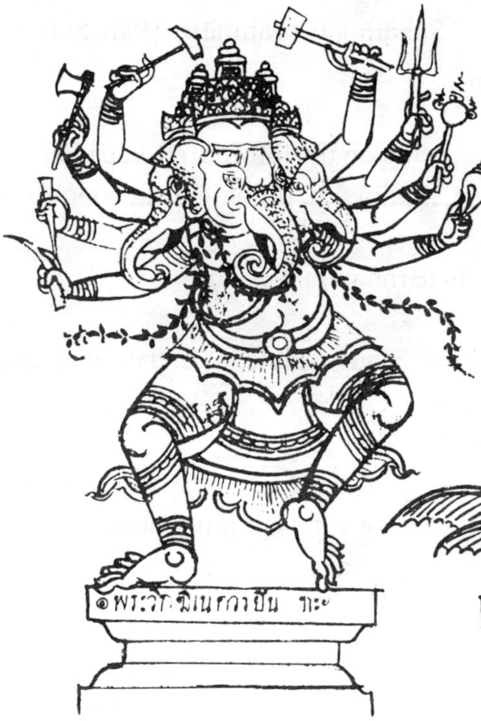
๏พระวิฆเนศวรยืน

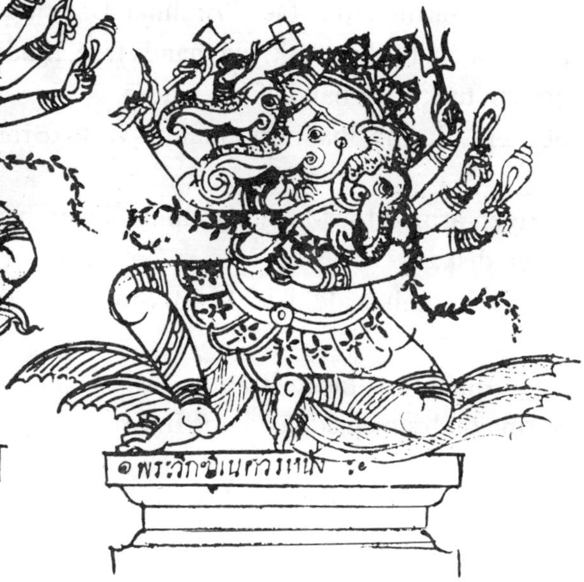

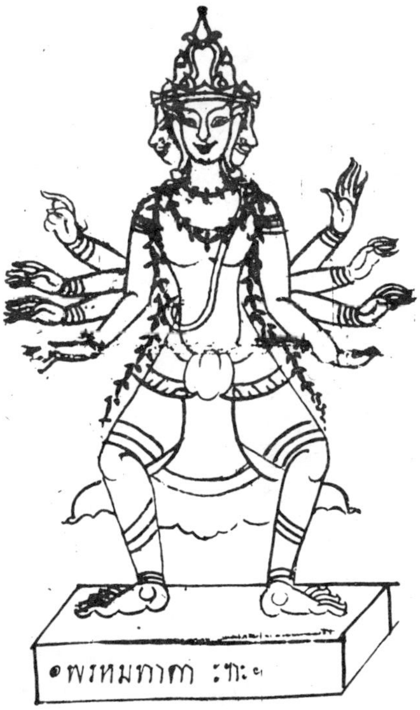
๏พรหมทาศ

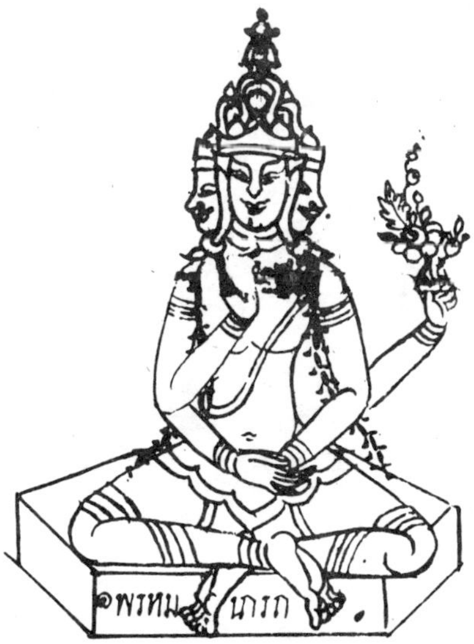

32. Eight-armed four-faced Brahmā sahāṁpati. Standing, eight legs. R.h. trident, hammer, —, trident, l.h. flaming disk, conch, circle, mudrā.
Sarma 37a braḥ saḥhaḥptībrhm | ‹‹B. Sahāṁpati brahmā››. [Pāli Sahampati brahmā].

33. Fourteen-armed four-faced Brahmā. Dancing on the left foot. R.h. trident, hammer, conch, broken tusk, two hands free, mudrā, l.h. flaming disk, conch, circle, broken tusk, two hands free, mudrā.
See 215, Sarma 36a. brhm maḥheśvr | ‹‹Brahmamaheśvara››.

34. Sixteen-armed four-faced Brahmā. Seven heads visible. R.h. hare in each, l.h. triple disk.
Sarma 6a braḥ śrrddhisid || ‹‹B. Śraddhāsiddha (?)››.

35. Ten-armed four-faced Brahmā. All the ten arms have a lotus-bud.
Sarma 6b braḥ śrrddhāsid || ‹‹B. Śraddhāsiddha››.

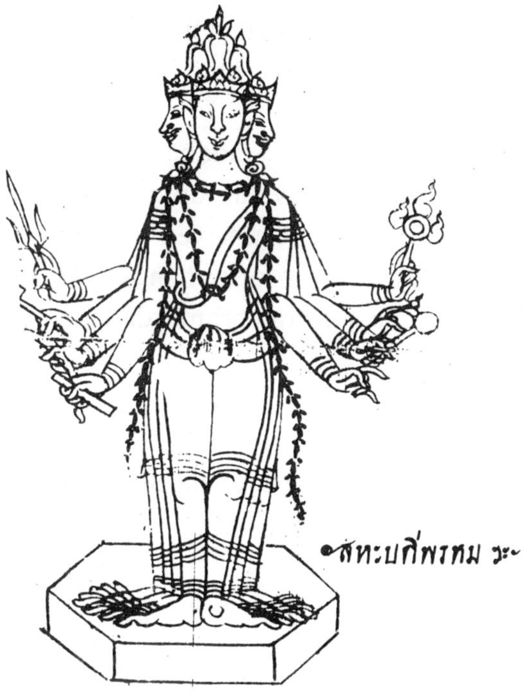
สหะบดีพรหม

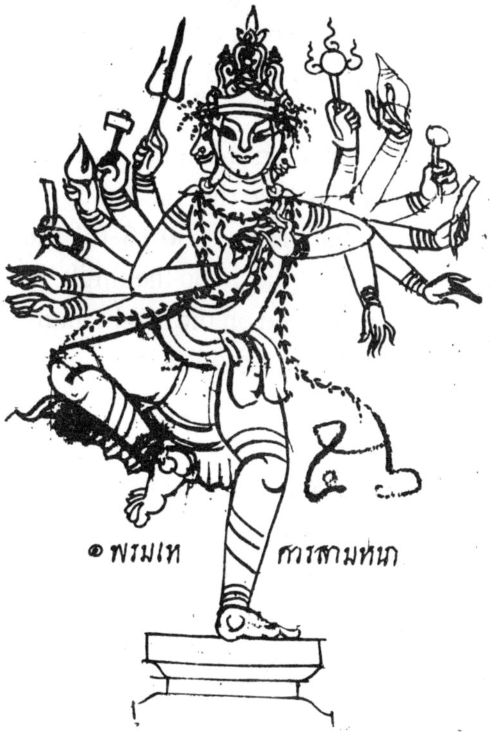
พรมเท

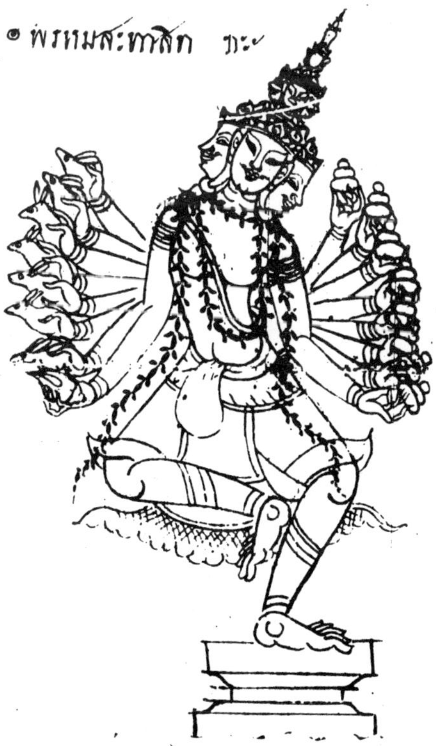
พรหมสะหาสิก

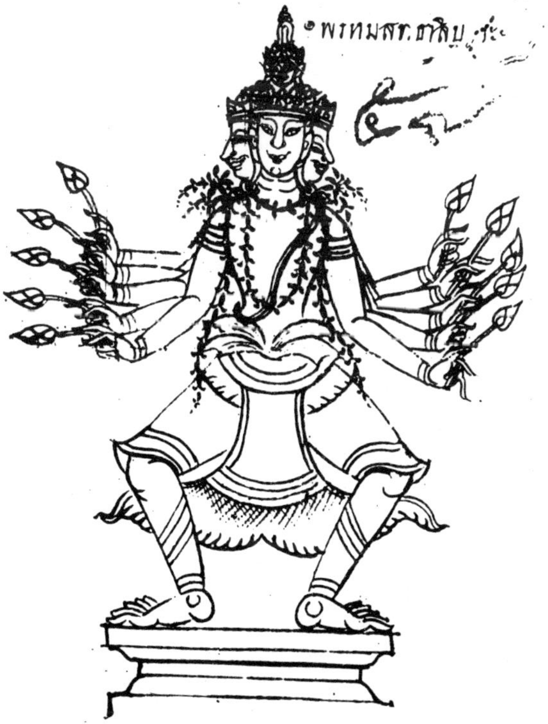

36. Twentyfour-armed eight-faced Brahmā śraddhādeva. R.h. trident, hammer, disk, short baton, other hands have no attributes, l.h. flaming disk, conch, hammer(?), short baton, broken tusk, other hands are without symbols.
Cf. 107, 218, Sarma 34b braḥ brhm' sddhādib I ‹‹B. Brahmā Śraddhādeva››.

37. Twenty-armed eight-faced Brahmā śraddhādeva. Śraddhādeva = Manu Vaivasvata the husband of Śraddhā in the Bhāgavata-purāṇa 9.1.11. See Mahābhārata 1.60.13 for the husband of Śraddhā. R.h. seven hold the bow, mudrā, placed on the thigh, mudrā. L.h. hold the arrow, three hands hang down, one placed on the thigh, mudrā. See 219, Sarma 34a braḥ brhmăsddhādeb I ‹‹B. Brahman Śraddhādeva››.

38. Nārāyaṇa on a lion, with Bhūdevī and Śrīdevī.
Cf. 181, Sarma 24 braḥ nrāyn' drṅ siṅhbhāhn' I ‹‹B. Nārāyaṇa siṁhavāhana››.

39. Six-finger deity.

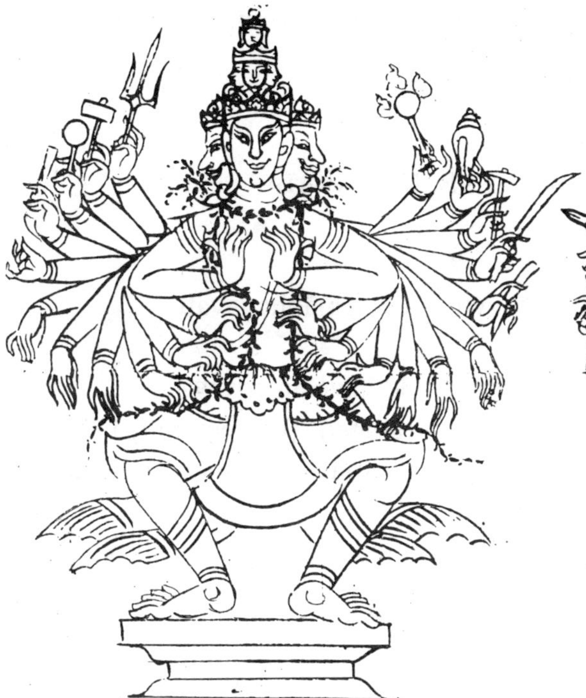

๑ พรหมสกตาทิพ ฯะ

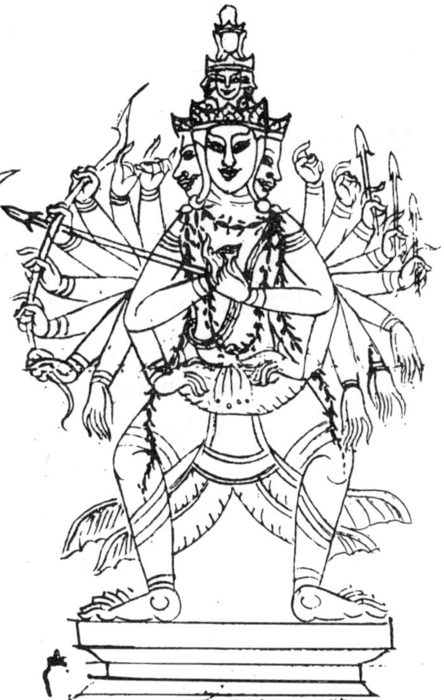

๑ พรหมสกตาเทพ ะฯะ

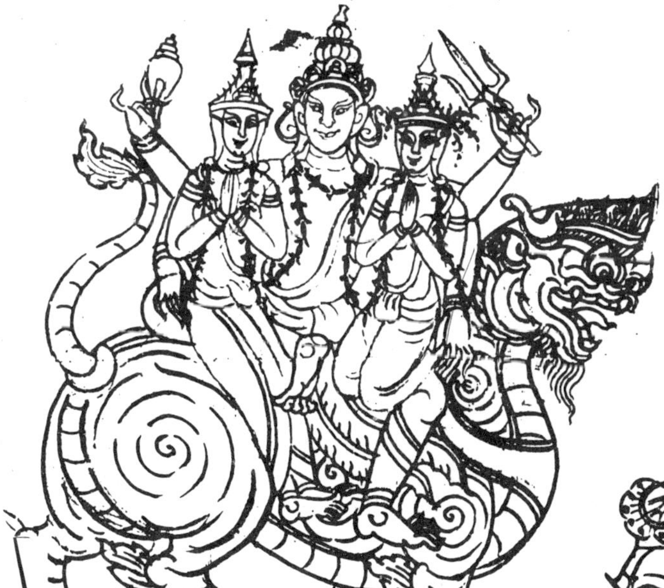

๑ พระเภกายทรงสิงคภาหะณะ

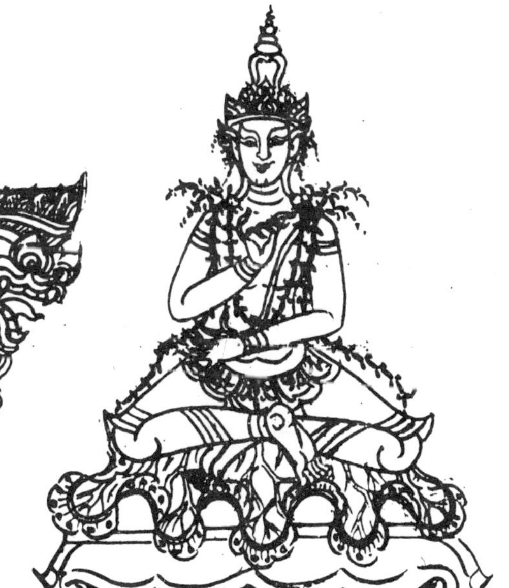

๑ พระชาแมมมีจตุสิละหกบ่วาทะ

40. Lakṣmī, holding a lotus-bud in the left hand.
See 220, Sarma 23a braḥ lakmī gōēa aṅg śītā I ‹‹B. Lakṣmī under the form of Sītā››.

41. Maheśvarī.
See 221, Sarma 23b braḥ mheśvārīy' I ‹‹B. Maheśvarī››.

42. Umā bhagavatī.
See 126, 222, Sarma 23c braḥ umābhgvtī I ‹‹B. Umābhagavatī››.

43. Īśvara. Right hand holds a bow, the left should have an arrow.
See 241, Sarma 38a rāmāvaḥTāl gōēa braḥ rāmbed' [correct *deb*] Prāb nāsūr nāi rāmkieryTi' I ‹‹Rāmāvatāra. He is Rāmadeva who vanquishes the asura Rāvaṇa in the Rāmakīrti››.

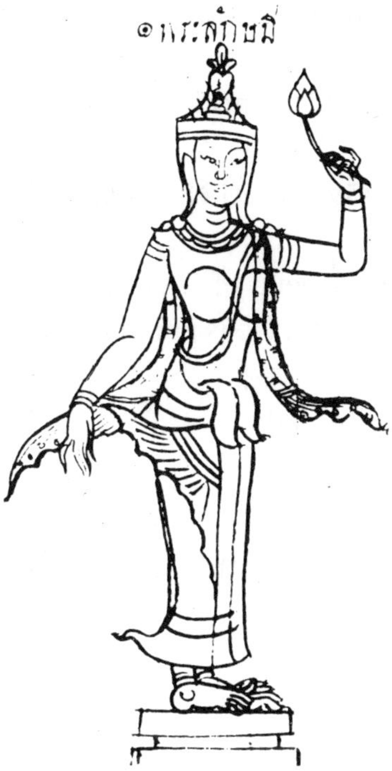
๑ พระลักษมี

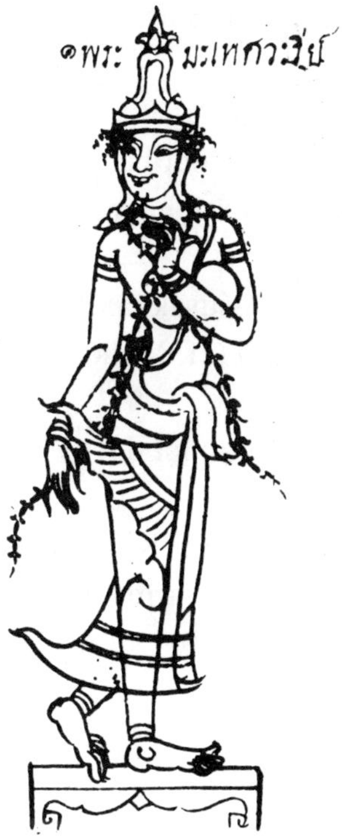

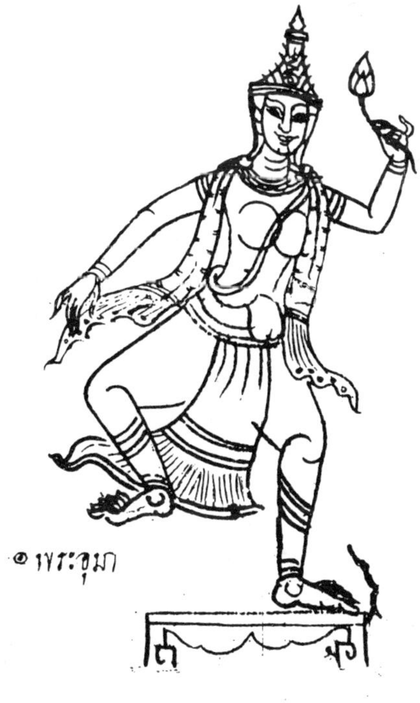
๑ พระอุมา

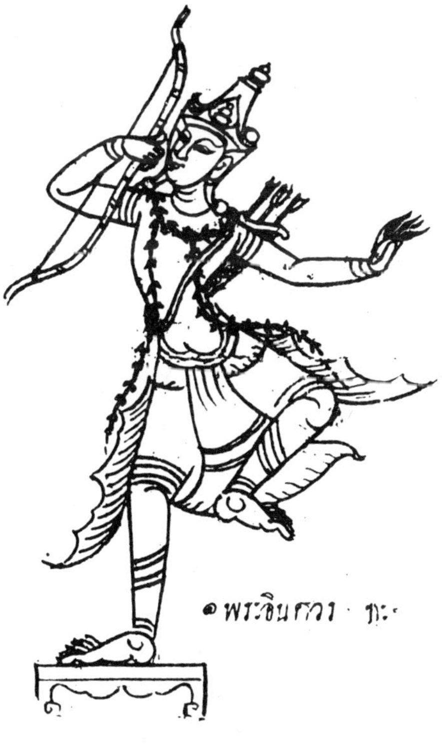

44. Siddhikarma. Two deities sitting in salutation, superposed in the interlàce of serpents.
See 109, 224, Sarma 33 braḥ debkrrm' Praḥ siddhi I ‹‹B. Devakarmasiddhi››.

45. Six-armed Nārāyaṇa devakarma. Four hands hold the neck and tails of the nāga and the two front hands are in mudrā.
Sarma 32a braḥ naḥrāyn' nndukkh I ‹‹B. Nārāyaṇa [et] Nandukkha (?)››.

46. Ṛṣi Deva Paśusakha. Paśusakha is the śūdra husband of Gaṇḍā, the servant of the seven ṛṣi (cf. Mahābhārata 93.22, 51, 104, 135). He is popular in South-east Asia.
Sarma 3b braḥ ṛṣī devpś II ‹‹B. ṛṣi Devapaś[usakha]››.

47. Ṛṣi Kalaikkōṭṭu (K. is Tamil for Ṛṣyaśṛṅga).
See 137, 161, Sarma 2b braḥ ṛṣī kaḥlaiykoṭ II ‹‹B. ṛṣi Kalaikkōṭṭu››.

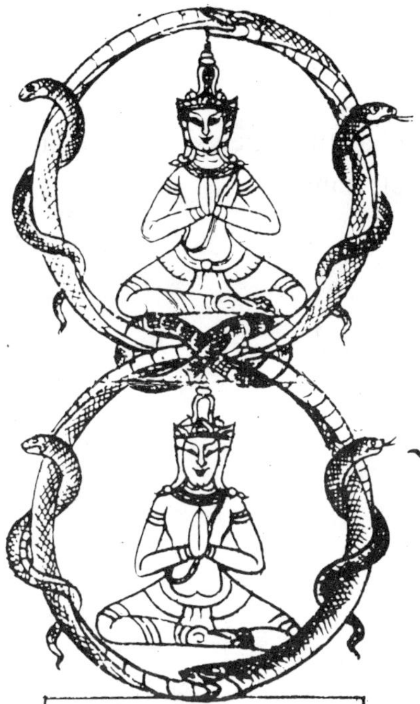

๏พระสิทธิกรรม ทะ๑

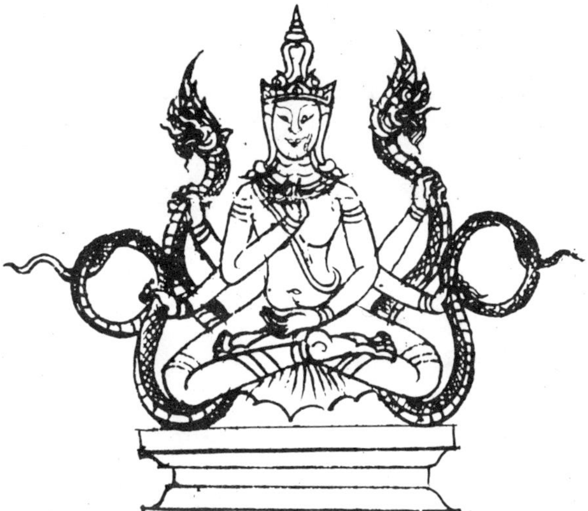

๏พระนภายเทพกรรม ะ๒

๏ ฤๅษีเทวะยักษ์ ทะ

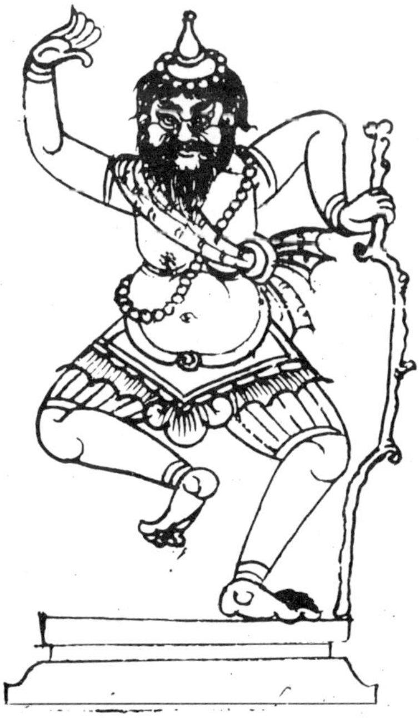

๏ ฤๅษีกะไลยโกฎ ทะ๑

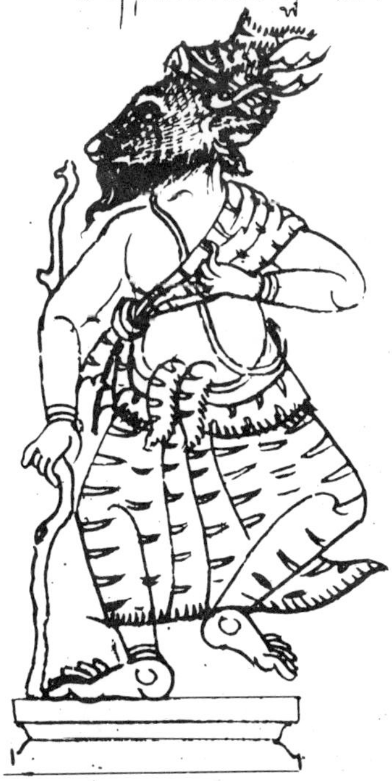

48. Ṛṣi with a fan.

49. Ṛṣi with a fan.

50. Six-armed Vighneśvara.
Sarma 12b terms it Kauñjarānaneśvara. He has three heads. R.h. elephant with 36 heads, elephant, conch. So also in the left hands.

51. Śivaputra. R.h. trident, l.h. flower.

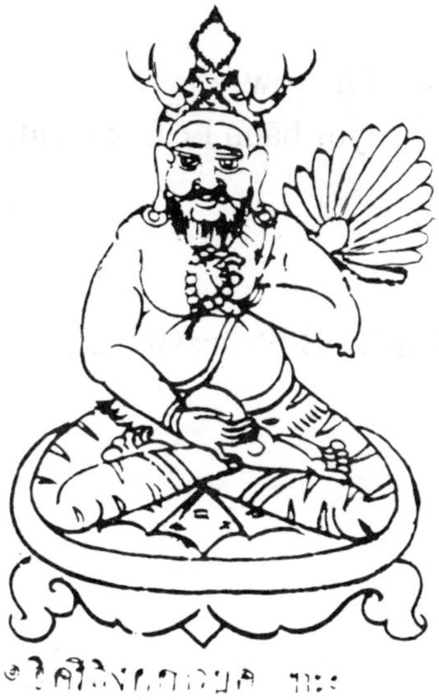

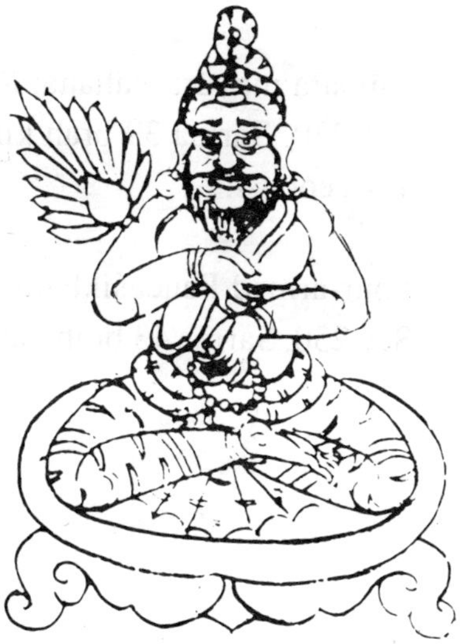

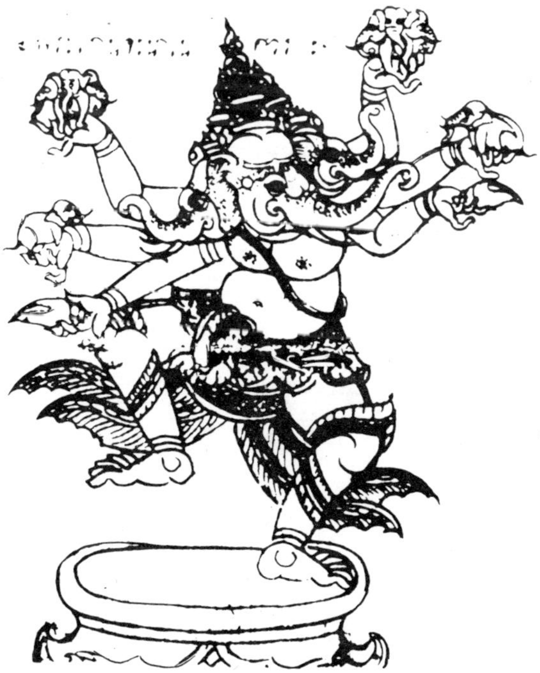

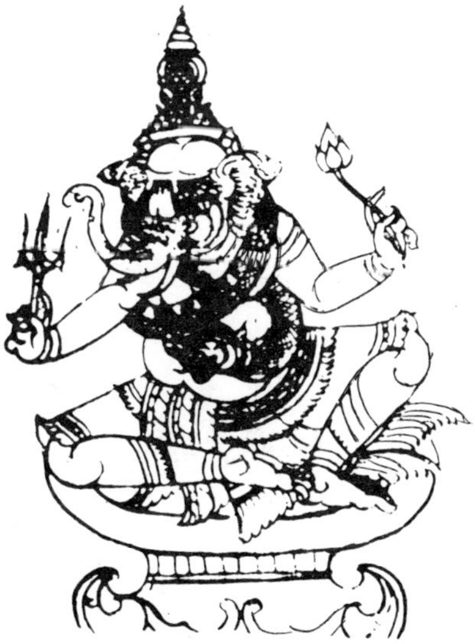

50. Six-armed Vighneśvara.
Sarma 12b terms it Kauñjarānaneśvara. He has three heads. R.h. elephant with 36 heads, elephant, conch. So also in the left hands.

51. Śivaputra. R.h. trident, l.h. flower.

48. Kūmara mayūra-vāhana. R.h. holds arrows, l.h. bow.
See 230, Sarma 39 braḥ khăndhkumār drṅ myur bāhṇ I ‹‹B. Skandakumāra on a peacock››.

49. Four-armed Pancaśikhara playing vīṇā.
See 230, Sarma 43 braḥ Pāñcaḥśiṅkhartīt biṇ I ‹‹B. Pañcaśikhara playing vīṇā››.

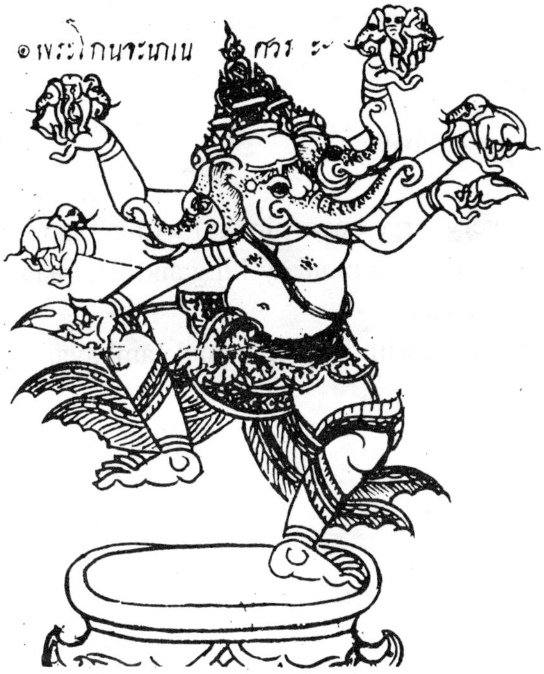

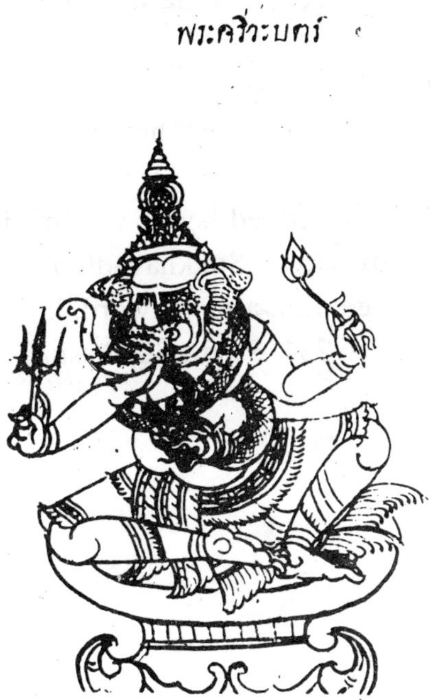

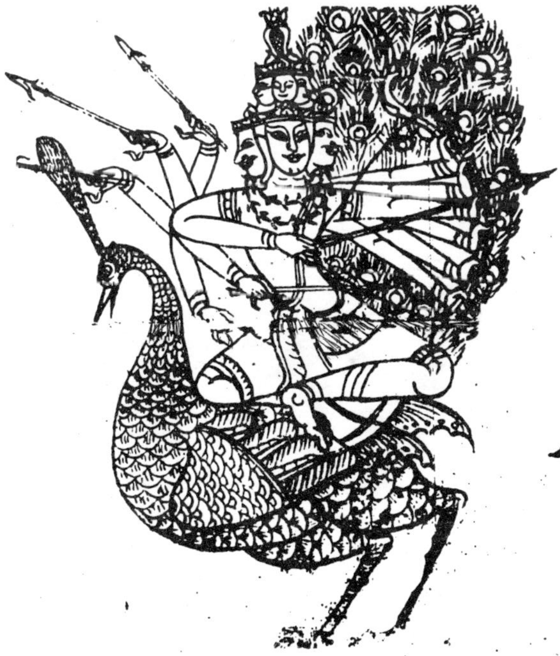

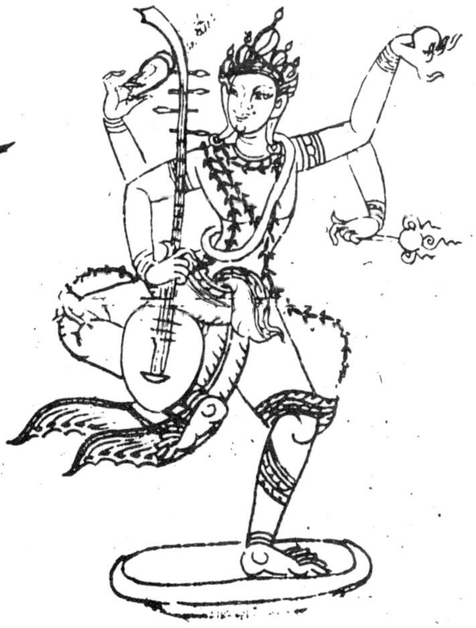

50. Eight-armed Īśvara becomes lord of the world after killing the yakṣa Kuṅkha (?).
See 102, 232, Sarma 46 braḥ iśvr I ‹‹B. Īśvara››.

51. Jāmbavant.
Sarma 42b jambhūvaḥrāj I ‹‹king Jāmbavant››.

52. Four-armed Īśvara who made a very large bow (pināka) with a bamboo given by ascetic Sukkhavaḍh. He is flanked by a monkey-king and a human personage. R.h. arrow, sword, l.h. bow, shield.
See 234, Sarma 30. Assimilates Rāma with Hanumān and Jāmbavant.

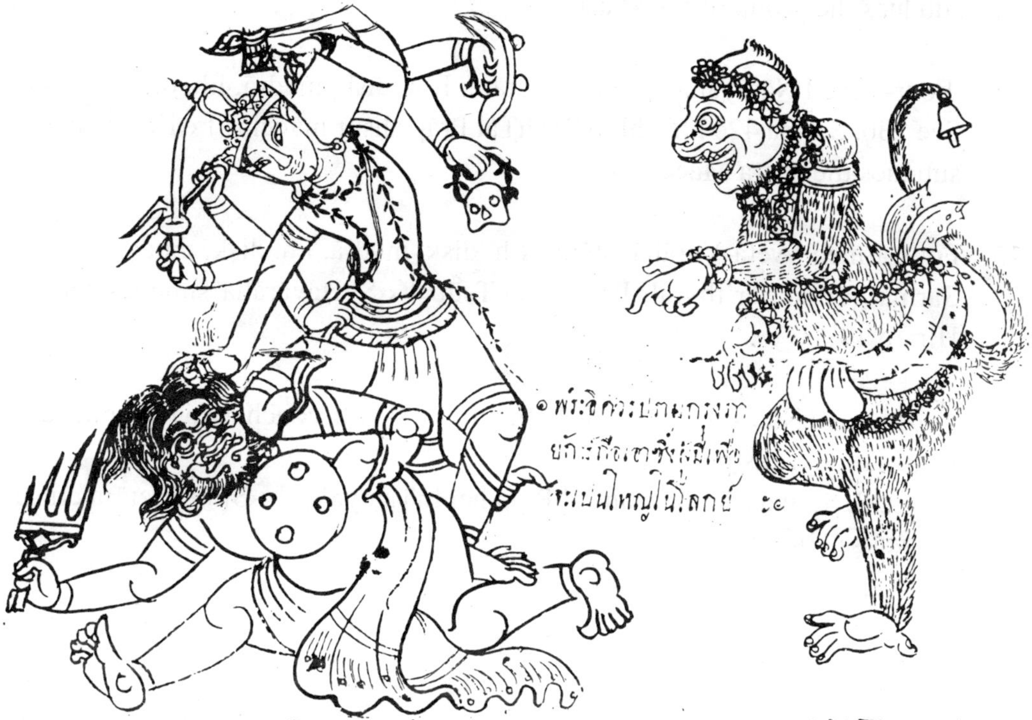

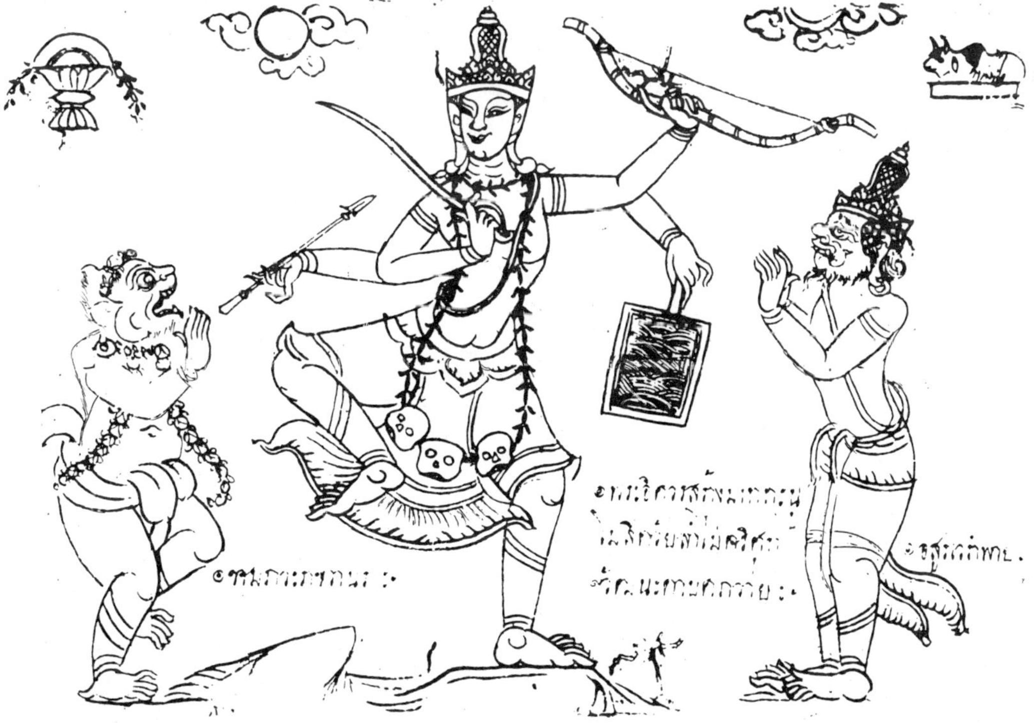

53. Four-armed Nārāyaṇa Matsyāvatāra. R.h. disk, mudrā, l.h. disk, mudrā. See 235, Sarma 42a măcchāaḥvaḥTāl Prāp hmū[1] sănkhaḥsūr | ‹‹Matsyāvatāra subdues the group of Śaṅkhāsura››.

54. Four-armed Nārāyaṇa Kacchapāvatāra. R.h. disk, mudrā, l.h. disk, mudrā. See 236, Sarma 42c khăchhjpā'vaḥTāl Prāp aḥsūr măcchā | ‹‹Kacchapāvatāra subdues the asura Maccha››.

55. Four-armed Śveta-Varāhāvatāra. R.h. disk, mudrā, l.h. disk, mudrā. Sarma 41b sveTr'thvrāh Prāp hiranTsūr | ‹‹Śvetavarāha subdues the asura Hiraṇya››.

56. Four-armed Narasiṁāvatāra. R.h. flaming disk, l.h. conch, two lower hands tear apart Hiraṇyakaśipu.
See 238, Sarma 31 siṅh'vaḥTāl Prāp herănTaḥ yăkṣ | ‹‹Siṃhāvatāra crushing the yakṣa Hiraṇya››.

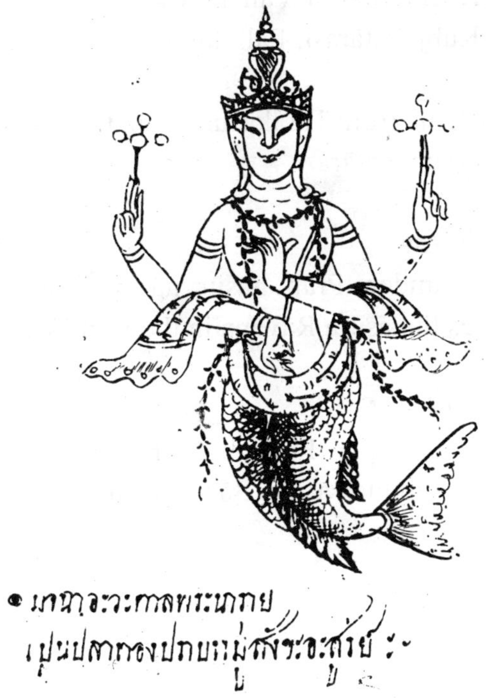

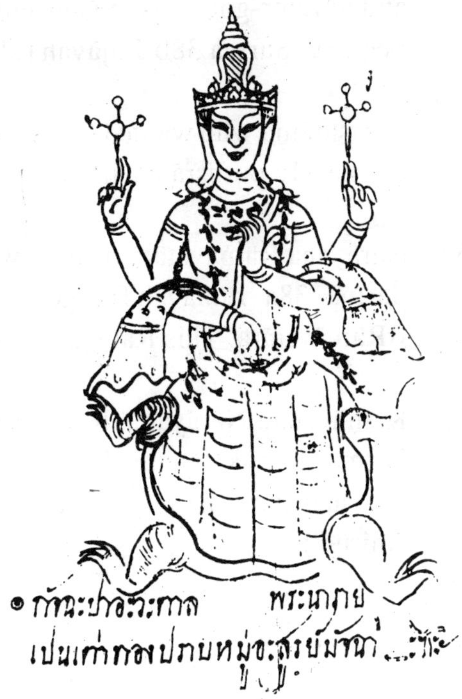

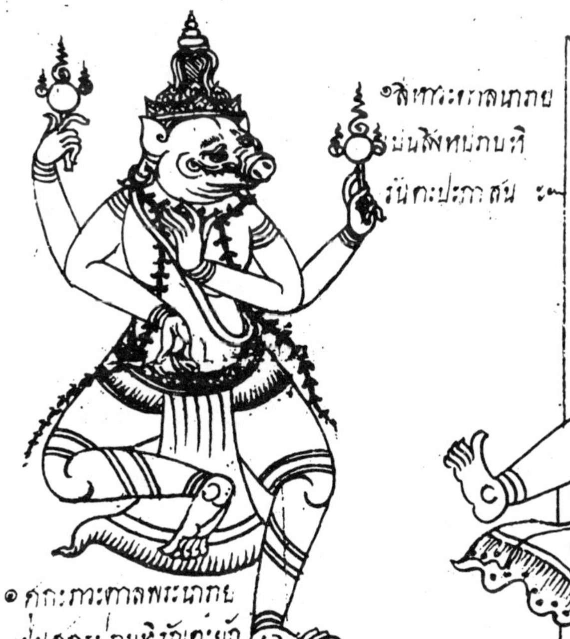

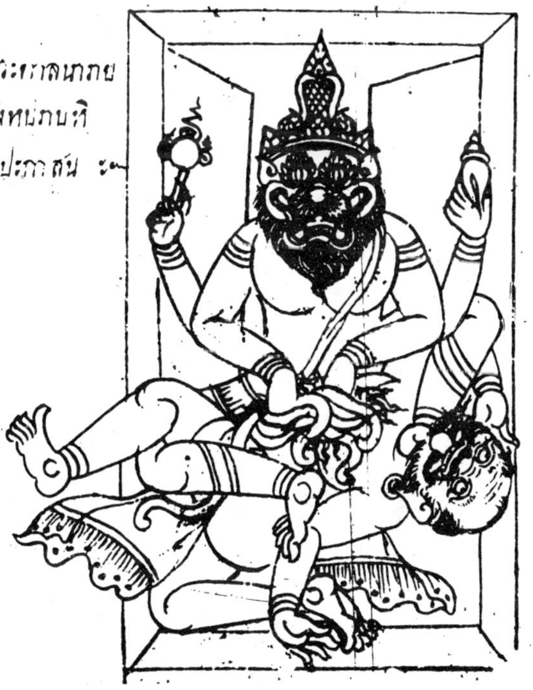

57. Kubjāvatāra Nārāyaṇa, who conquered Tāravān Brāhmaṇa carrying a parasol and a water-gourd, is the current representation of Vāmanāvatāra.
See 239, Sarma 38b JujjāvaḥTāl I ‹‹Kubjāvatāra››. Pāli kujja

58. Paraśurāma who wanted to take away Umā from Tārakāsura. R.h. free, l.h. axe.
Sarma 41c puruṣrāmāaḥTāl I ‹‹Paraśurāmāvatāra››.

59. Nārāyaṇa Rāmāvatāra. R.h. bow, l.h. arrow.
Sarma 38a rāmāvaḥTāl gōēa braḥ rāmdeb Prāb nāsūr năi rāmkieryTi' I ‹‹Rāmāvatāra. This Rāmadeva subdues the asura Rāvaṇa in the Rāmakīrti››.

60. Kṛṣṇāvatāra Nārāyaṇa. R.h. free, l.h. disk.
Sarma 38c kiśaḥṇuvaḥTāl gōēa prmcăk-ṛṣṇ Prāp bnāsūr naï anirud I ‹‹Kṛṣṇāvatāra; he is Paramakṛṣṇa who subdues asura Bāṇa in [the legend of] Aniruddha››.

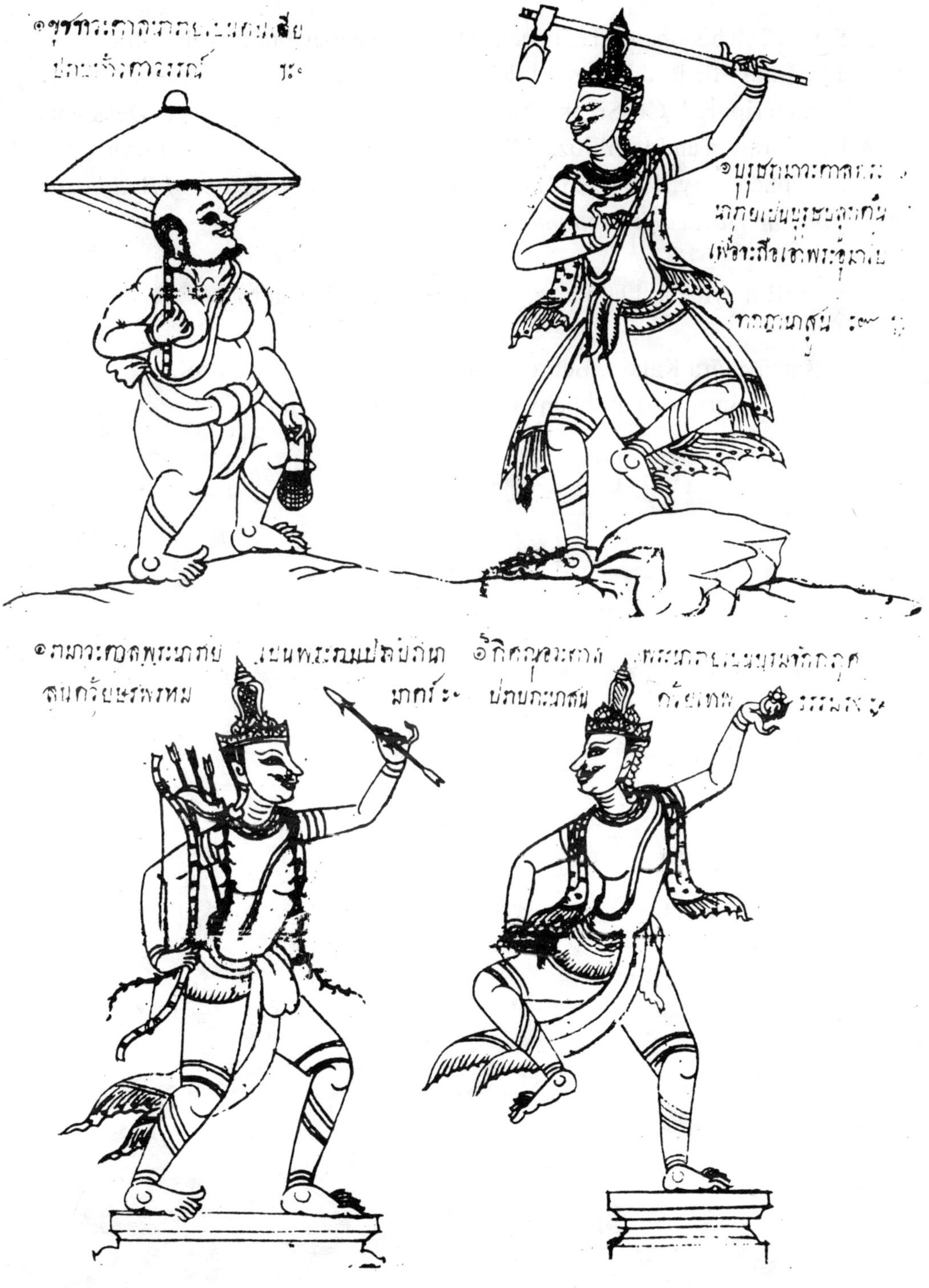

๏ พุทธวระกาลพระนารายเปนพระเจ้าฯ

61. Four-armed Buddhāvatāra Nārāyaṇa. R.h. circle, l.h. flower, two main hands open.
Sarma 28b buddhāvaḥTāḷ boeca caḥ thōēa au joeṅ braḥ śivaḥ limṅg' Taiaḥsūrah Trīpūrāṁ "B. Buddhāvatāra destined to regain the śivaliṅga carried away by asura Tripura." Cf. Śivapurāṇa 2/5.4-5, Kāñcīpurāṇa 30 (R. Dessigane, P.Z. Pattabiramin and J. Filliozat, *Les légendes çivaïtes de Kāñcipuram*, Publ. IFI n^{0} 27, Pondichéry, 1964, p.37) and R.C. Dvivedi, *The Origin of Buddhism*: *a tale from the Haracaritacintamani*.

62. Śiva. R.h. trident, l.h. noose, two main hands in mudrā.

63. Daśamāvatāra Kalkin. Behind him is a horse with a parasol.
See 245, Sarma 40 dusaḫaḫvaḫTāl I ‹‹tenth avatāra››.

๑ พกธวาะกาลพระนากยเปนพระเศิลาะ
สื่อชาซึ่งพระศรีวะลิงค์แค่ชสูระกรีปก ระ๙

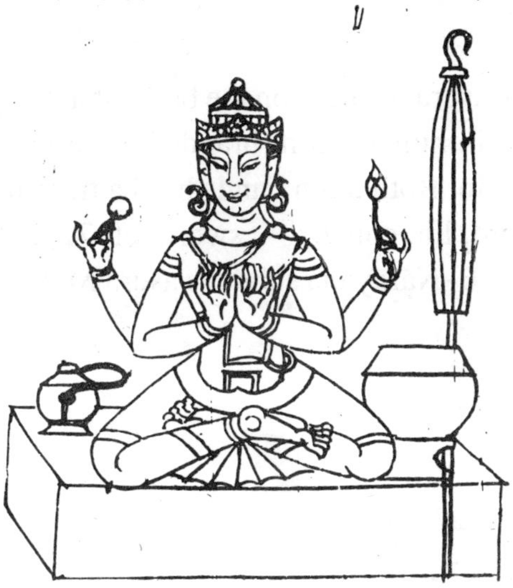

๒ พระศิวา ระ๒

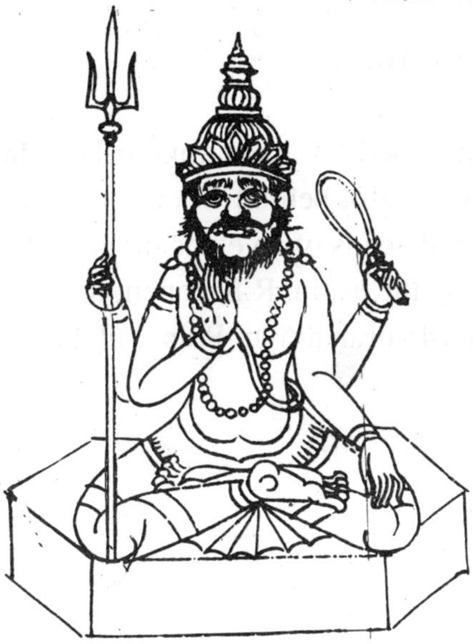

๑ กละกึ่งวะกาลย์ ระ๙

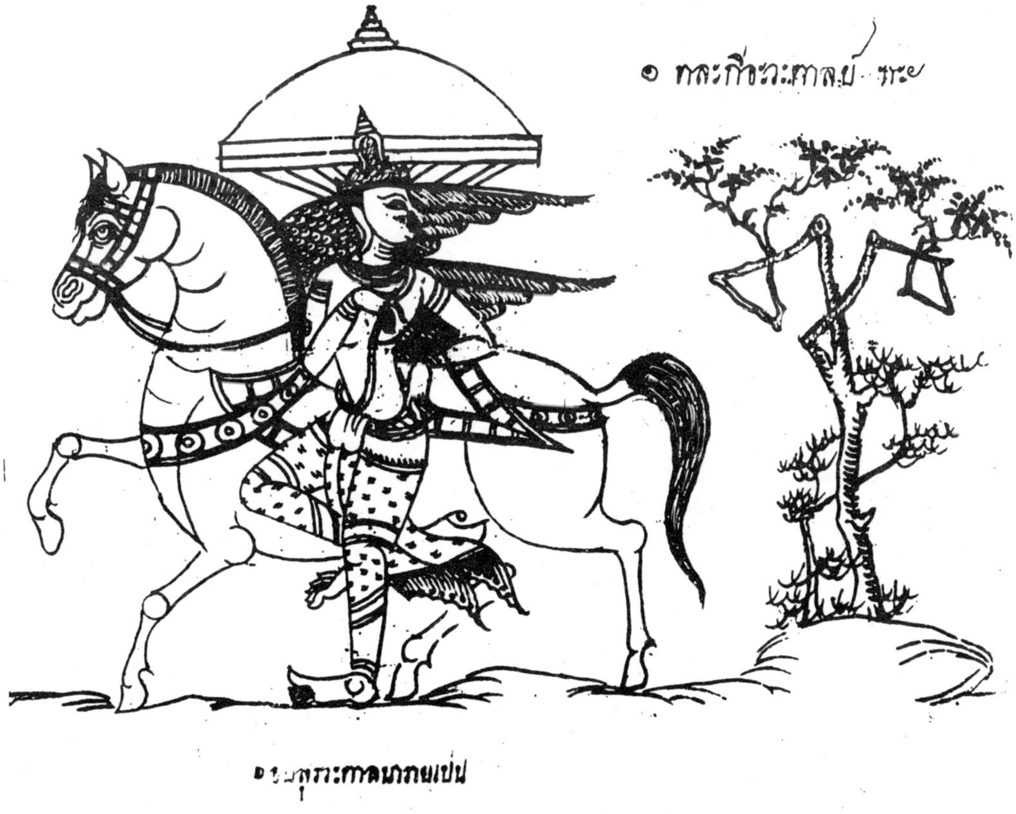

๑ ะ สุระกาลนากยเปน

64. Nārāyaṇa becomes a danceuse to entice Brahmā.
See 122, Sarma 20a braḥ nrāyn' cāp raḥpāṃ ‹‹B. Nārāyaṇa dancing››.

65. Nārāyaṇāvatāra.

66. Eight-armed Nārāyaṇa vanquishes Mahiṣāsura. Dances on the body of a decapitated buffalo, behind whom is a person in human form brandishing a sword. Severed heads of an elephant and a buffalo. Both main hands hold a trident attacking the asura. R.h. conch, disk, sword, l.h. conch, —, sword, cf. 72, 248. Sarma 45 braḥ nrāyn' Prāp asū[r]mhit | ‹‹B. Nārāyaṇa subdues asura Mahiṣa.››

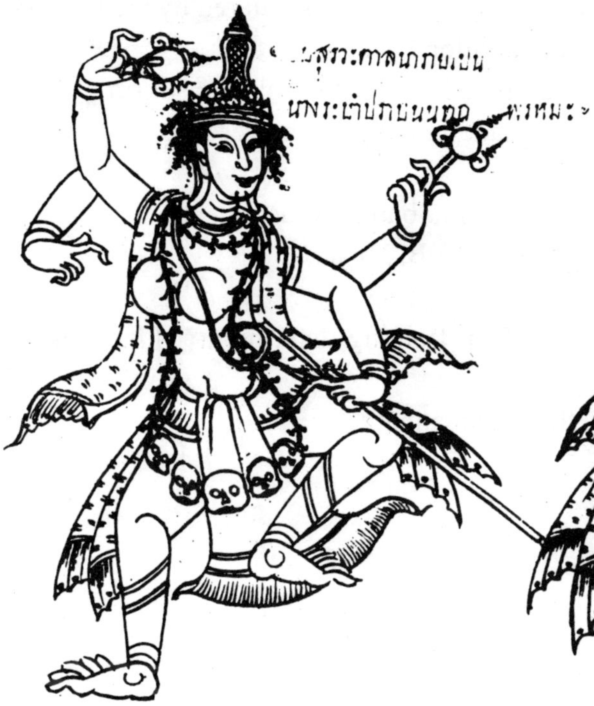

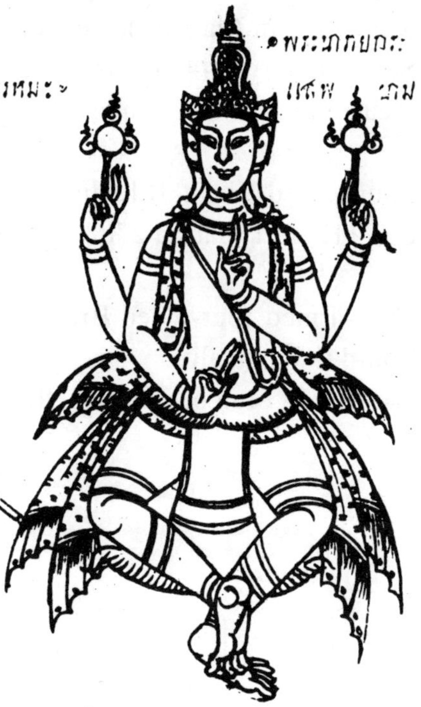

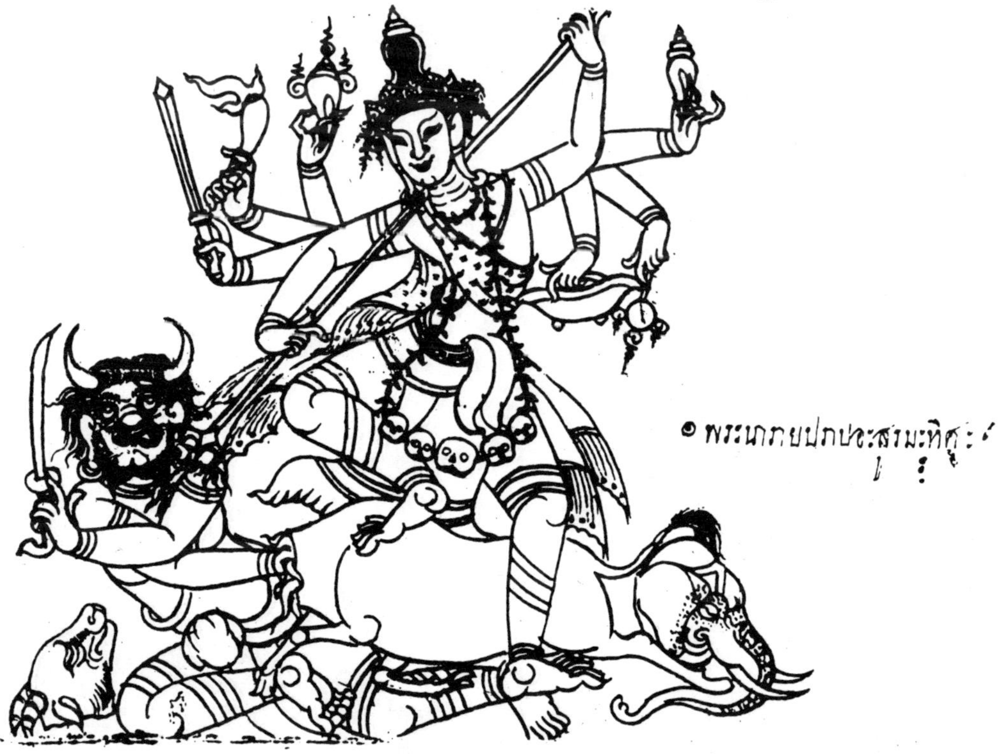

TRIMŪRTI

67. Four-armed Īśvara on Himavān. Seated on a rock sheltered by the tree sukrom. R.h. tambour (ḍamaru), free, l.h. antelope, free.
See 249, Sarma 44 braḥ iśyr srāṅ^{2} braḥ himbān nai rm^{1} maï^{2} sukrm | ‹‹B. Īśvara created the Himavant under the shade of the sukrom tree.”

68. Four-armed Viṣṇu. R.h. disk, conch, l.h. baton, lotus.
See 112, 251, Sarma 27b braḥ visṇu | ‹‹B. Viṣṇu››.

69. Four-armed four-faced Brahmā. R.h. flaming disk, mudrā, l.h. book, water-gourd (kamaṇḍalu).
Sarma 27a braḥ brhm nārth “B. Brahmannātha’.

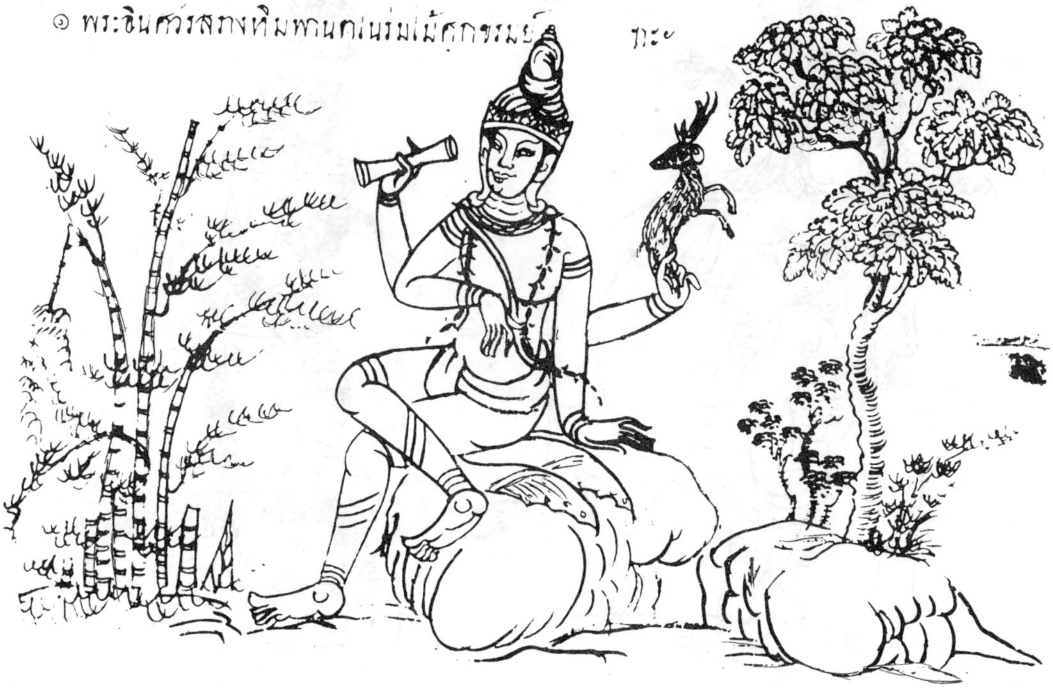
๑ พระอินศวรสกงหิมพานตเนร่มไม้ศุกขรมย์
พระ

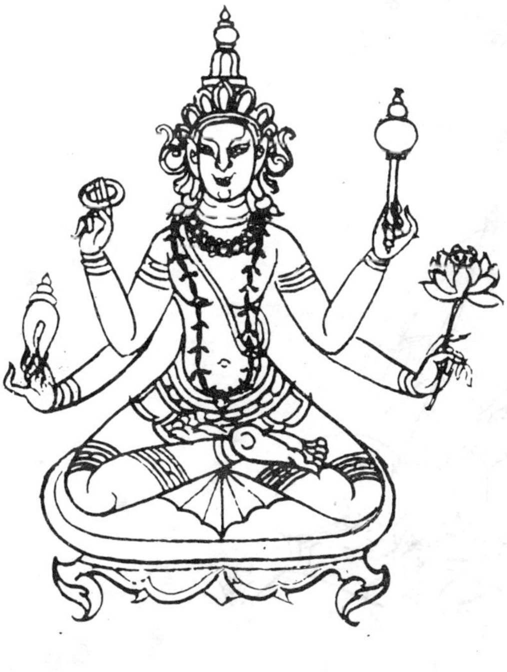

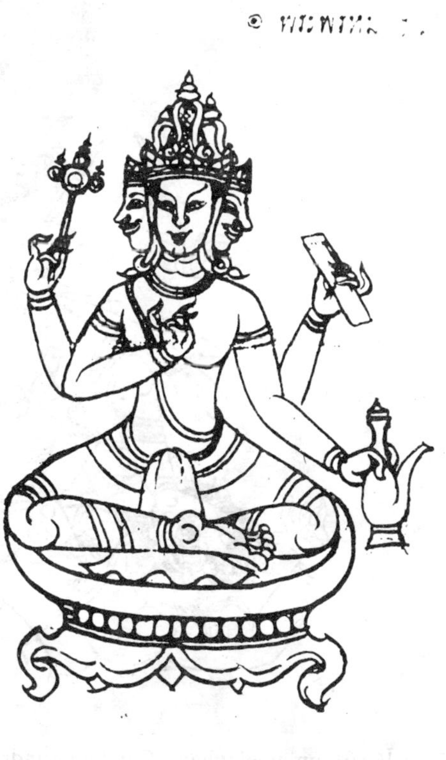
๑ พระพรหม

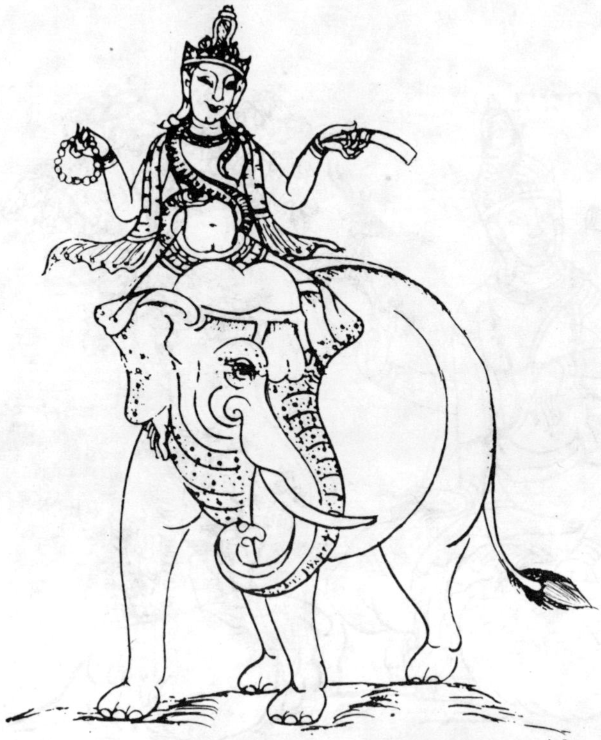

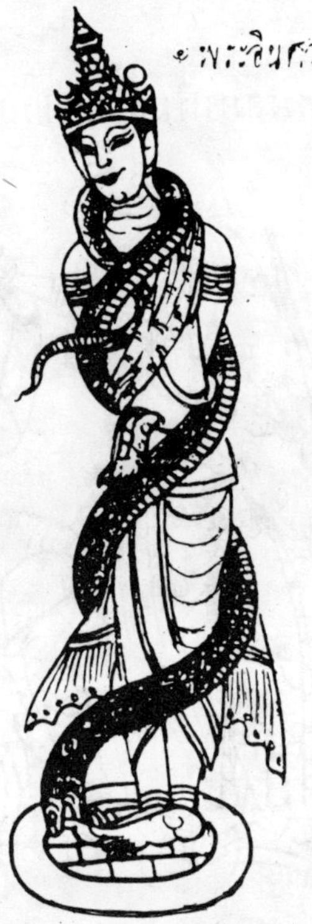

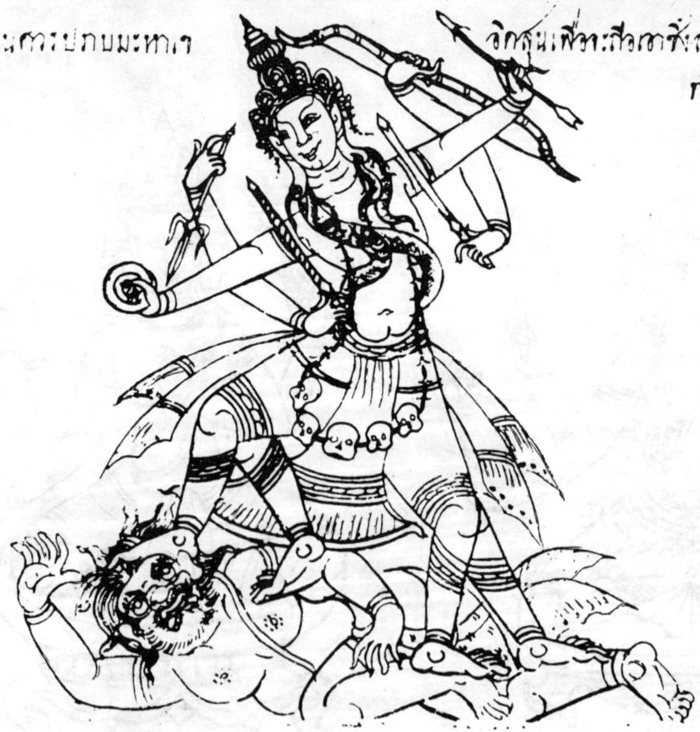

70. Īśvara on an elephant. Can he be Indra?
71. Īśvara entwined by a serpent.
72. Īśvara subdues Mahiṣāsura. R.h. trident, noose, serrated weapon, l.h. bow, arrow, sword. See 255.

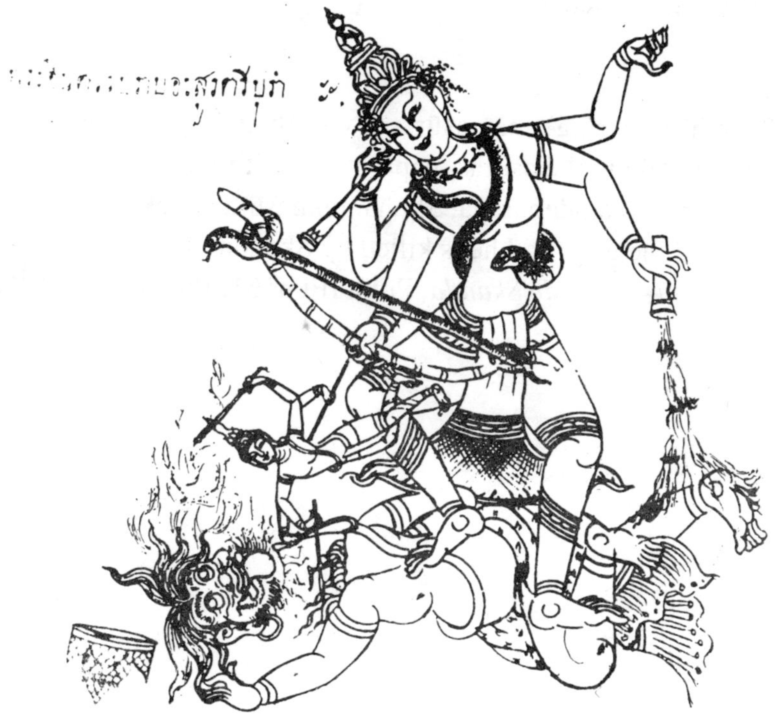

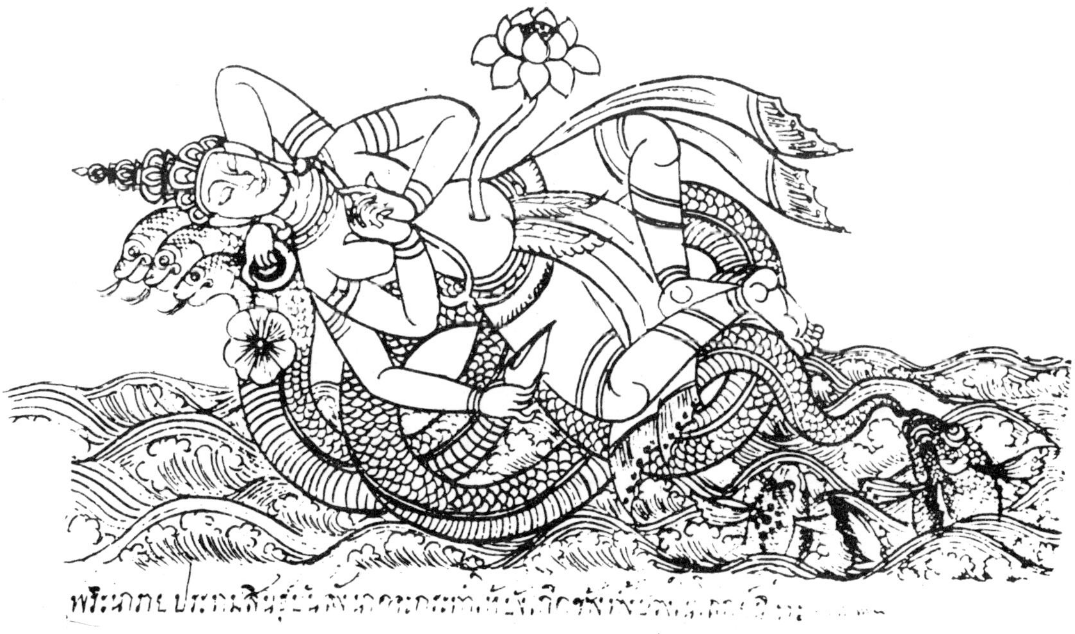

73. Īśvara slaying Tripura asura. Tripurāntaka.
74. Nārāyaṇa lying on nāga with a lotus emerging from the navel.

75. Nārāyaṇa slaying Ekadanta.

76. Drahriṅg.
Sarma 29 braḥ draḥ riṅg' măt asūr săTv' pāb tvy² pvṅ¹ jōēeak pāj | ‹‹B. Drahriṅg' (?) attacking the asuras, pāpasattvas with noose››. According to the southern version of Skandapurāṇa, Siṁhamukhāsura attacks beings having tied up Vīrabāhu and the gods and he is killed by Skanda. (cf. R. Dessigane et P.Z. Pattabiramin, *La légende de Skanda*, Publ. IFI n⁰ 31, Pondichéry, 1967, p.152-157).

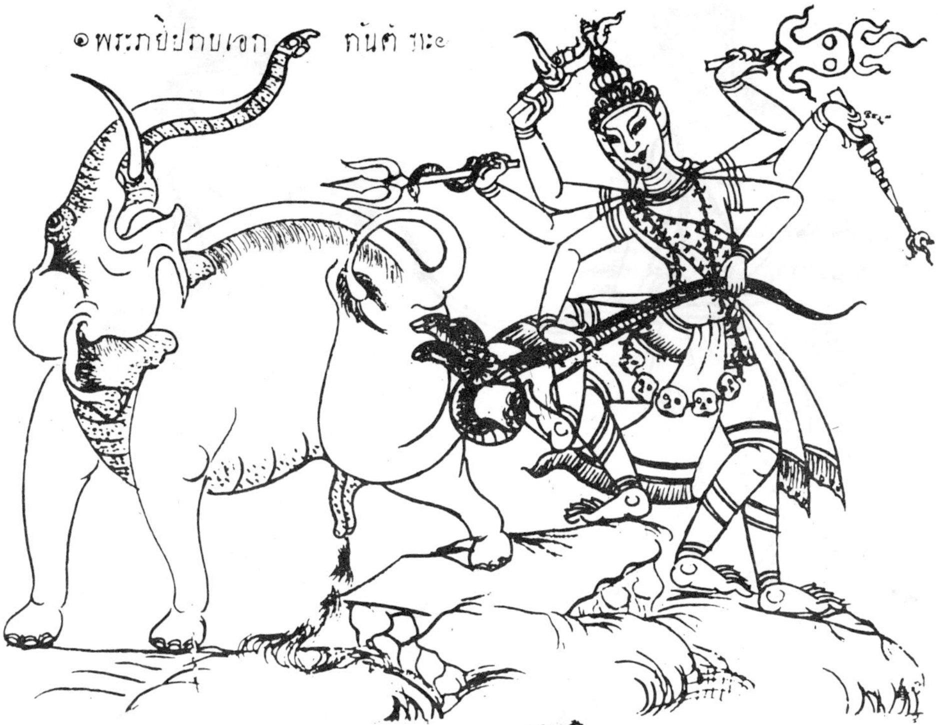
๏ พระภยิ่ปกบเอก กันต์

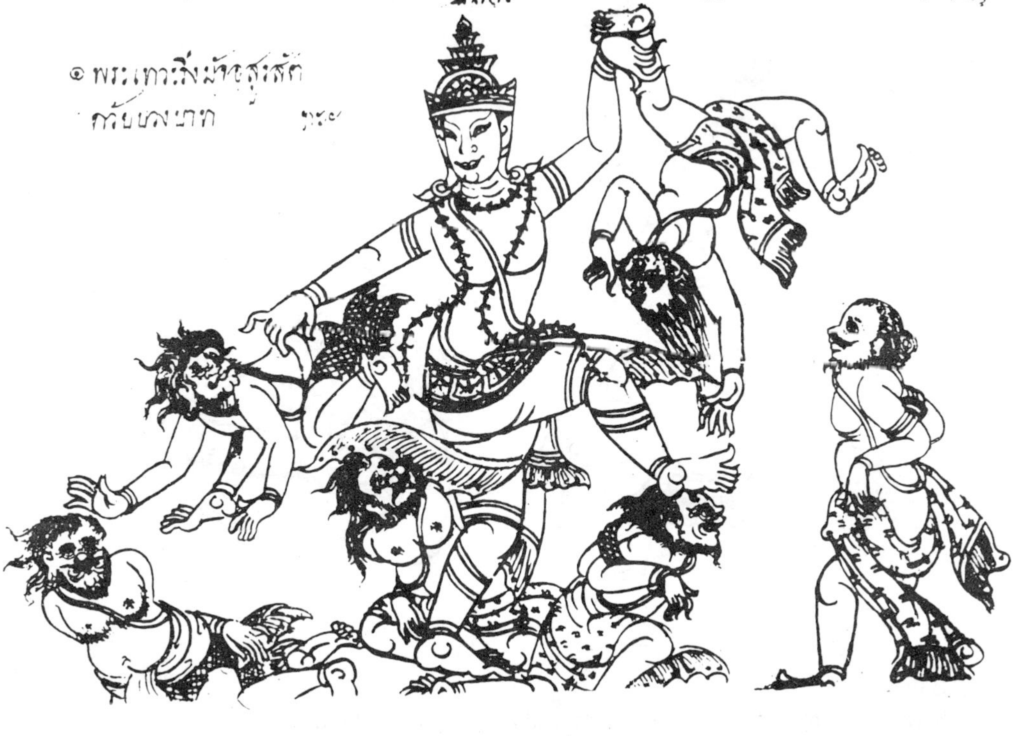
๏ พระเทวะสิงมัจสุรสัก
กับบงปาก

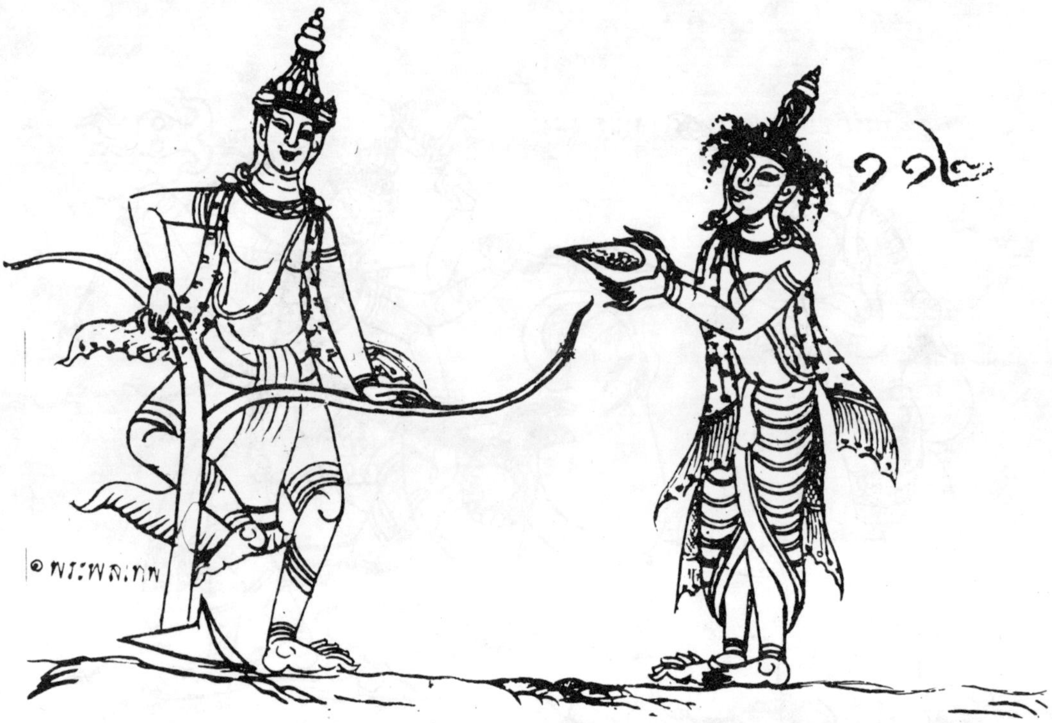

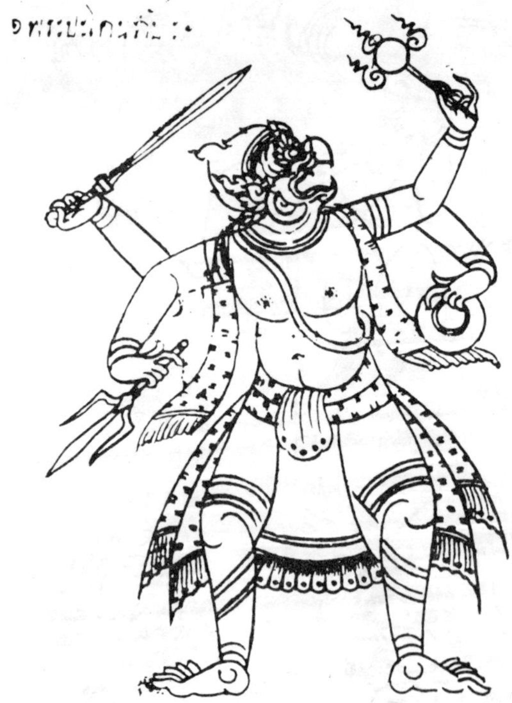

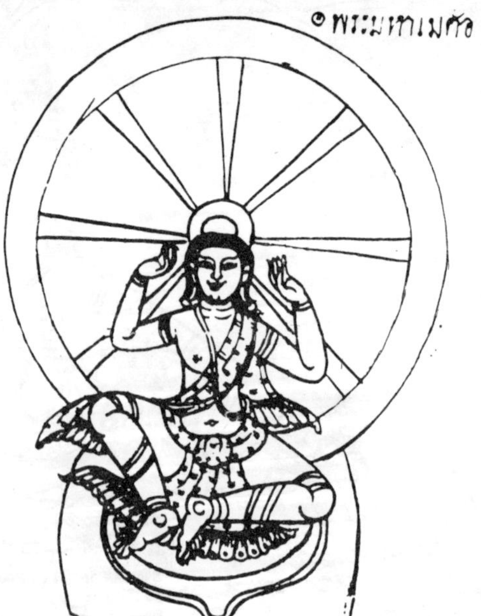

77. Baladeva.
    Sarma 3a braḥ bldeby' thaïnā || ‹‹B. Baladeva working hard››.
78. Nang Devī.
79. Calotap?
80. Mahāmesa?

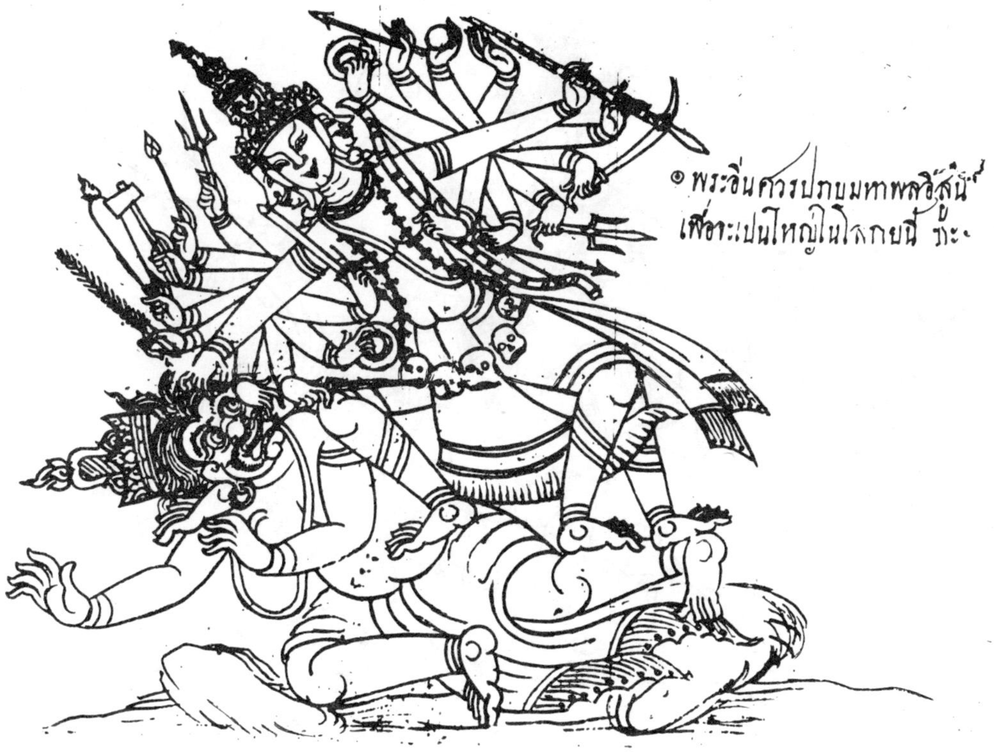

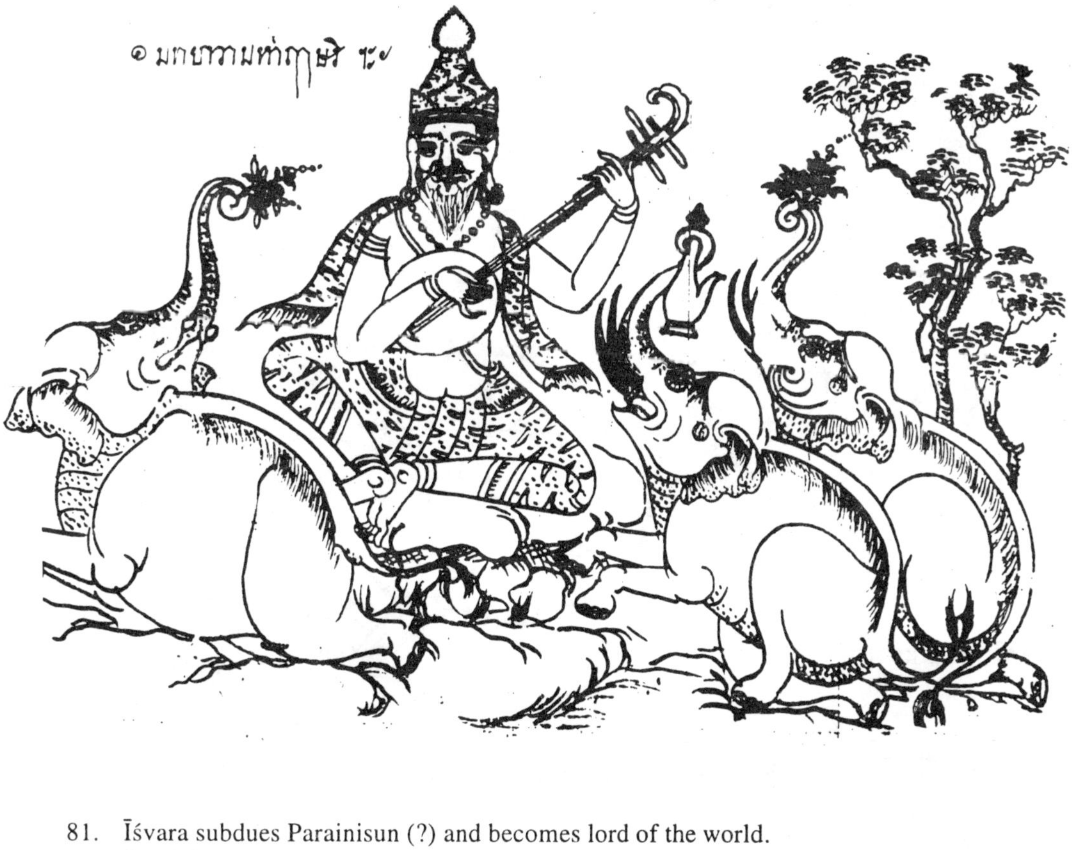

81. Īśvara subdues Parainisun (?) and becomes lord of the world. See 264.
82. Elephants come to listen to maharṣi —. See 265.

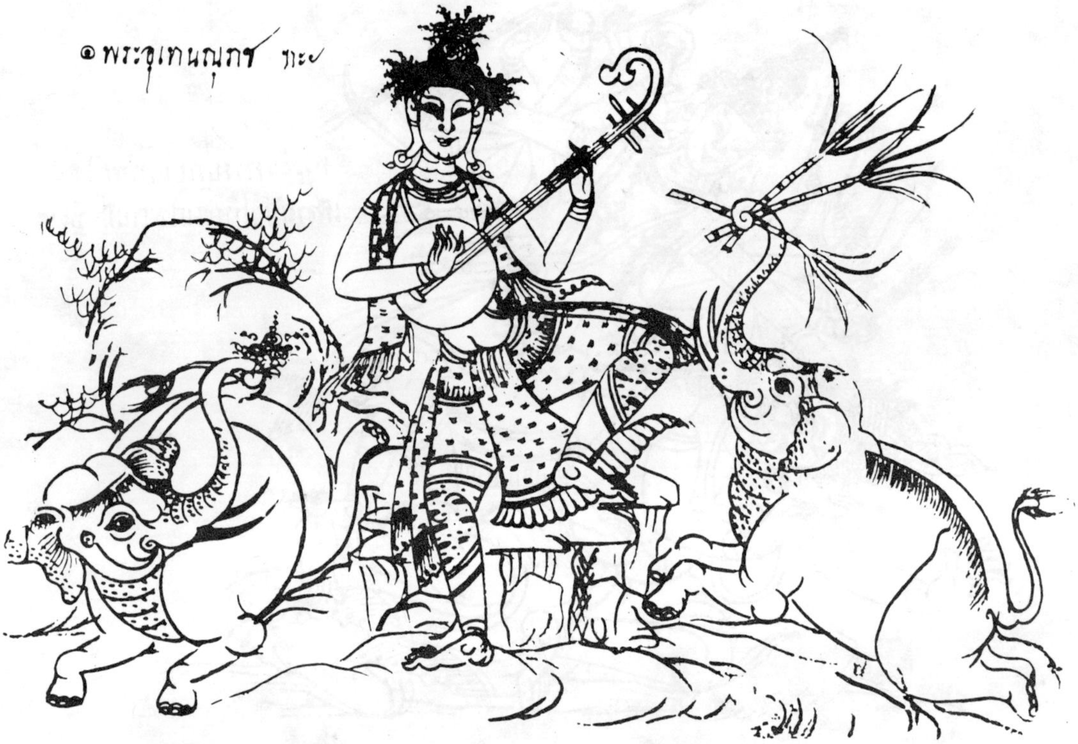

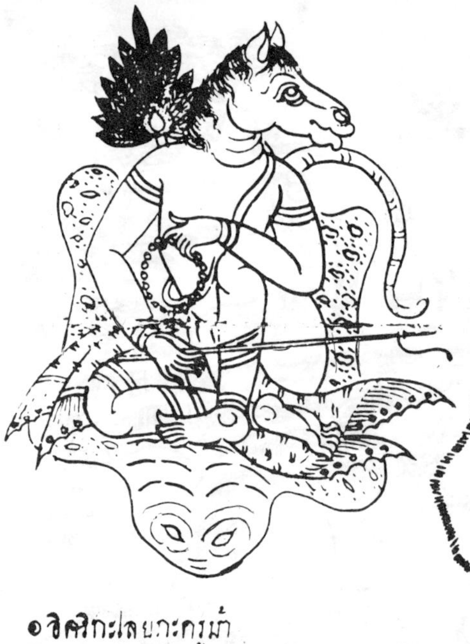

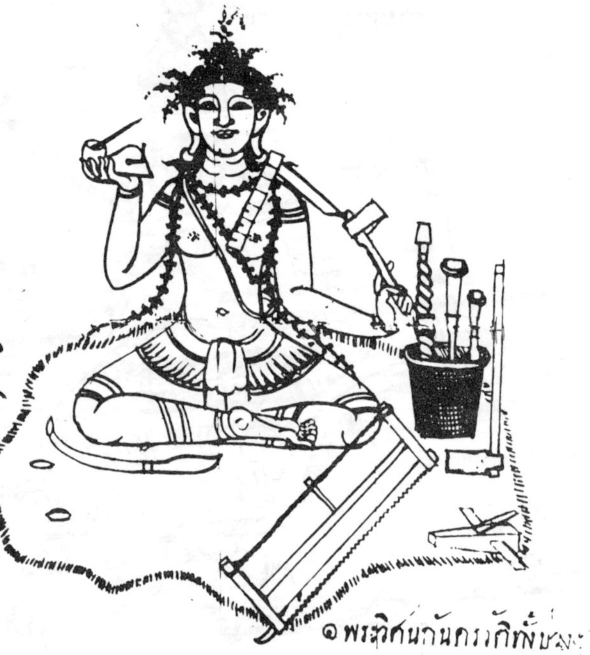

83. Uthenurāja? playing vīṇā surrounded by elephants.
84. Kasiryaga?, guru of horses.
85. Viśvakarmā .

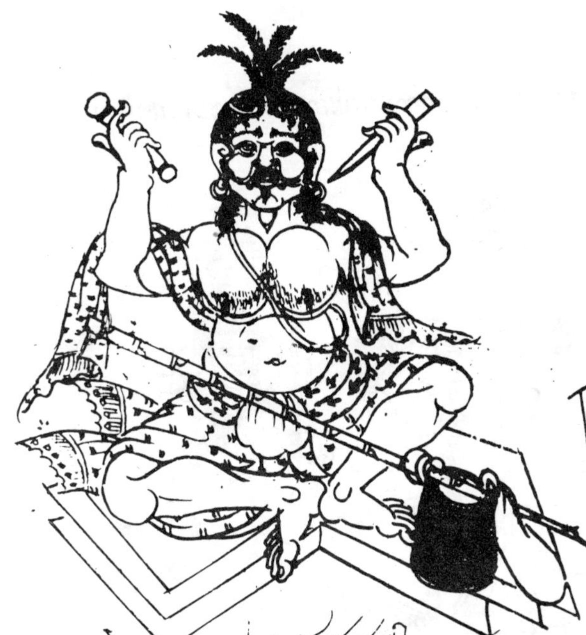

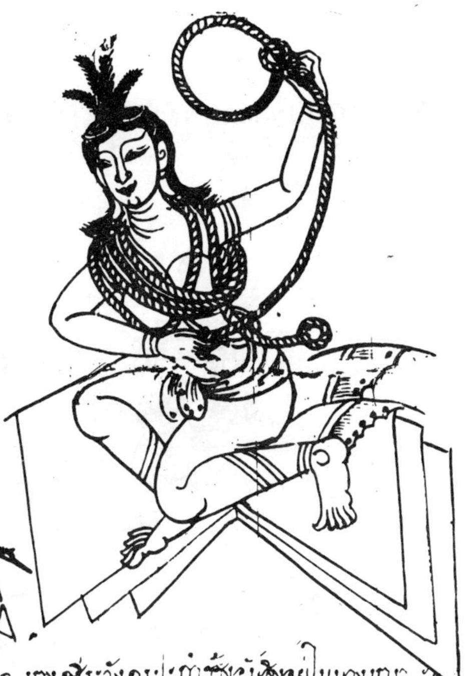

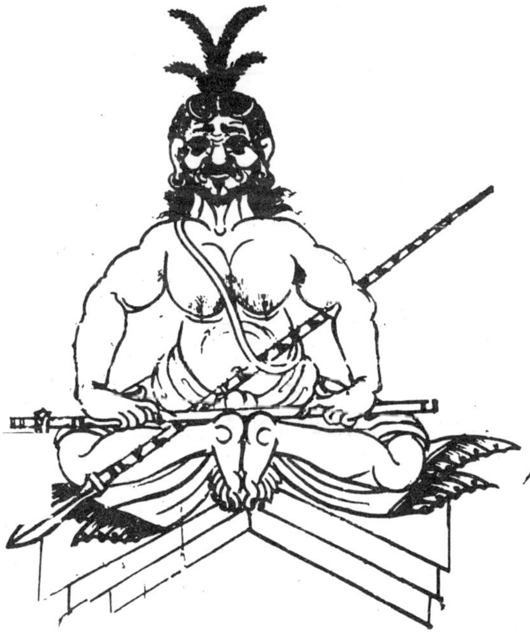

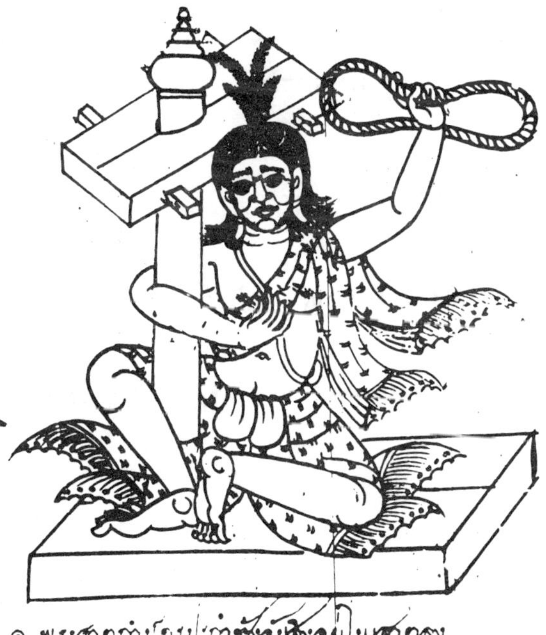

86. Trainer of elephants in Suotalung
87. Goddess of elephants who controls them with a cord.
88. Trainer of elephants in Yashore.
89. Trainer of elephants in Suotalung.

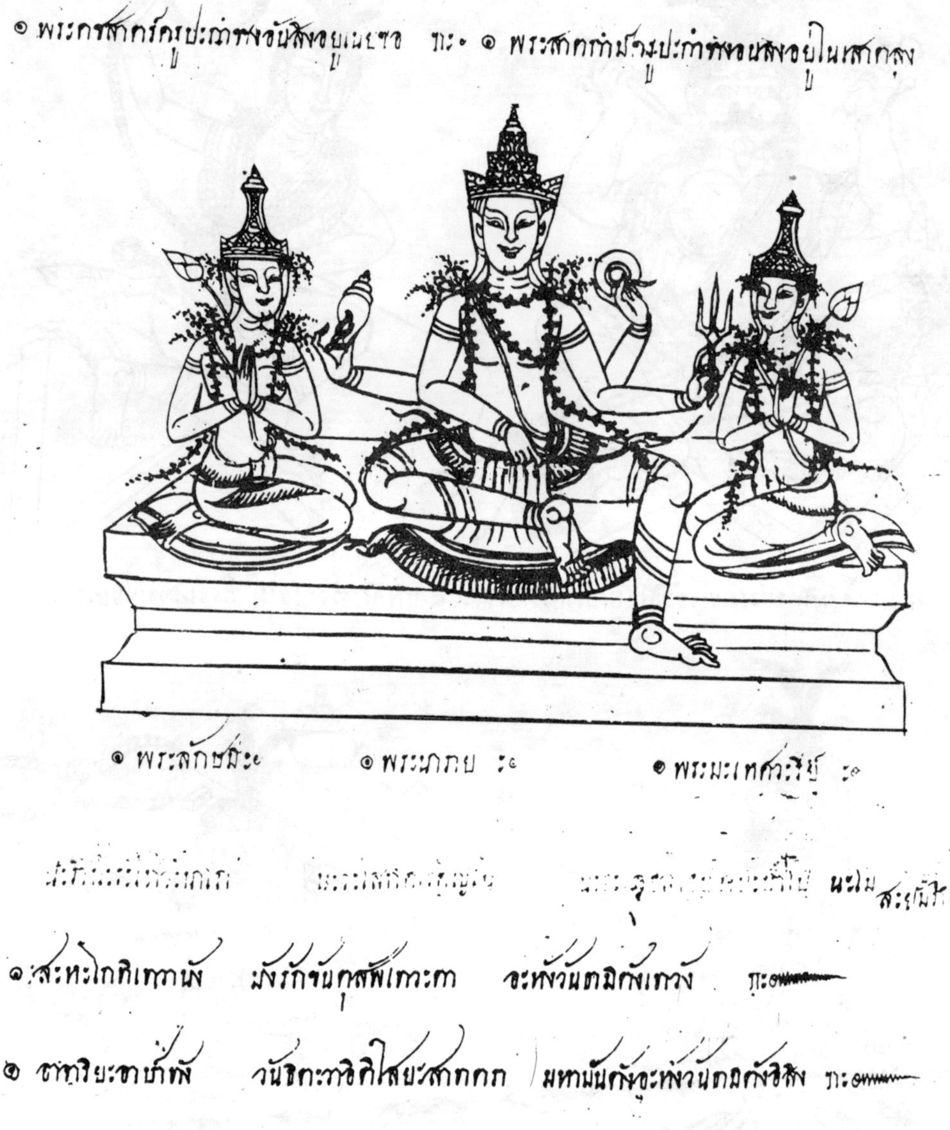

90. Nārāyaṇa flanked by Lakṣmī and Maheśvarī. See 273.

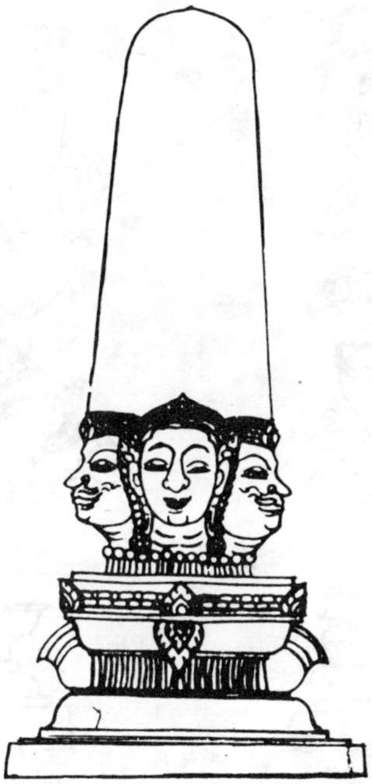

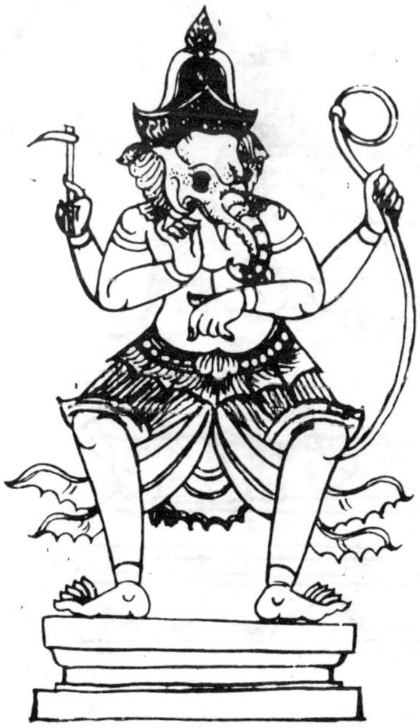

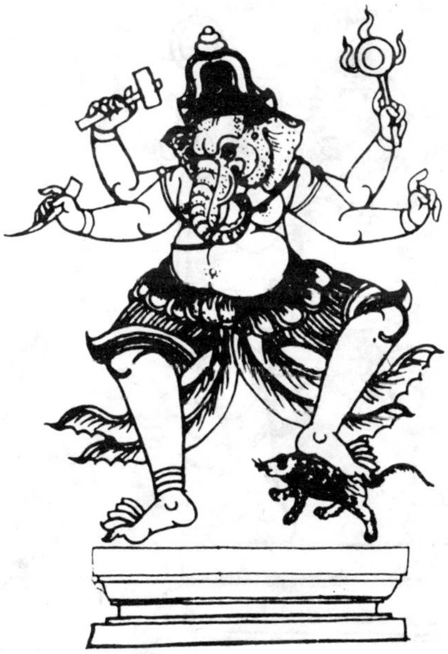

SECOND PANTHEON

91. Svāyambhuva-nātha. See 1.
92. Four-armed Mahāvighneśvara with an awl (?) and noose. See 28.
93. Four-armed Mahāvighneśvara, with left foot on rat. See 32.

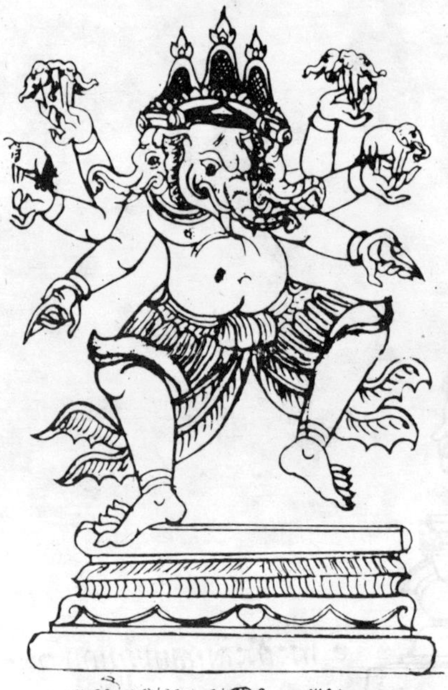

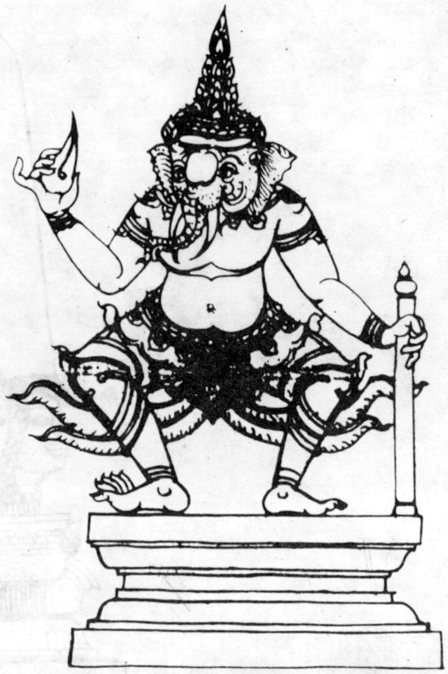

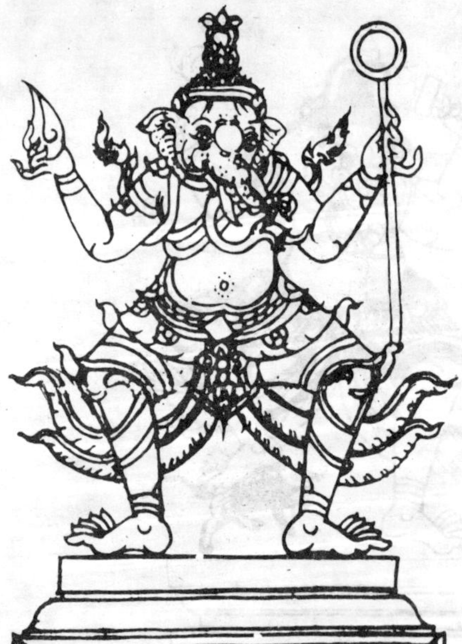

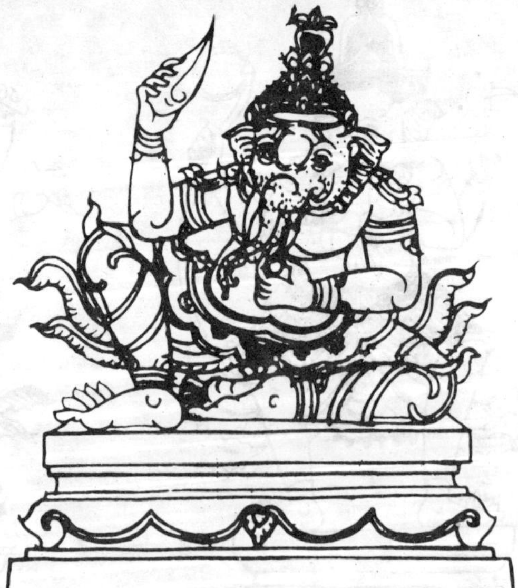

94. Six-armed Mahāvighneśvara with three visible heads. See 31.
95. Devakarma. See 29.
96. Mahāvighneśvara.
97. Devakarma. See 30.

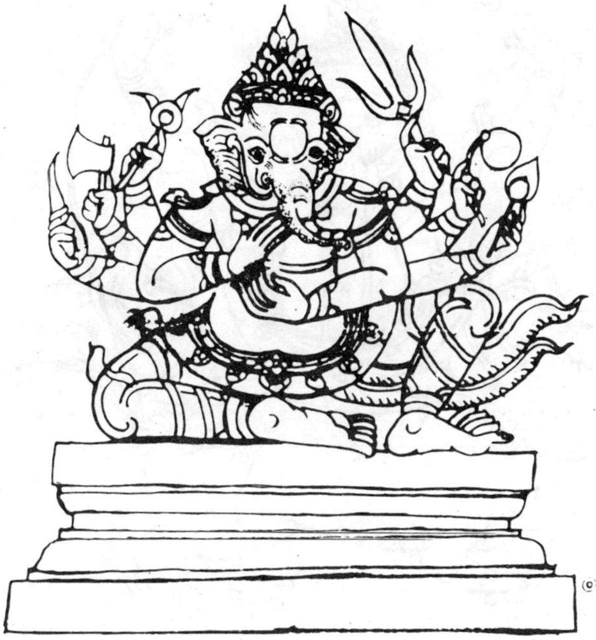

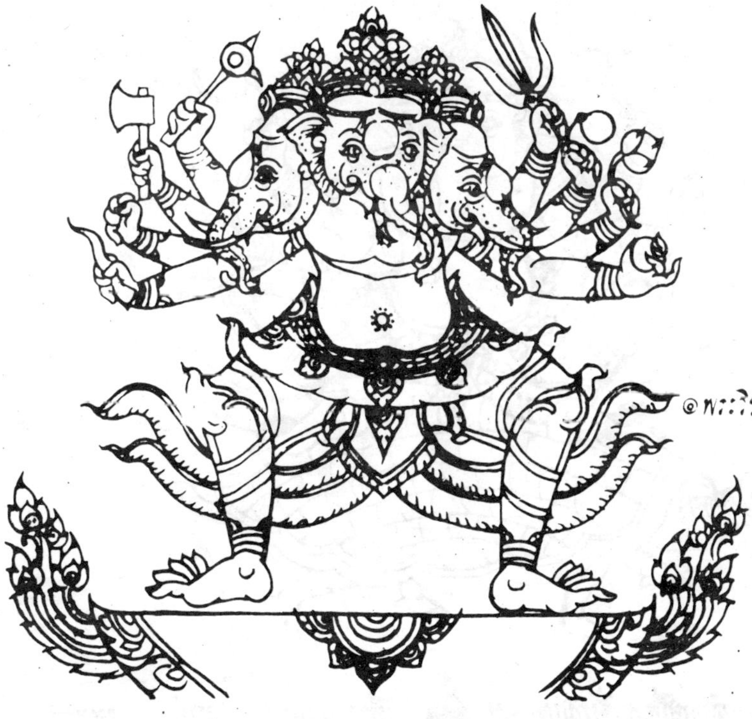

98. Eight-armed Vighneśvara. Sarma 7b.
99. Eight-armed Vighneśvara. See 23.

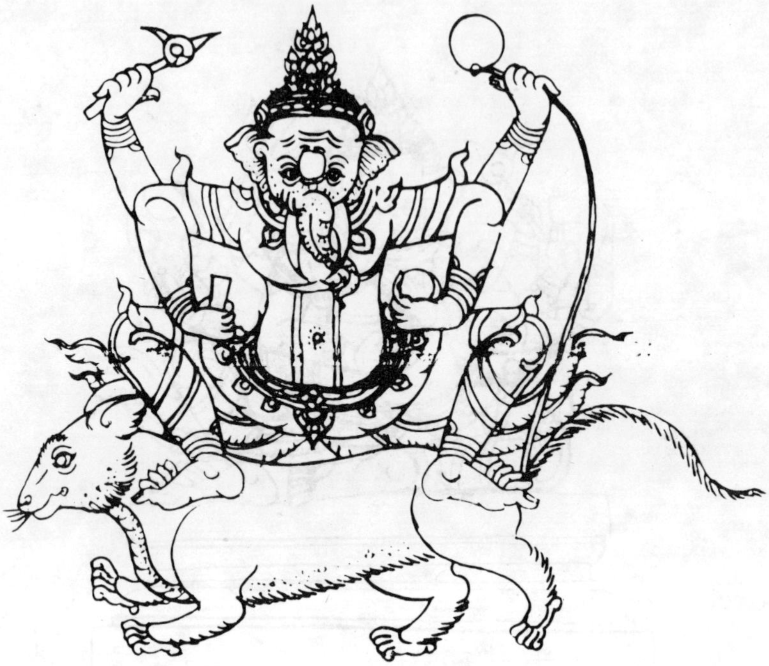

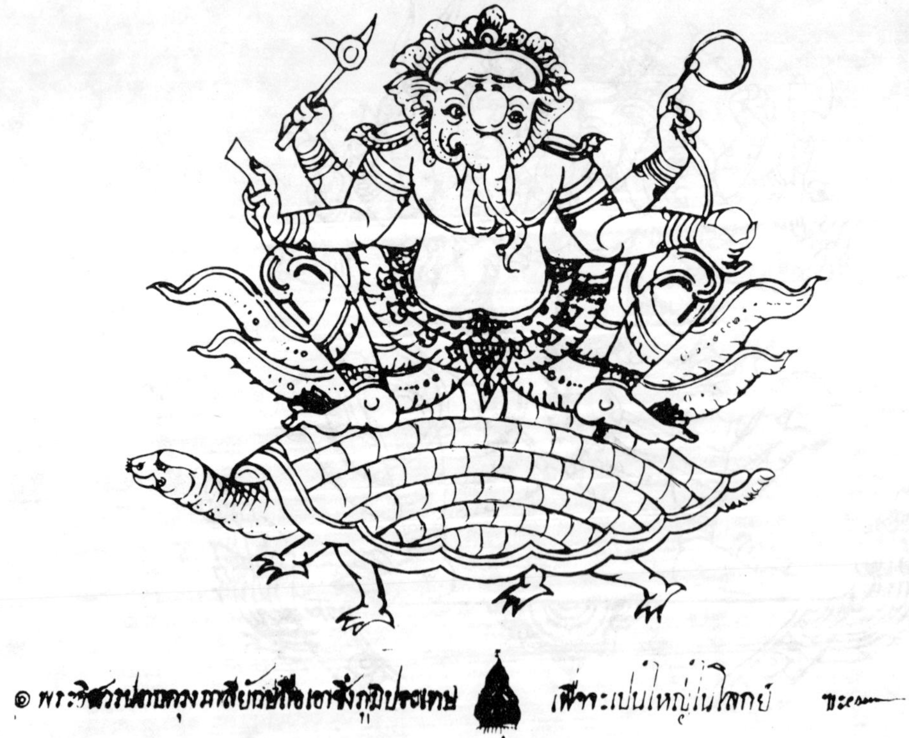

100. Four-armed Mahāvighneśvara on his rat. See 23.
101. Four-armed Mahāvighneśvara on a tortoise. See 24.

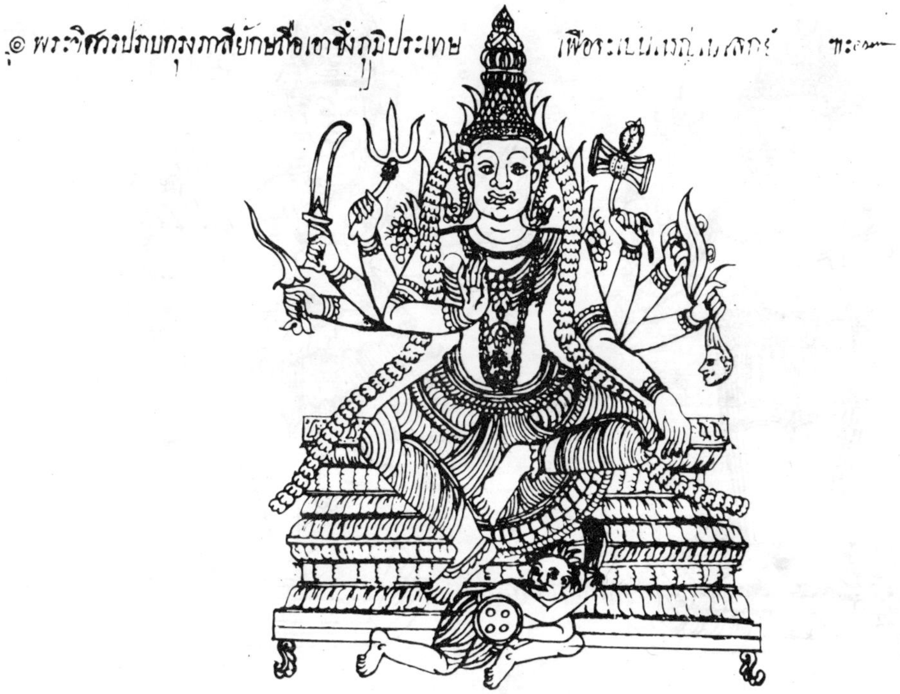

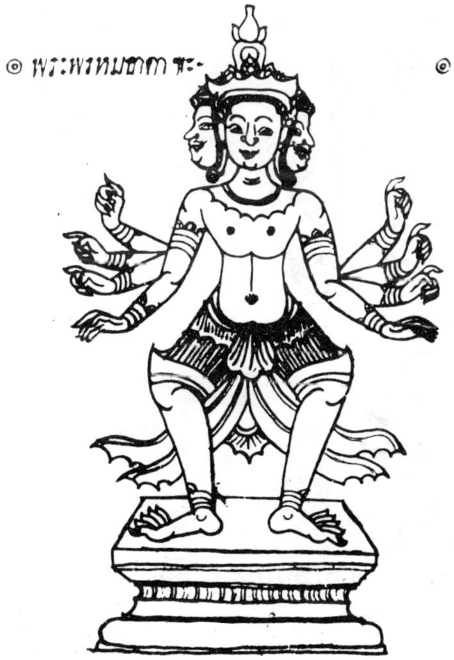

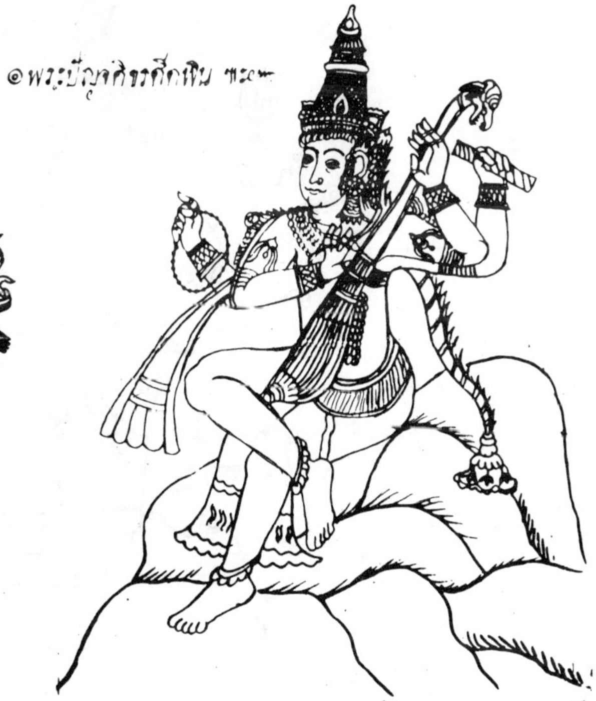

102. Eight-armed Īśvara seated on Kumbha-yakṣa armed with sword and shield. See 50.
103. Eight-armed Brahmā Dhātā. See 30.
104. Pañcaśikha playing vīṇā. See 49.

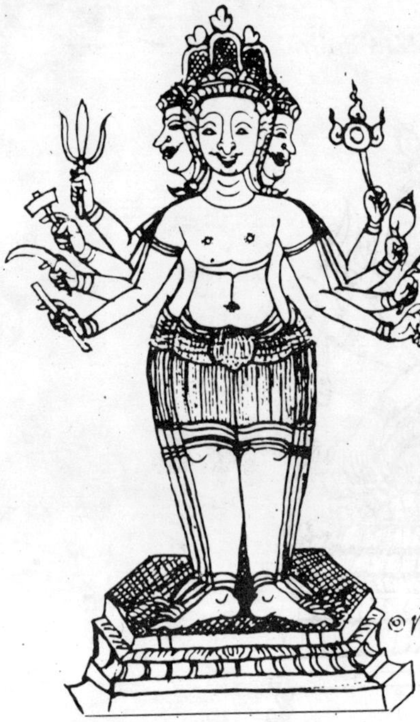

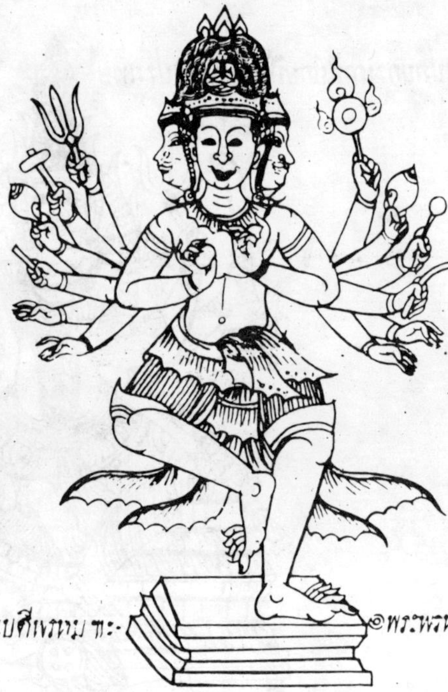

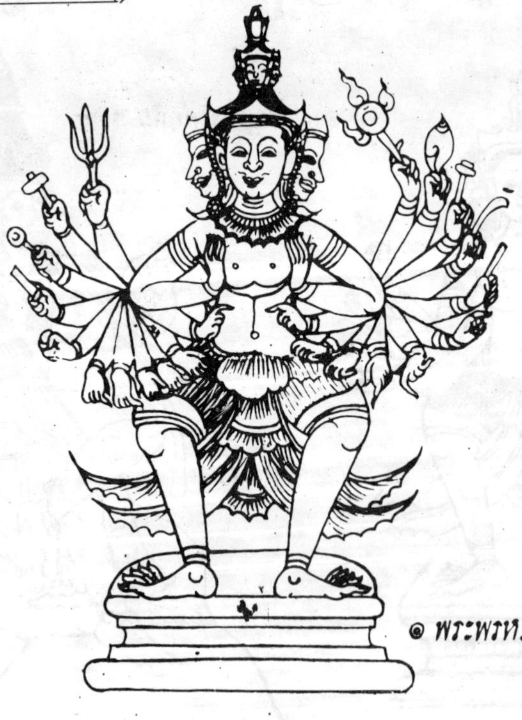

105. Eight-armed Sahāṁpati Brahmā. See 32.

106. Fourteen-armed Brahmā-Maheśvara. Dancing on the left foot. R.h. trident, hammer, conch, baton, two hands free, mudrā. L.h. flaming disk, conch, circle, sword, two hands free, mudrā. Sarma 36b braḥ brhm maḥheśvar | ‹‹B. Brahmamaheśvara››.

107. Twenty-armed eight-faced Śraddhādeva. See 36.

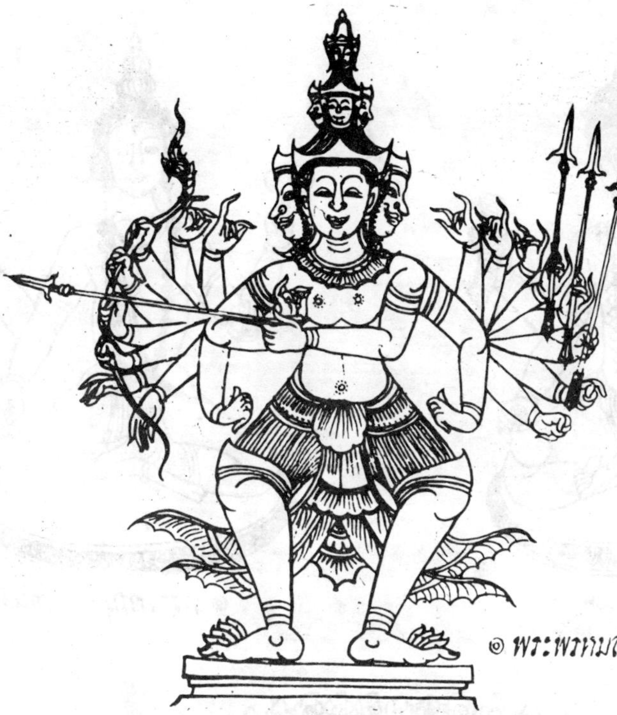

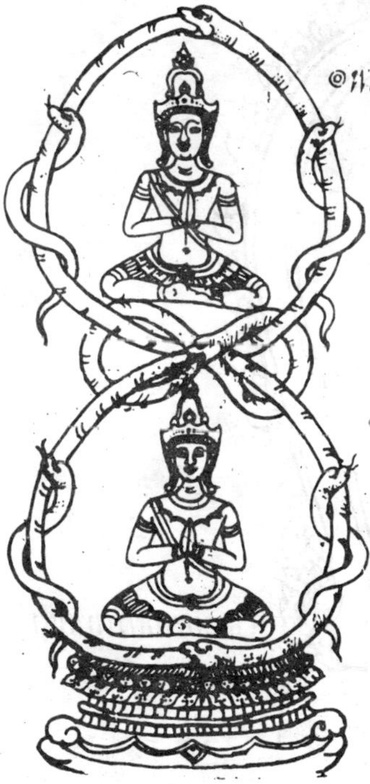

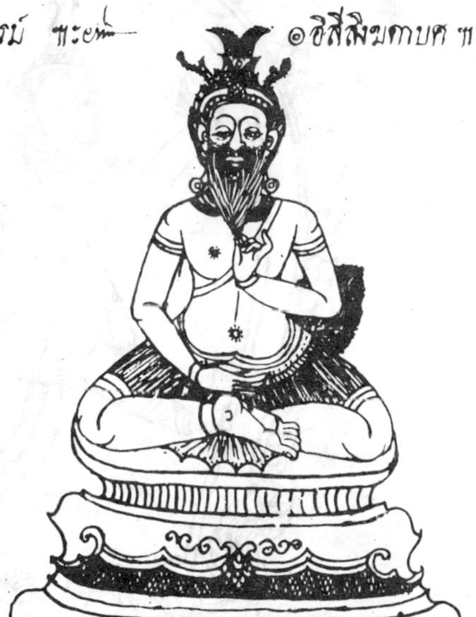

108. Brahmā śraddhādeva. See 37.
109. Deva-siddhi-karma. See 44.
110. Ṛṣyaśṛṅga tāpasa.
Sarma 5c braḥ iśrisiṅgh’ tāpś ‖ ‹‹The ascetic B. Ṛṣyaśṛṅga››.

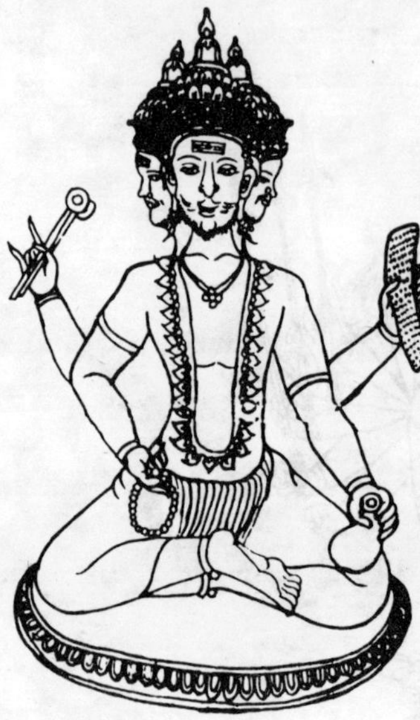

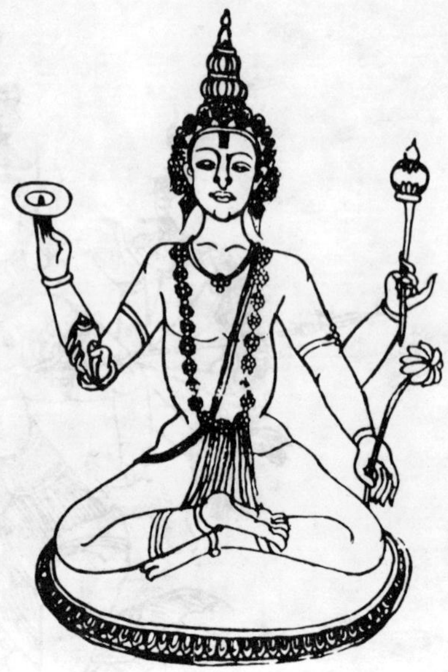

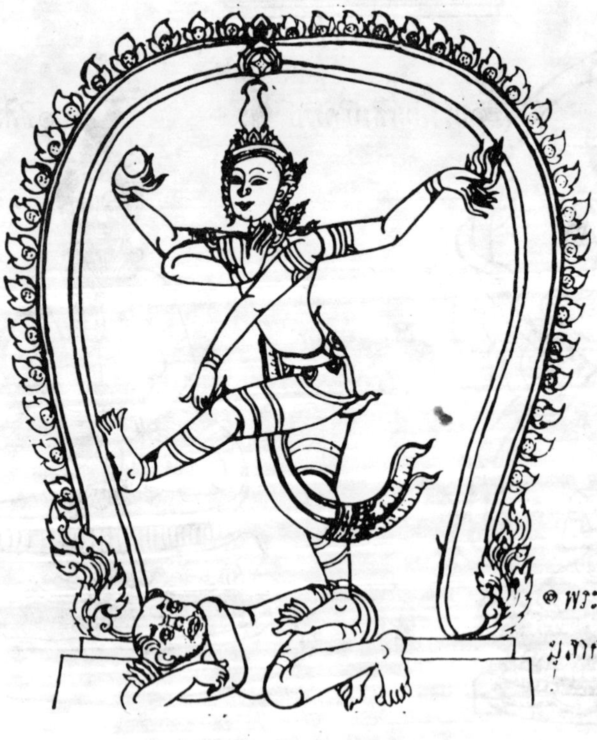

111. Four-armed four-faced Brahmā. See 82.
112. Four-armed Viṣṇu. See 65.
113. Four-armed Parameśvara trampling on Apasmāra-puruṣa. See 2.

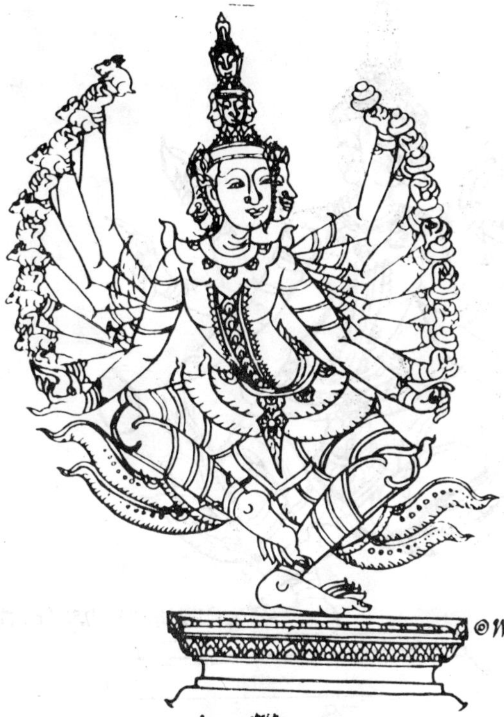

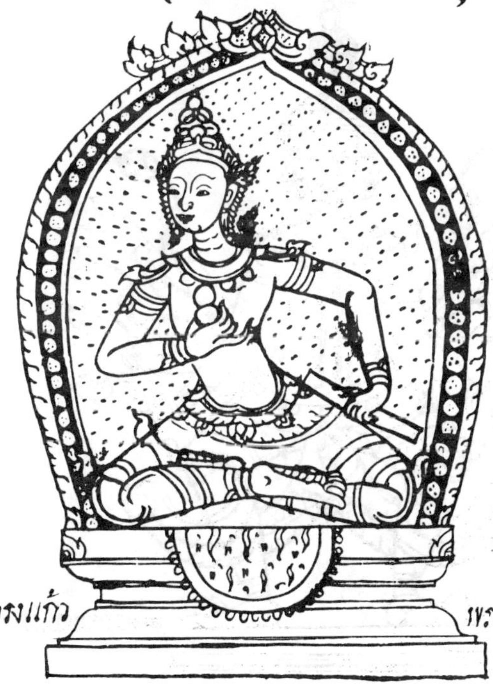

114. Sixteen-armed eight-faced Śraddhāsiddha (a form of Brahmā). See 34.
115. Parameśvara cakrapāṇi.

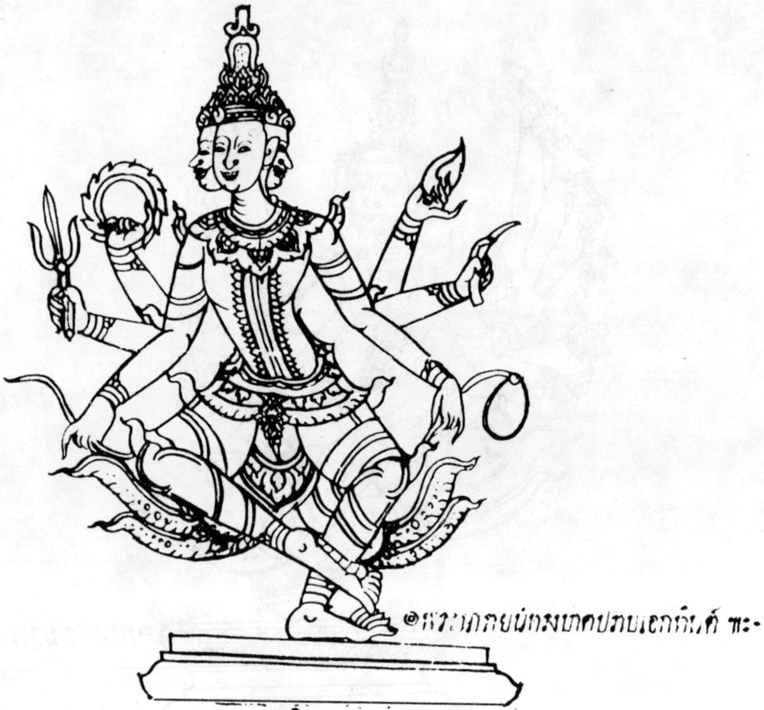

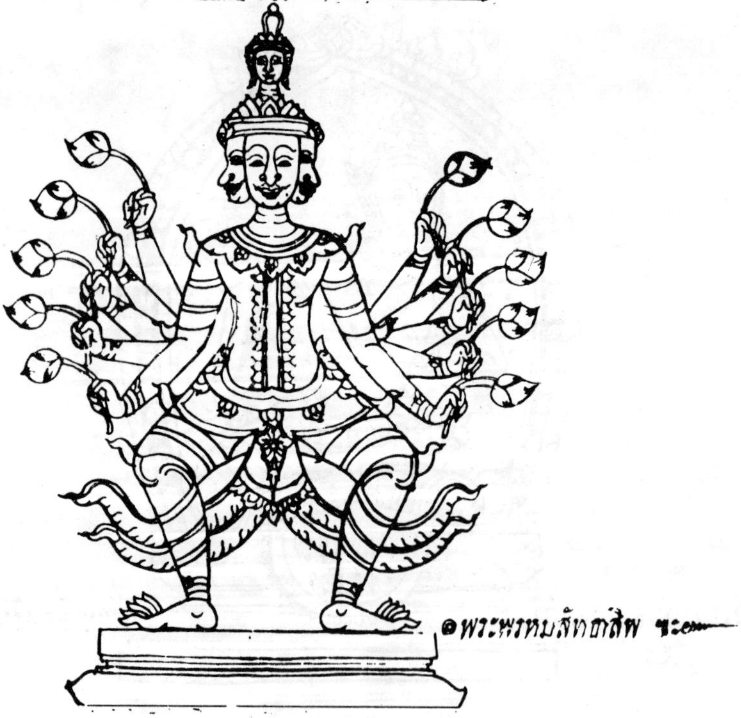

116. Six-armed Nārāyaṇa who subdues elephant Ekadanta. See 45.
117. Ten-armed four-faced Śraddhāsiddha (? form of Brahmā). See 35.

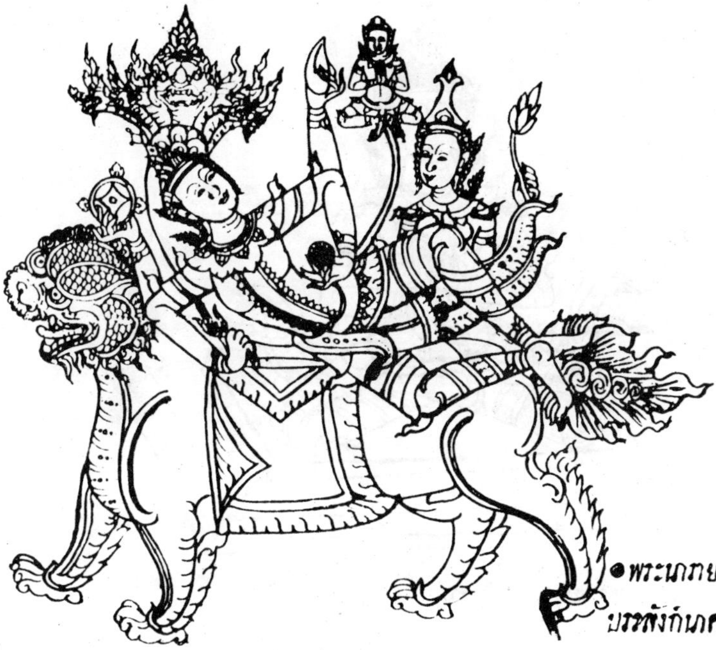

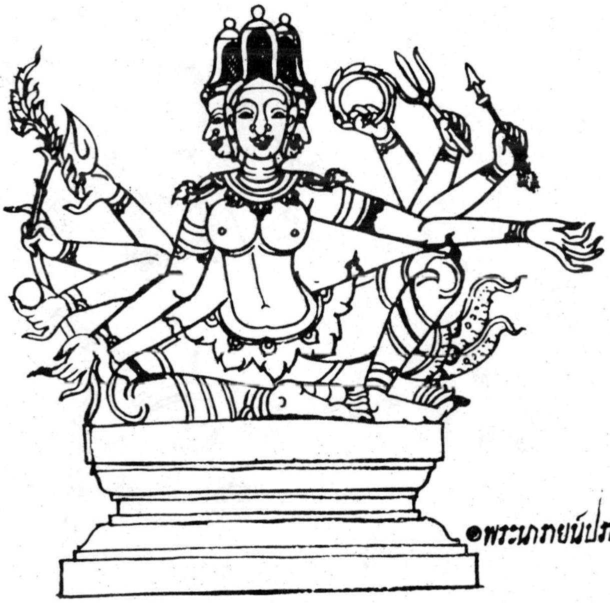

118. Nārāyaṇa lying on the nāga, accompanied by adoring Brahmā and Śrīdevī. See 21.
119. Eight-armed Nārāyaṇī. See 49.

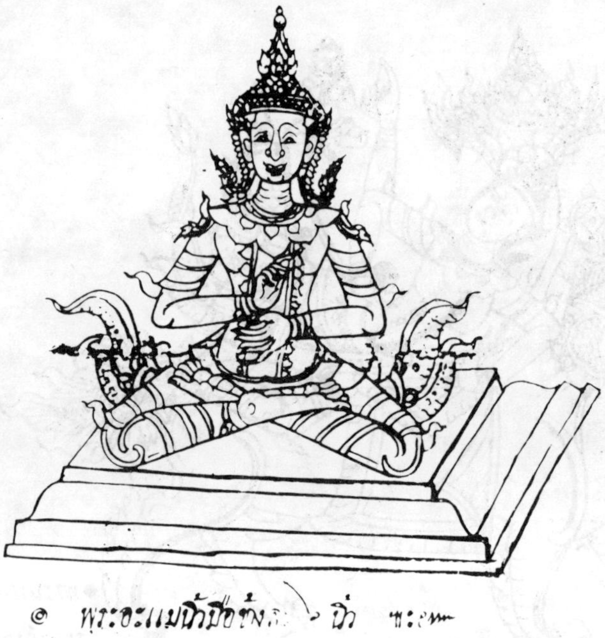

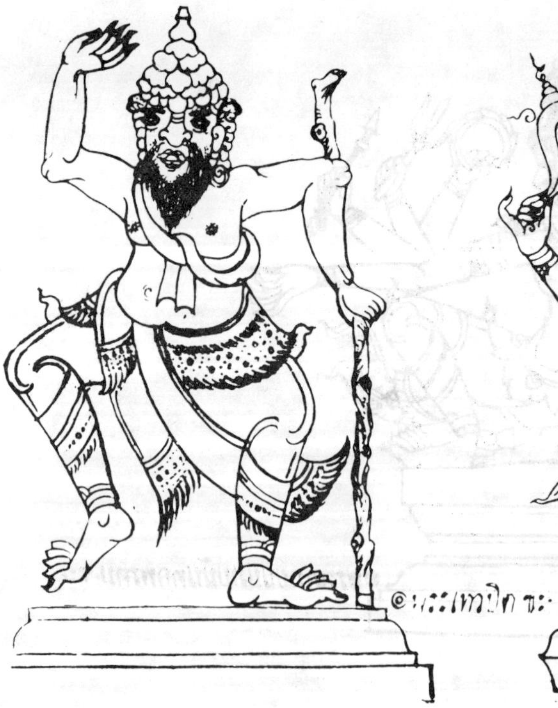

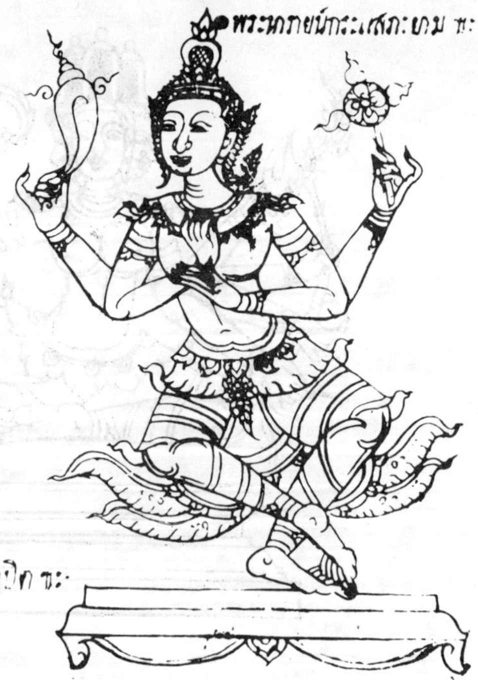

120. Six-finger deity. See 39.
121. Deva Paśusakha. See 46.
122. Four-armed Nārāyaṇa dancing. See 52.

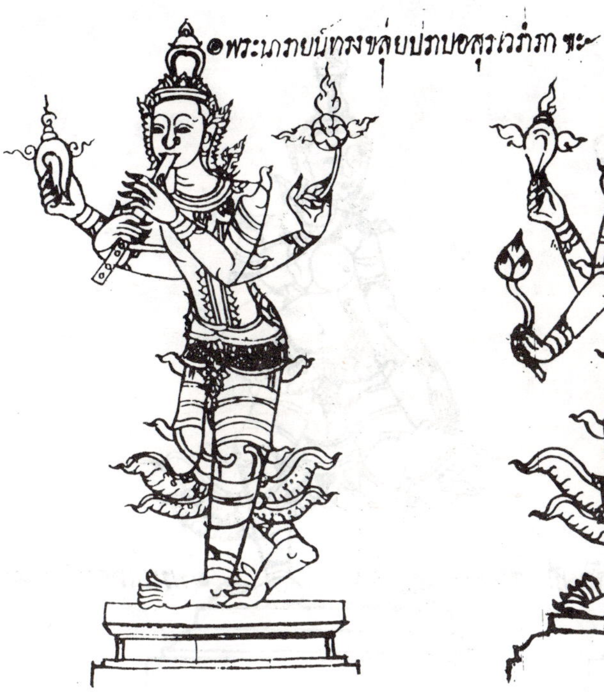

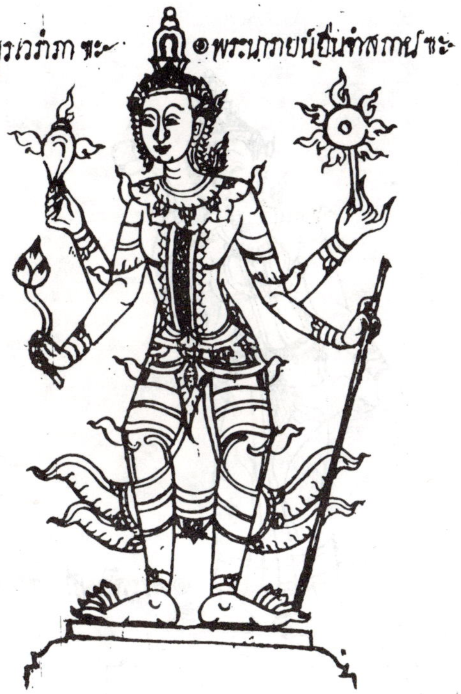

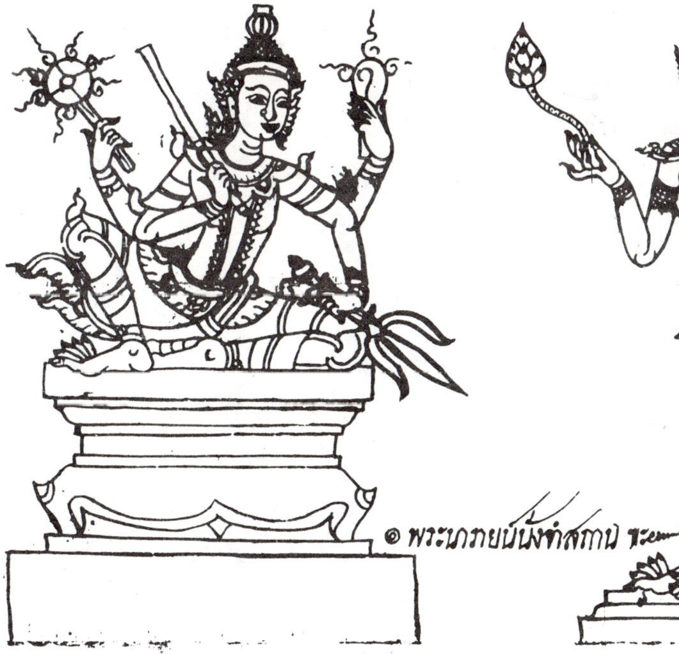

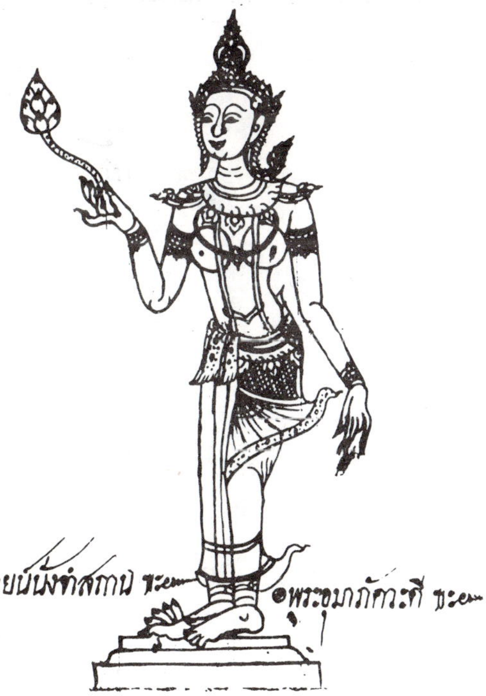

123. Four-armed Nārāyaṇa playing the flute. See 43.
124. Four-armed Nārāyaṇa standing upright. See 15.
125. Four-armed Nārāyaṇa seated. See 18.
126. Umā bhagavatī. See 42.

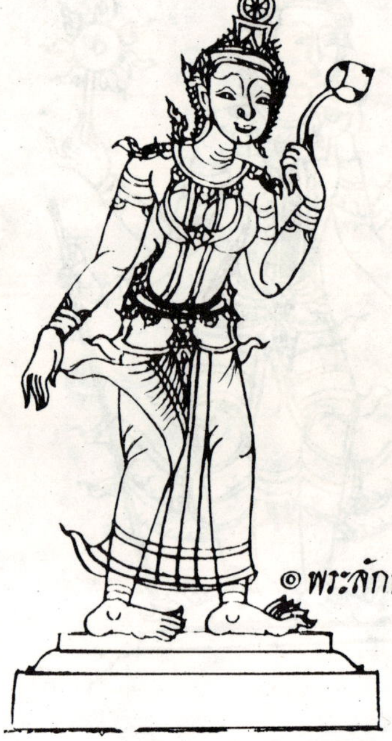

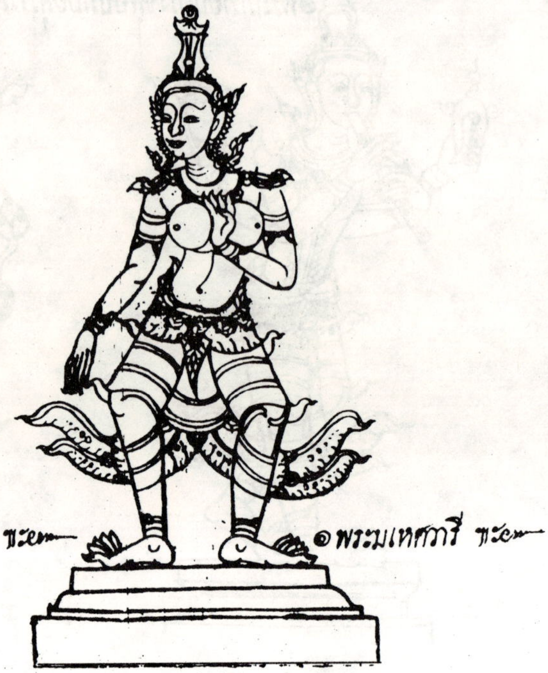

กลีบ

127. Lakṣmī. See 40.
128. Maheśvarī. See 41.

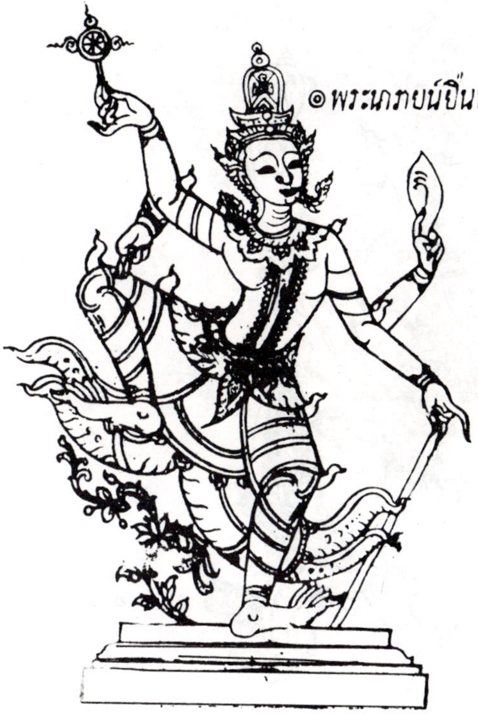

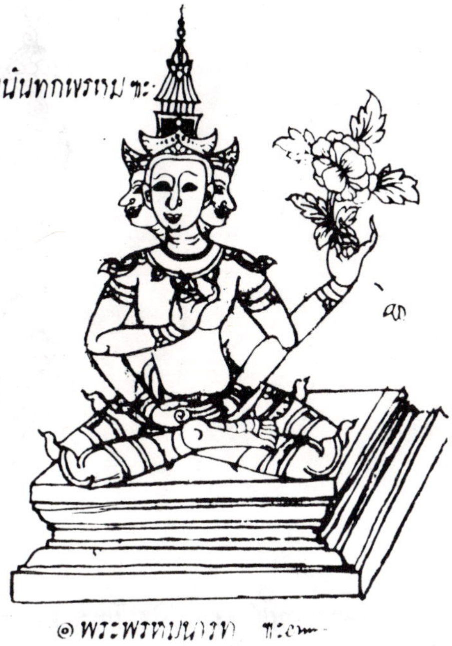

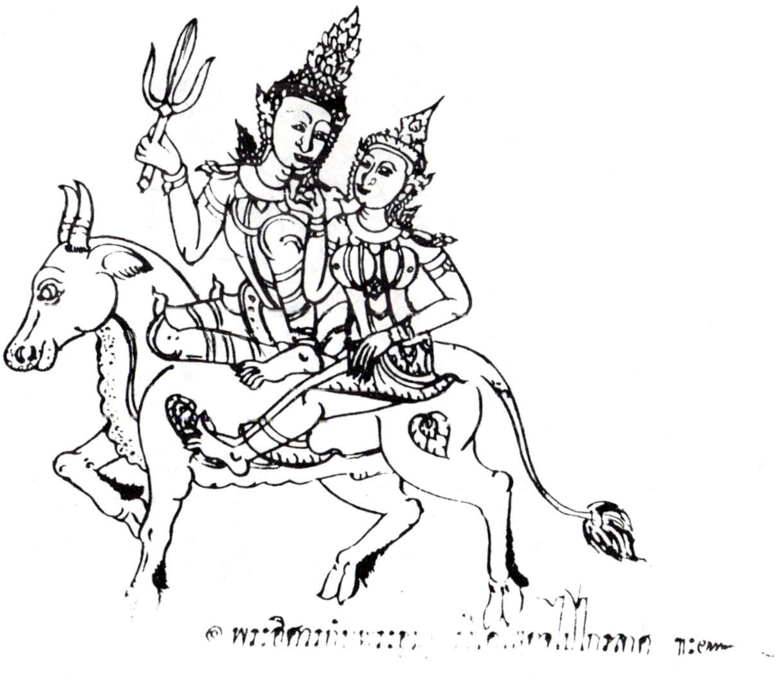

129. Four-armed Nārāyaṇa tames Nandukkha (?). R.h. flaming disk, free, l.h. conch, baton. cf. Sarma 22c and 32a.
Sarma 21b braḥ nrāyn' Prāp nndukkh | ‹‹B. Nārāyaṇa subdues Nandukkha(?)››.
130. Four-faced Brahma-nātha. cf. Sarma 26a braḥ brhmnārth | ‹‹B. Brahmanātha››.
131. Īśvara and Umā on Nandin on their way to Kailāsa. See 4.

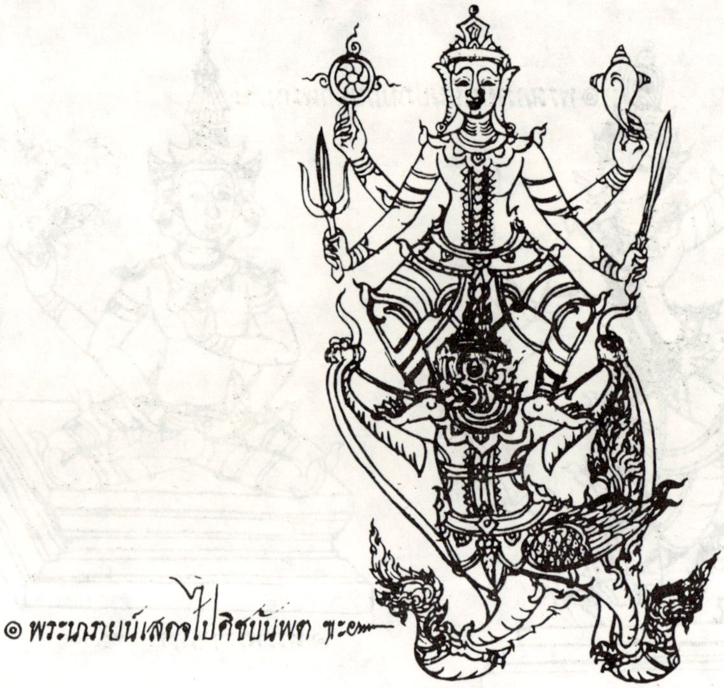

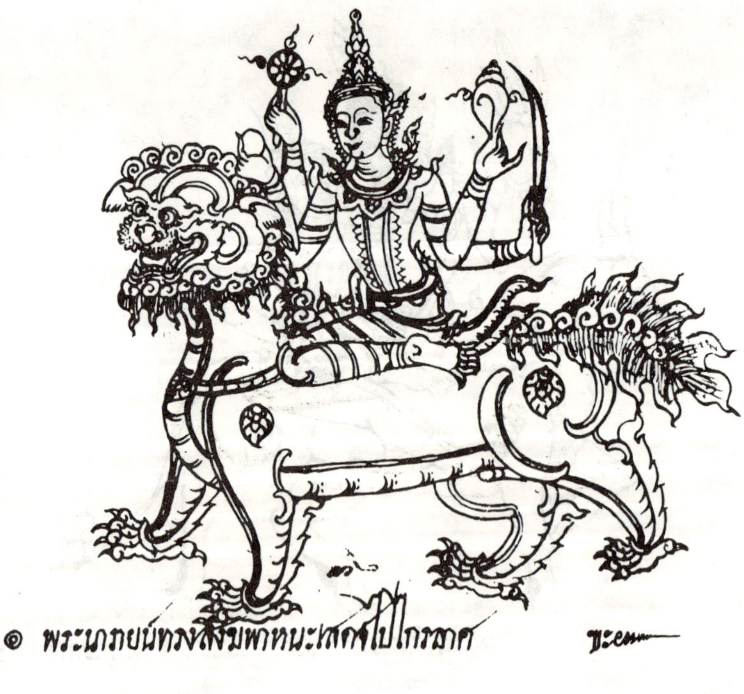

132. Four-armed Nārāyaṇa going to Vaikuṇṭha. See 8.
133. Four-armed Nārāyaṇa going to Kailāsa on a lion. See 10.

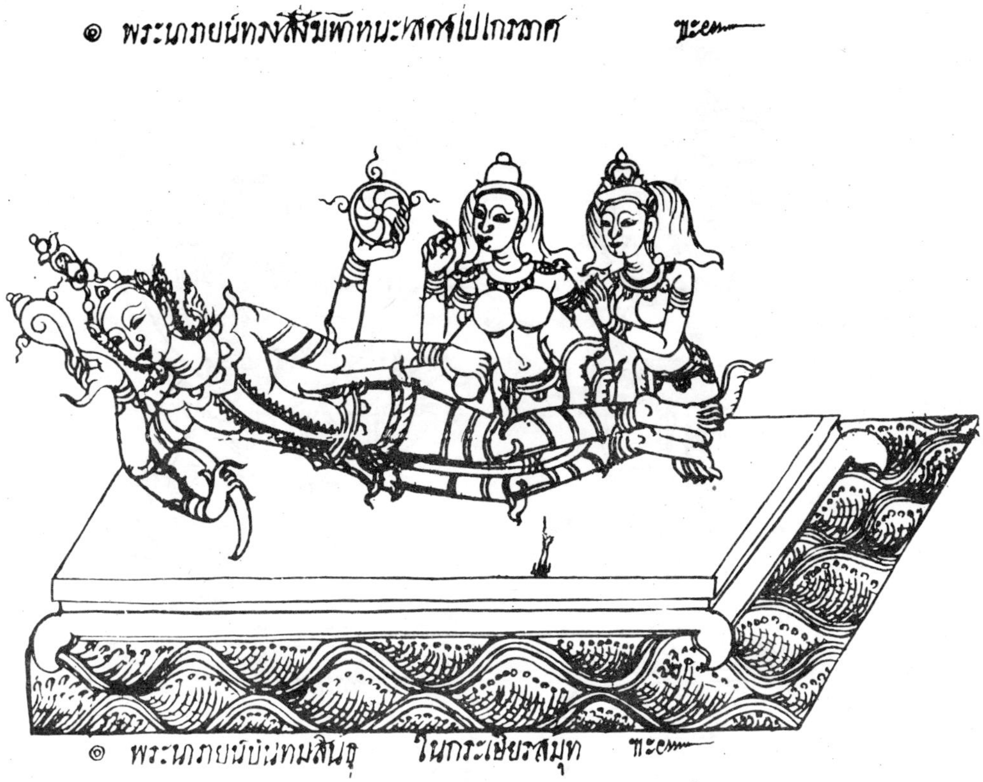

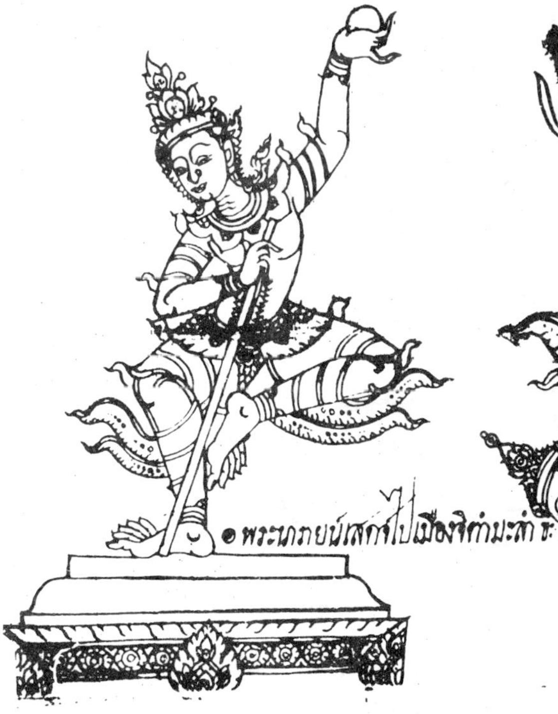

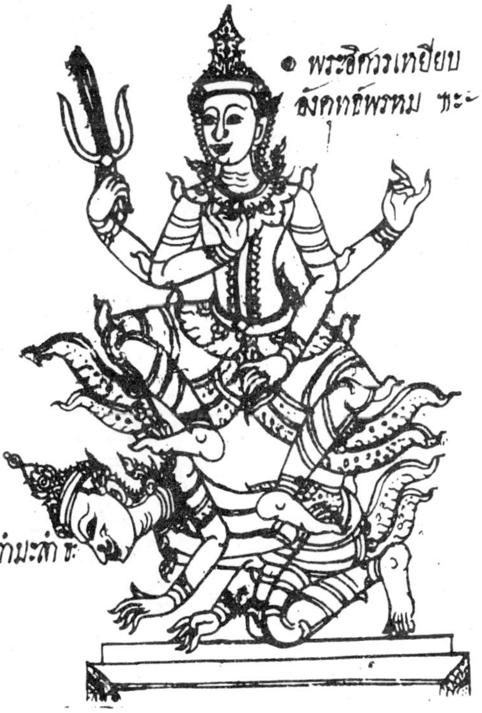

134. Four-armed Nārāyaṇa meditating afloat on the ocean, accompanied by Bhūdevī and Śrīdevī. See 20.
135. Nārāyaṇa going to Citramalā. See 16.
136. Four-armed Parameśvara subdues Andhaka. See 3.

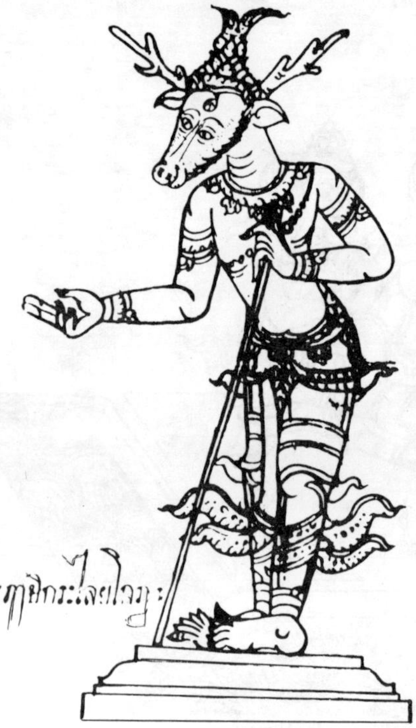

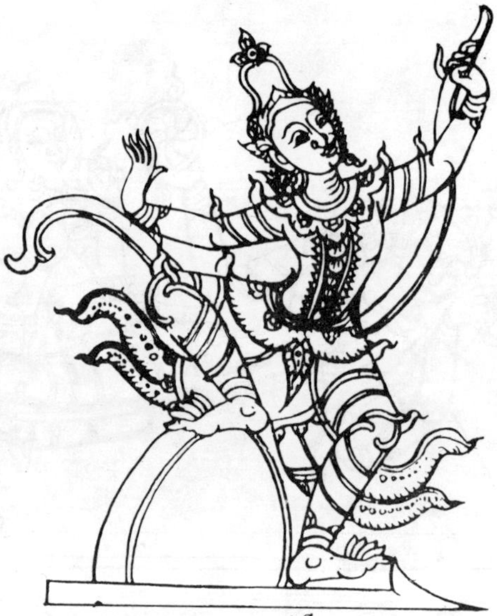

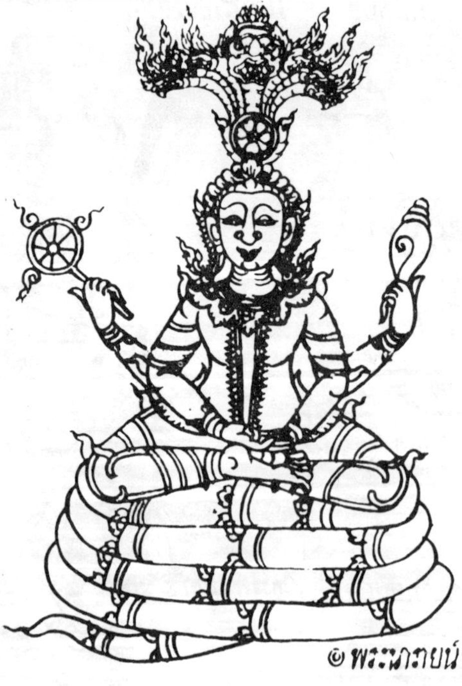

137. Ṛṣi Kalaikkōṭṭu/Ṛṣyaśṛṅga. See 47.
138. God of Ploughing.
139. Four-armed Nārāyaṇa meditating on a nāga. See 11.

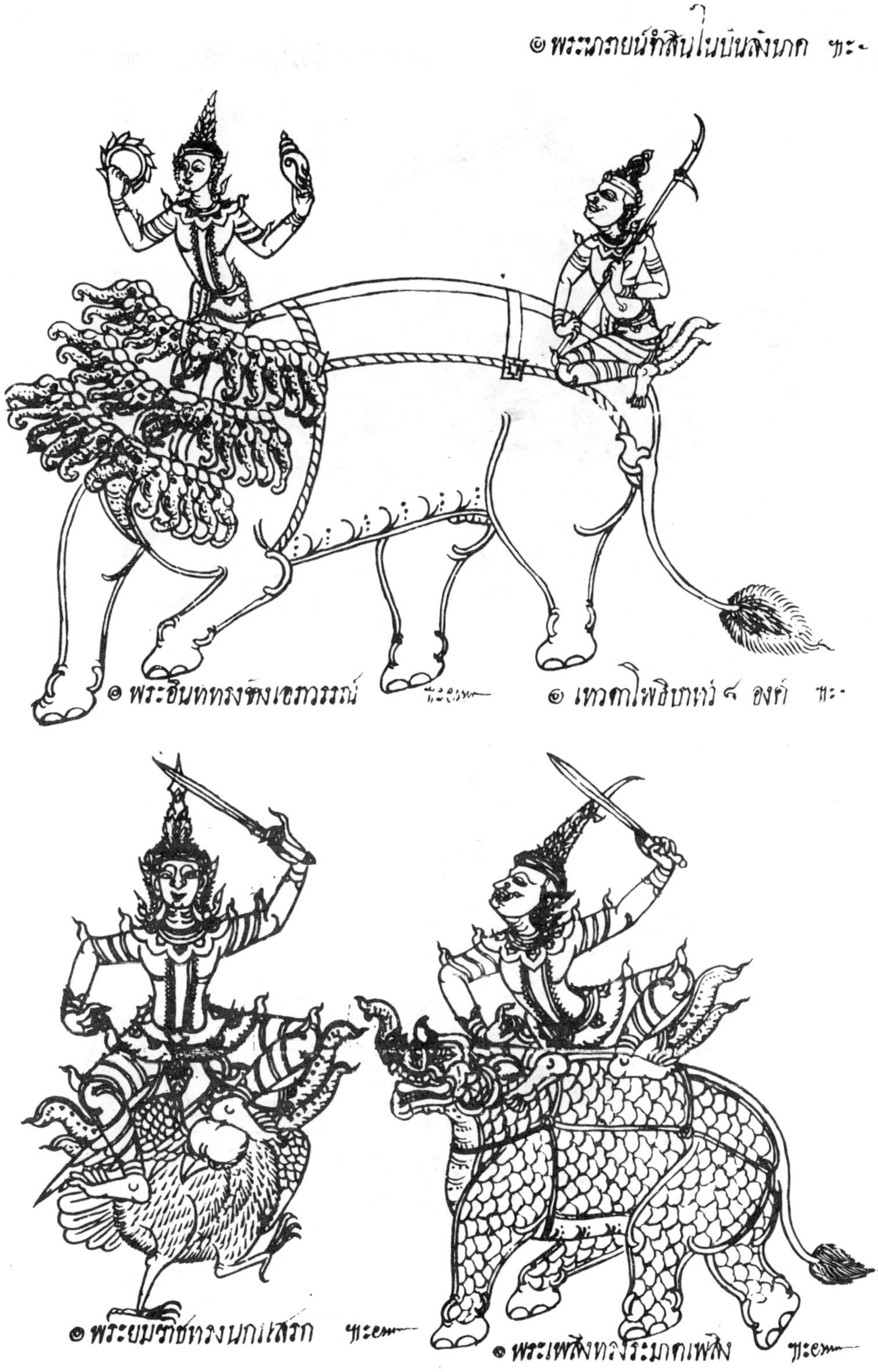

DIKPĀLAS

140. Indra on Airāvata. R.h. disk, l.h. conch, on an elephant with thirtythree tusks in three series of eleven superimposed. Elephant-driver on the rump. See 163, Sarma 35 braḥ indr cau² Bā² drṅ jāṅ² gj erāvrrṇ | ‹‹B. Indra, king of heaven, mounted on the elephant Airāvaṇa››.

141. Yamarāja on an owl. See 165.

142. ? on an elephant.

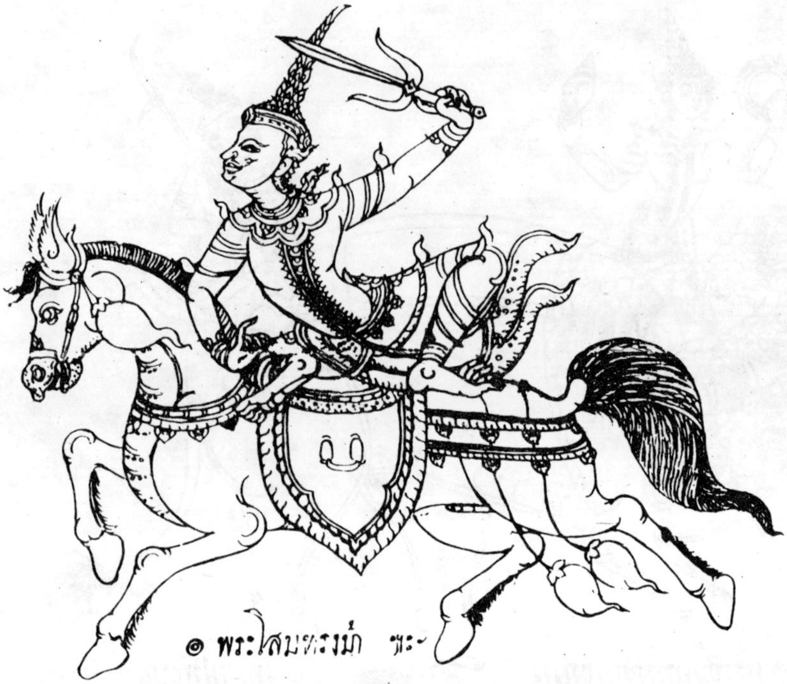

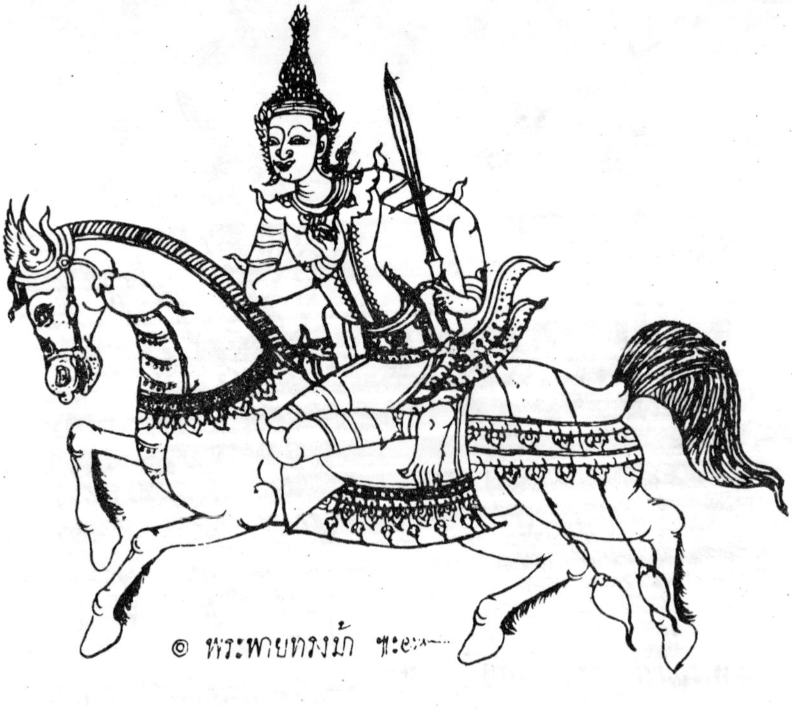

143. Candra on a horse. See 168.
144. Vāyu on a horse. See 169.

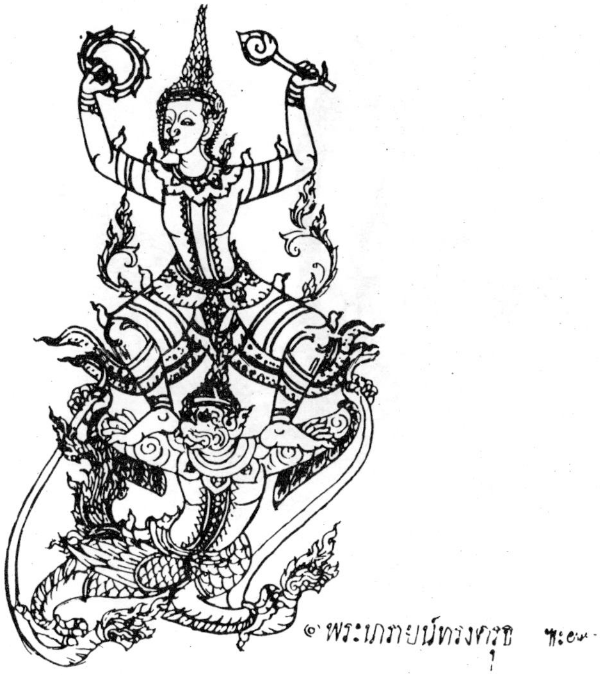

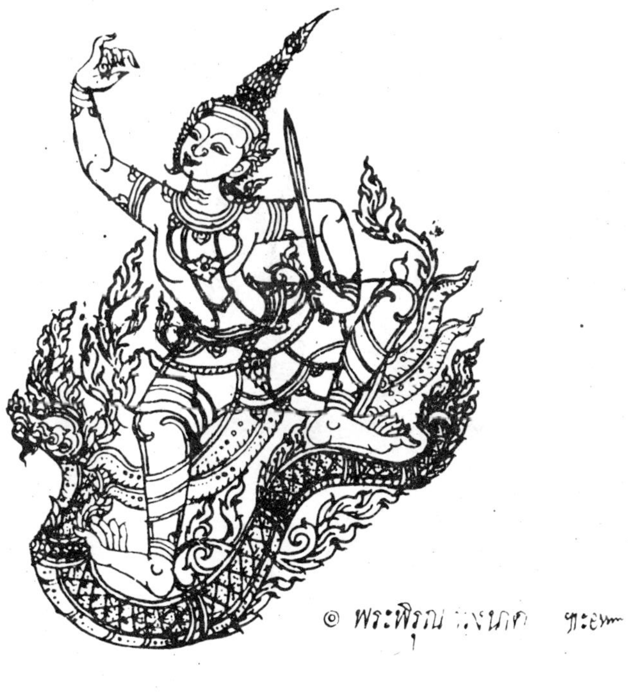

145. Nārāyaṇa on Garuḍa. See 166.
146. Varuṇa on a nāga. See 167.

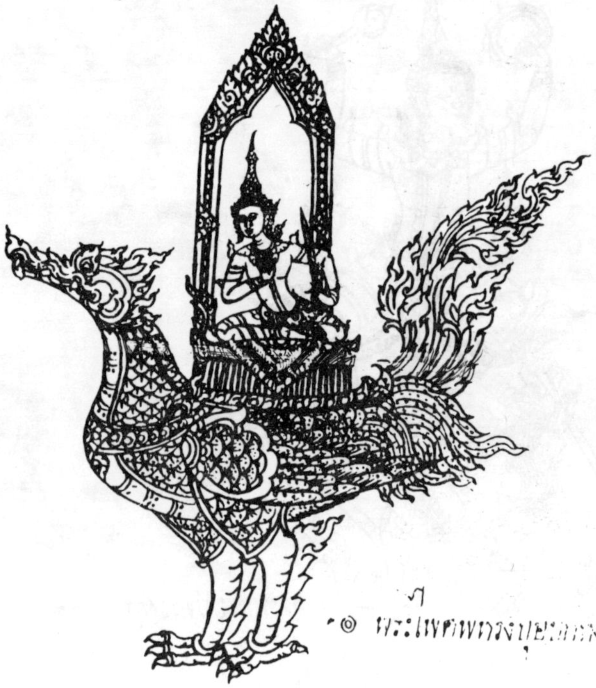

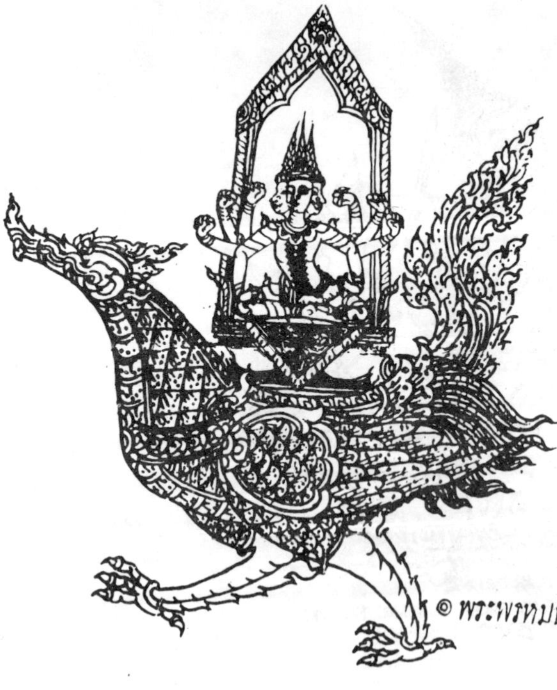

147. Agni on a peacock. See 164.
148. Brahmā on a haṁsa/goose. See 182.

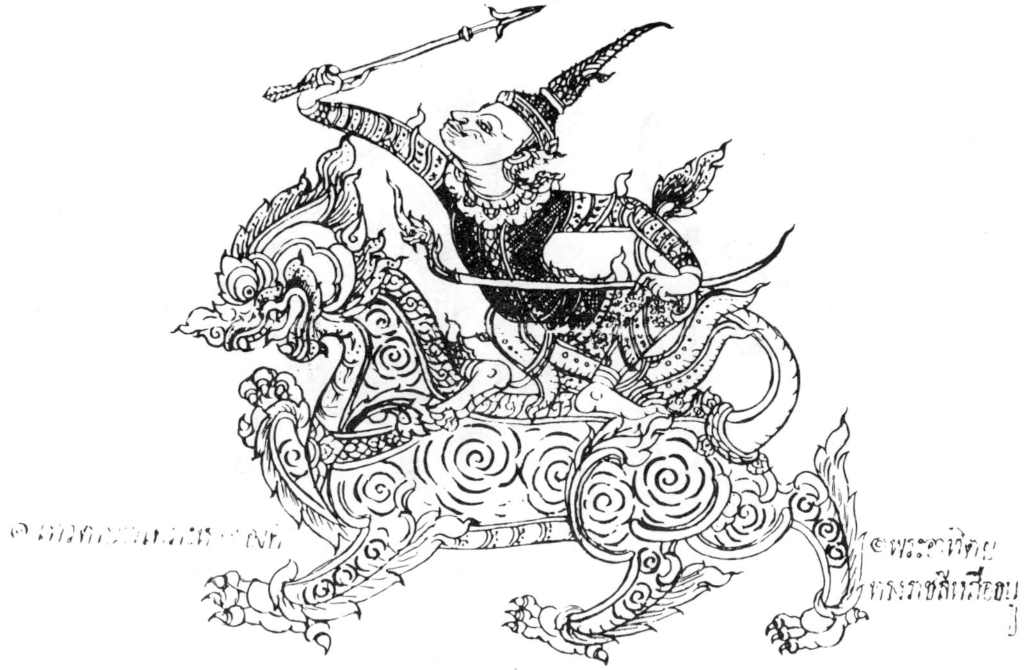

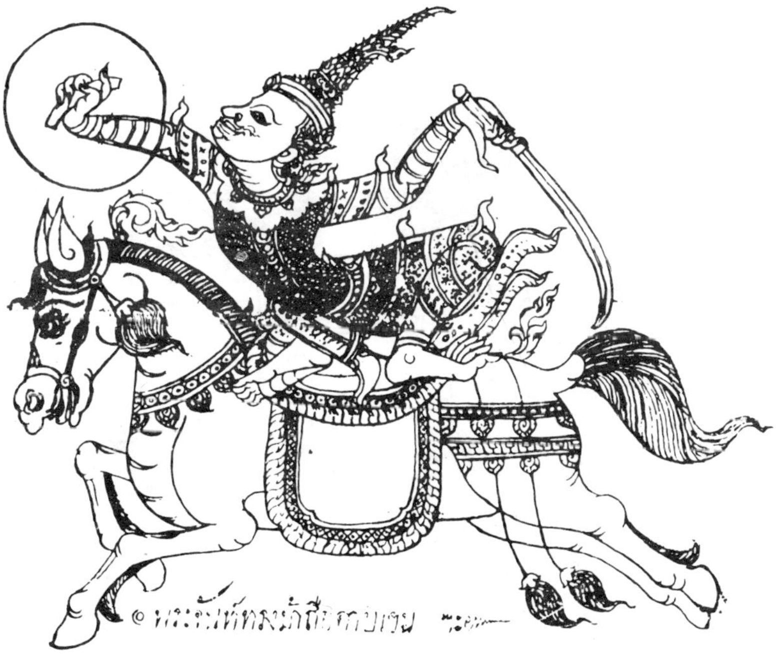

NAVA-GRAHA

149. Āditya /Sun on a lion, holding bow and arrow. See 171.

150. Candra /Moon on a horse, holding a sword and shield. See 172.

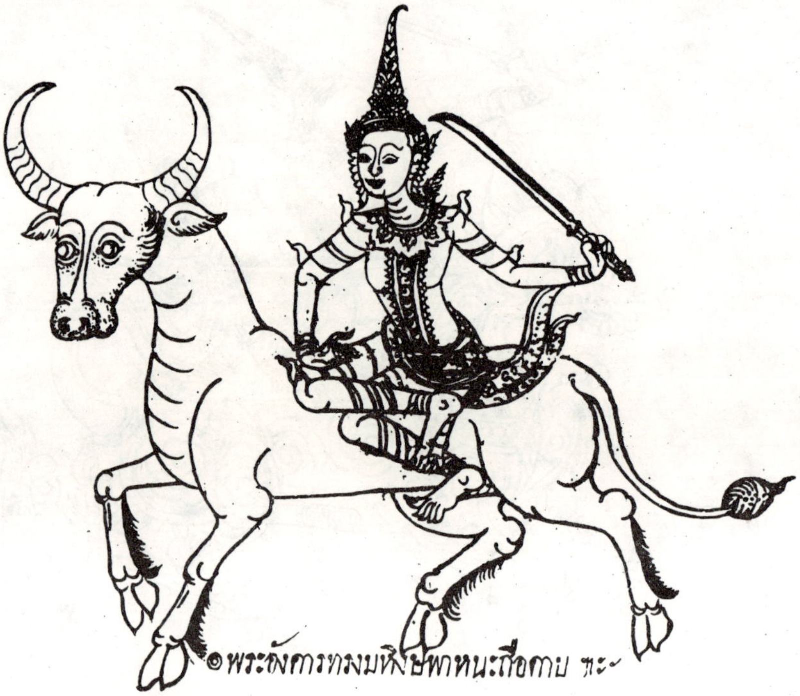

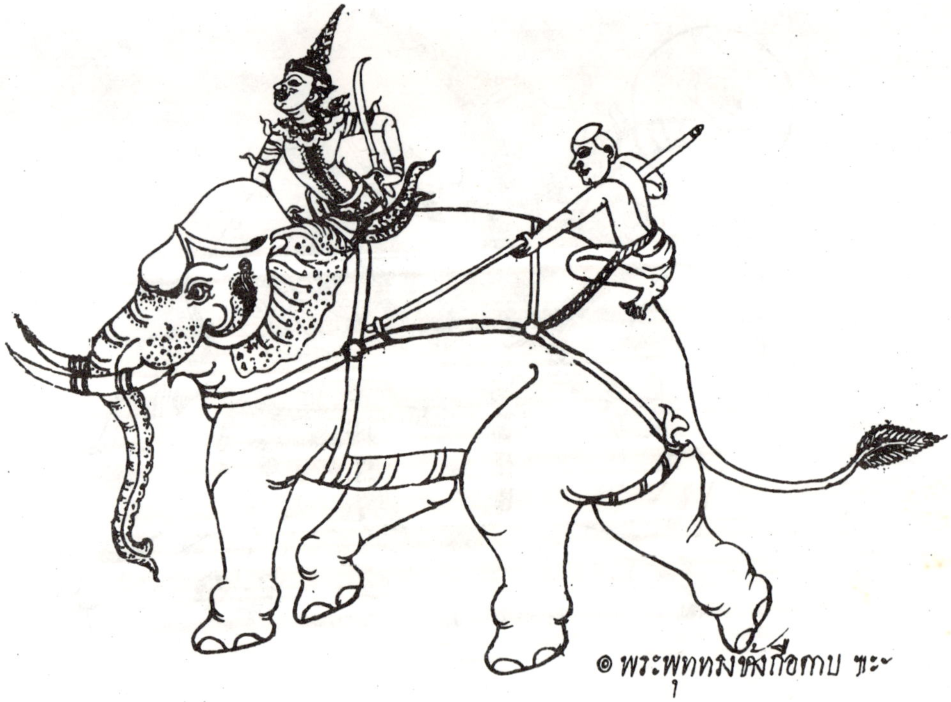

151. Aṅgāra on a buffalo, holding a sword. See 173.
152. Budha on an elephant, holding a sword. See 174.

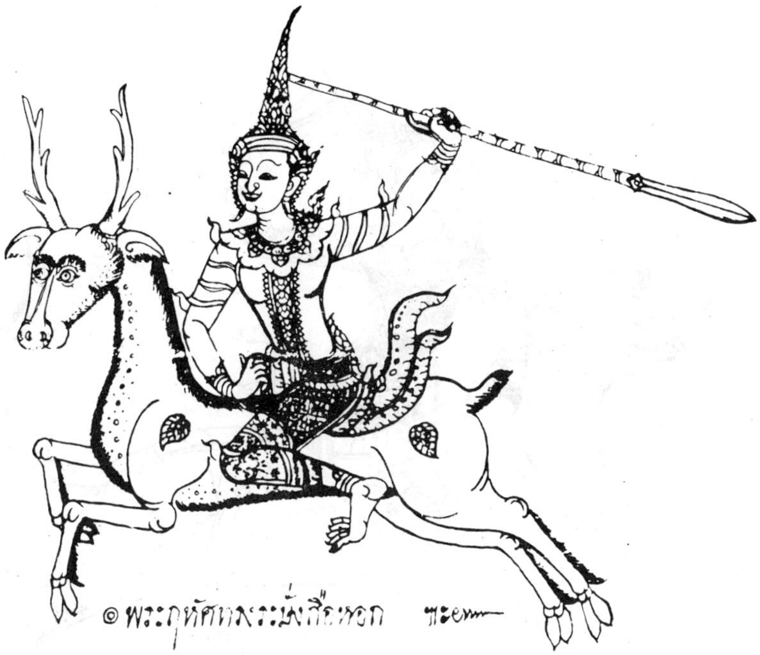

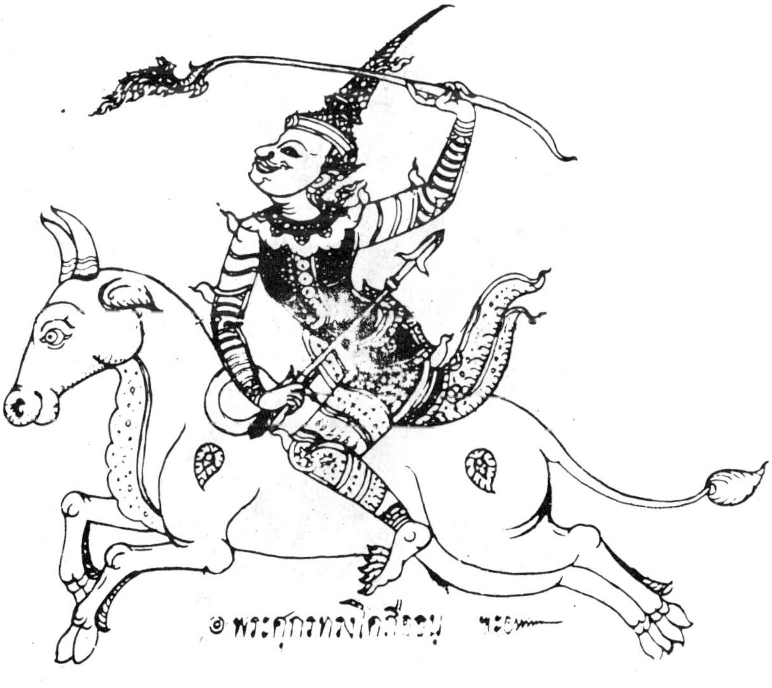

153. Bṛhaspati on a deer, holding a lance. See 175.
154. Śukra on a buffalo. See 176.

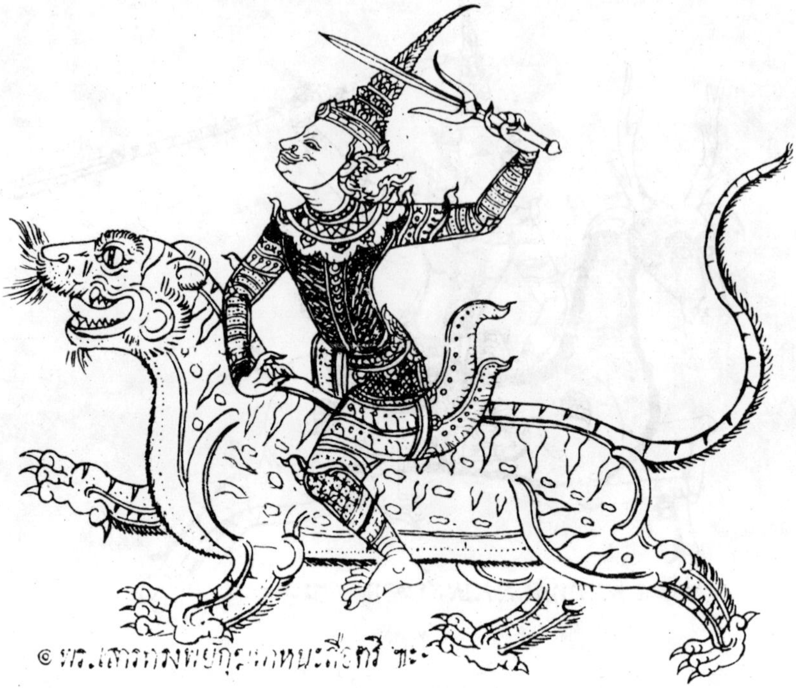

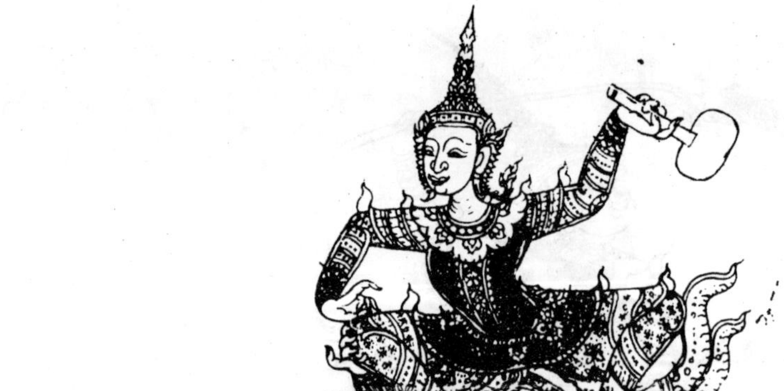

155. Śani on a tiger, holding a trident. See 177.
156. Rāhu on a yakṣa, holding an iron mace. See 178.

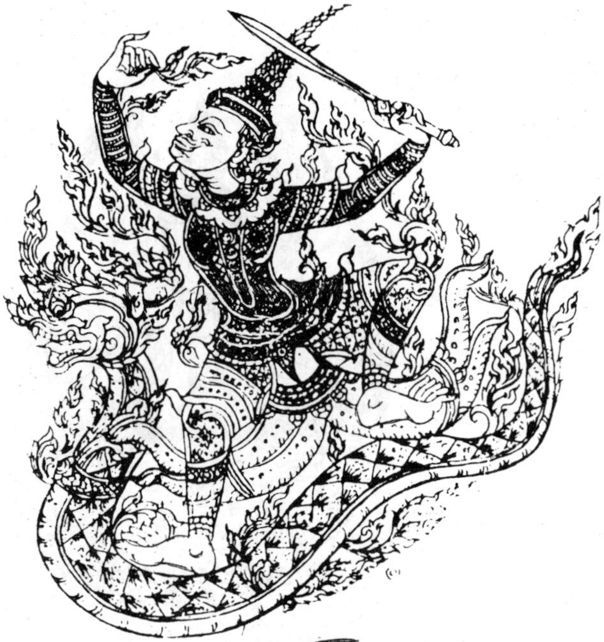

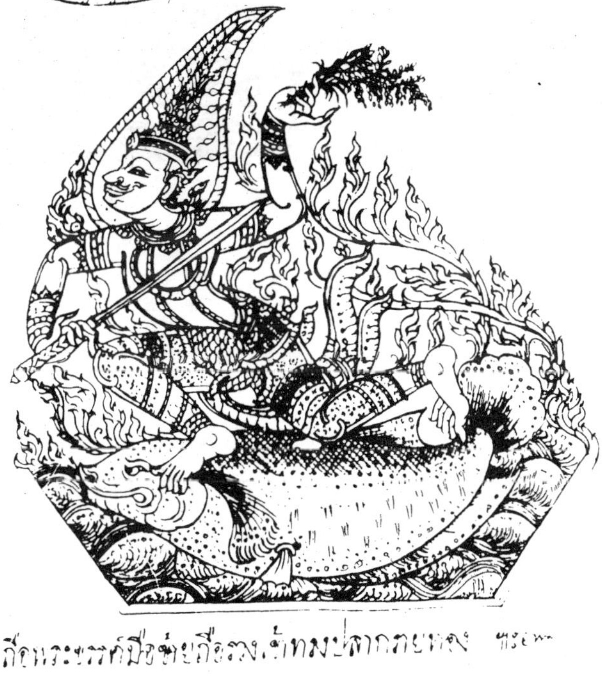

157. Ketu, on a nāga. See 179.

158. Mahājaya. See 170. Śiva rushing on a gold-fish Notopterus chitala. R.h. sword, l.h. ear of corn. Sarma 13b braḥ mhājaïy drṅ Plākrāy | ‹‹B. Mahājaya carried by the fish Notopterus chitala››.

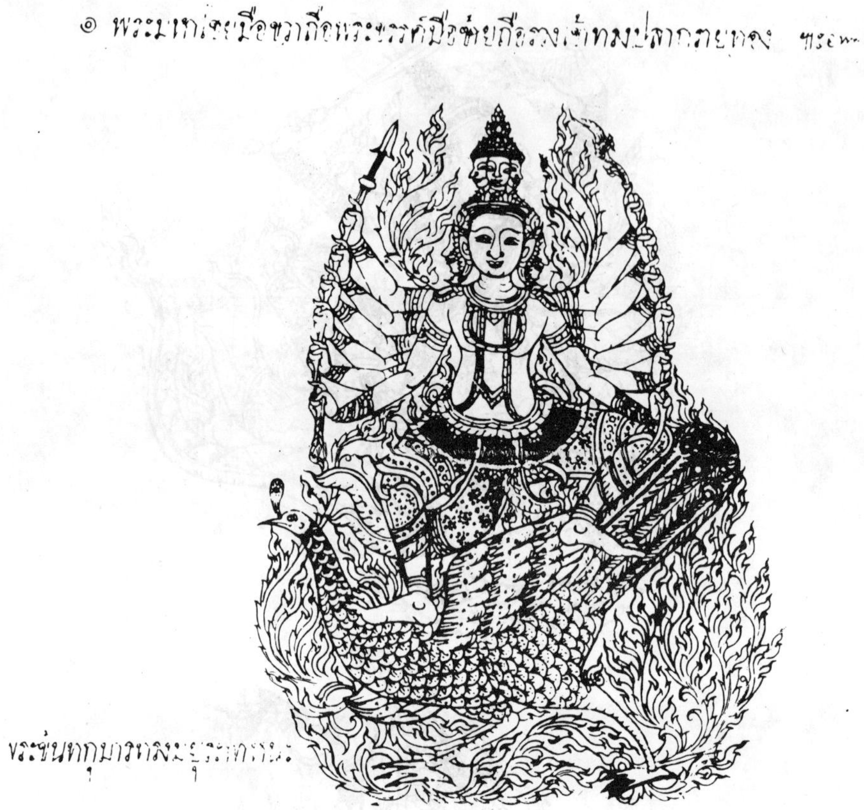

159. Skanda-Kumāra on a peacock. See 48.

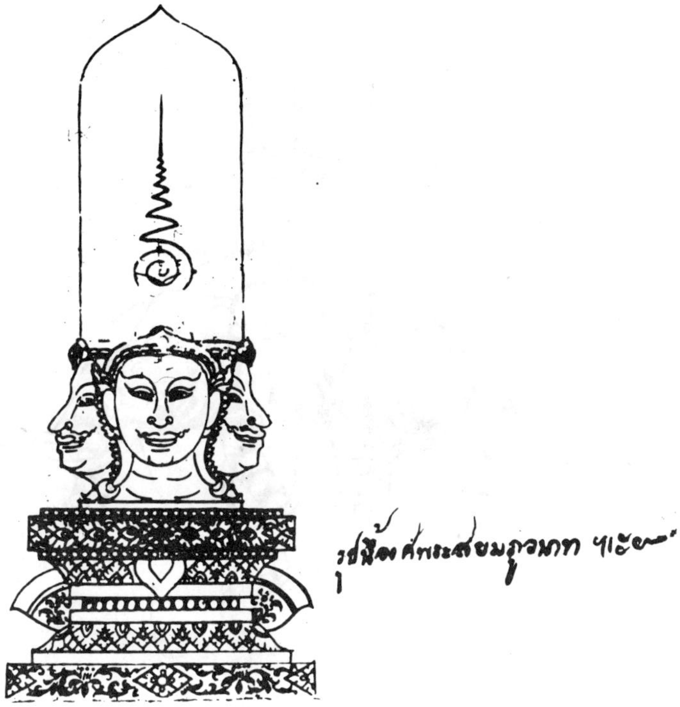

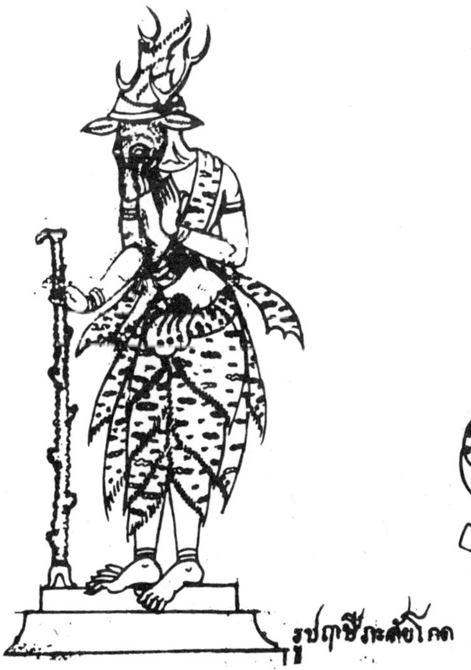

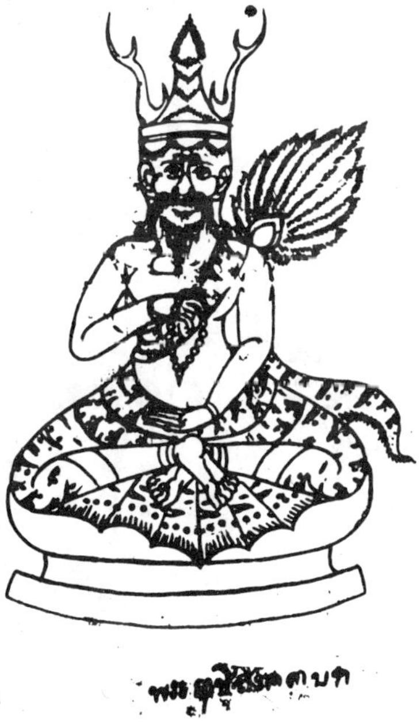

THIRD PANTHEON

160. Svāyambhuva-nātha. See 1.
161. Ṛṣi Kalaikkōṭṭu /Ṛṣyaśṛṅga. See 47.
162. Ṛṣi with a fan. See 48.

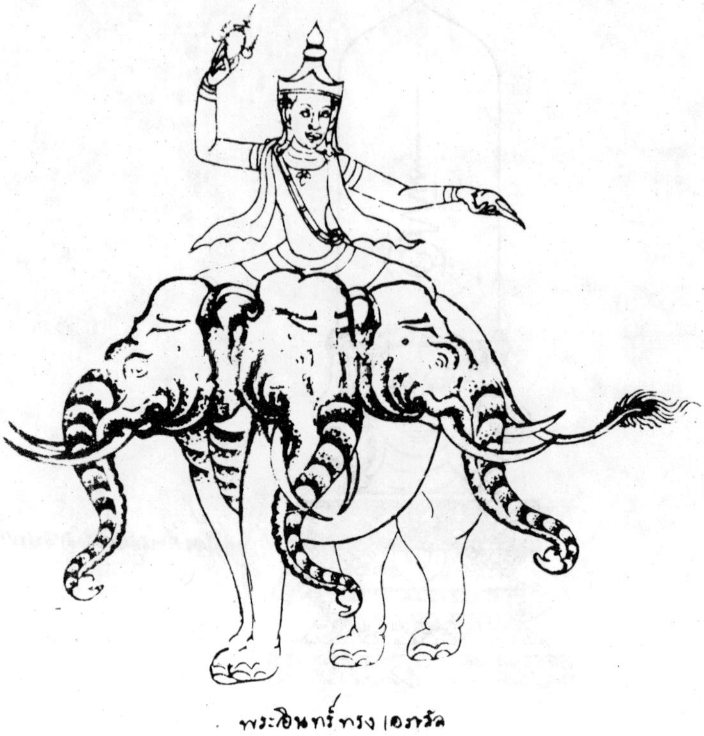

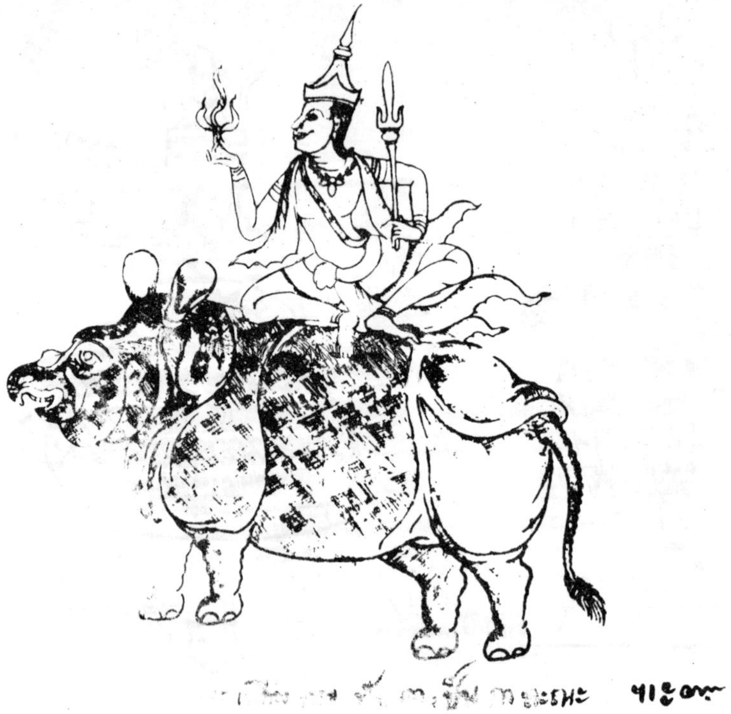

EIGHT DIKPĀLAS

163. Indra on three-headed Airāvata. See 140.

164. Agni on a rhinoceros. See 147.

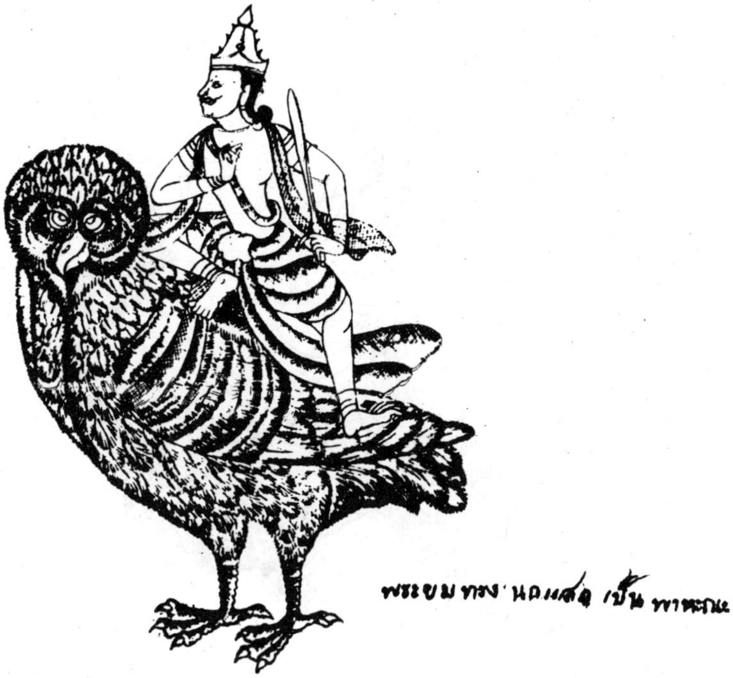

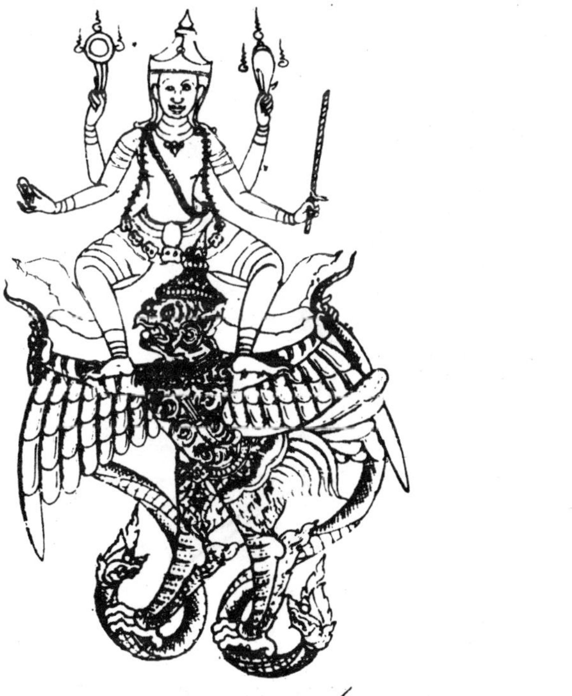

165. Yama on an owl. See 141.
166. Nārāyaṇa on garuḍa. See 142.

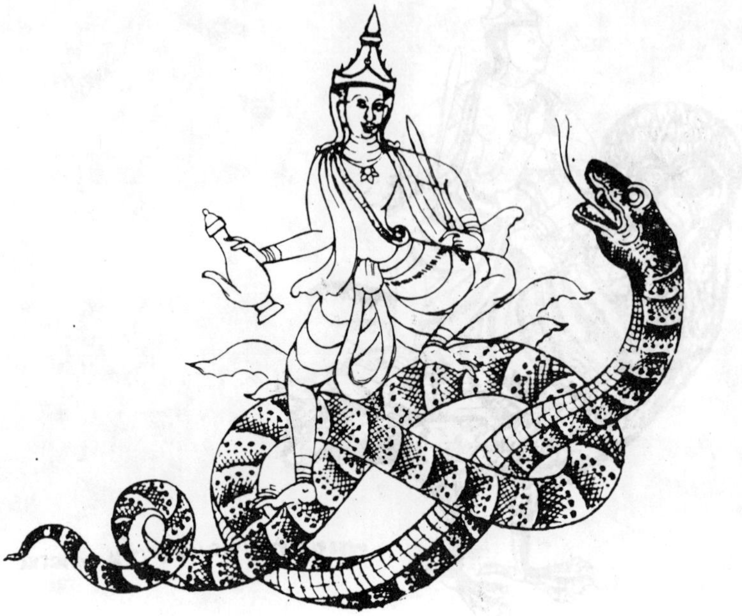

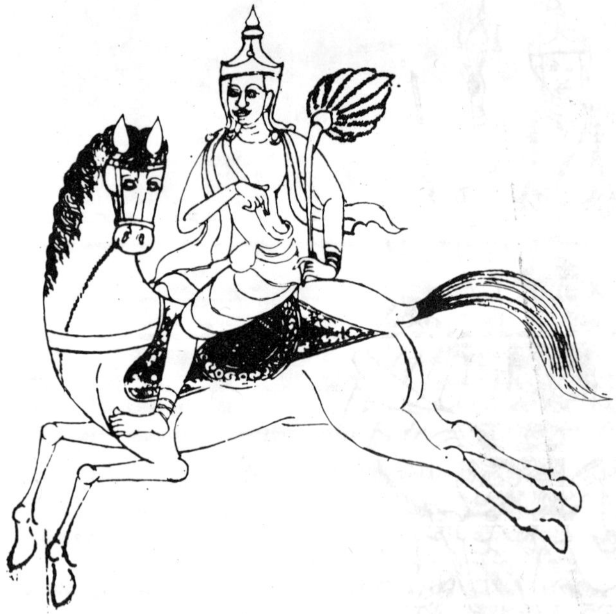

167. Varuṇa on a nāga. See 146.
168. ? on a galloping horse. See 144.

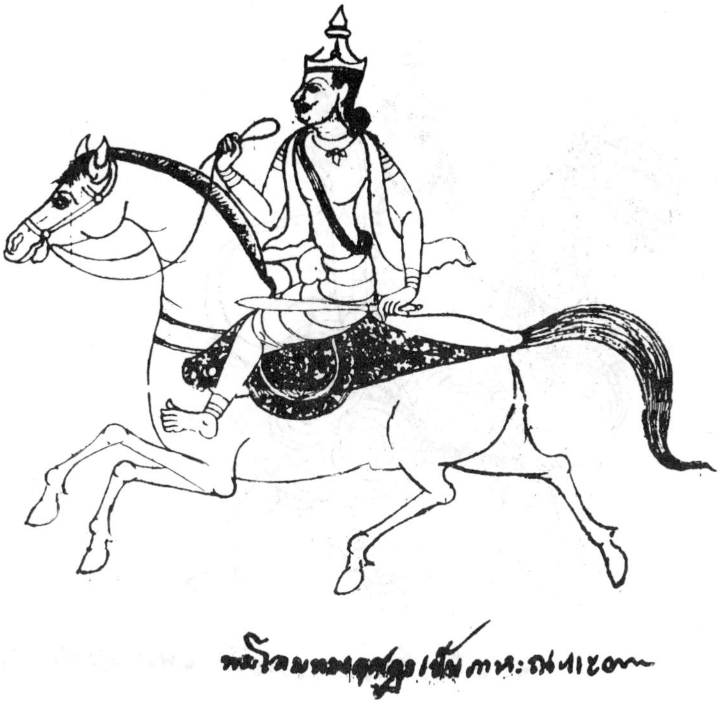

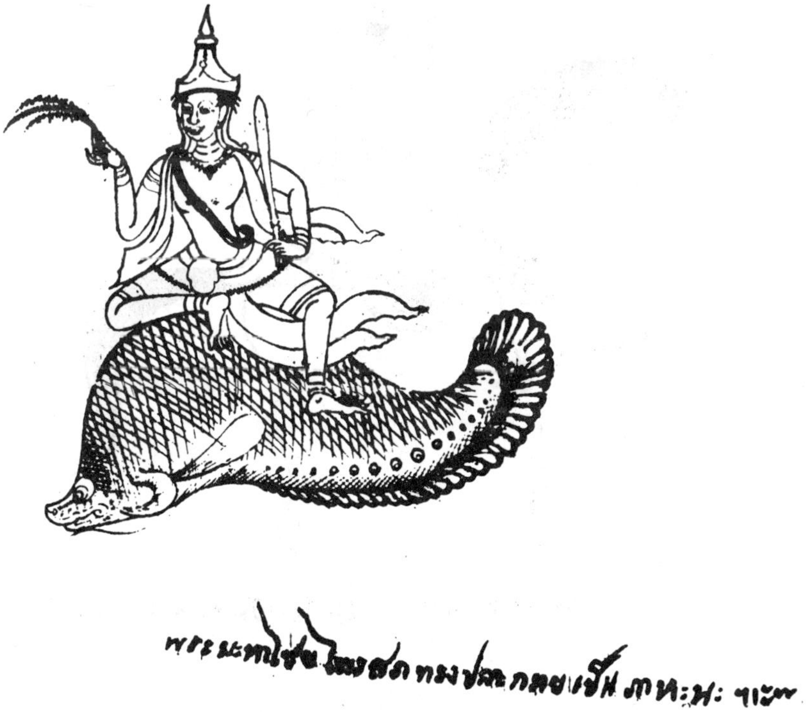

169. Vāyu on a horse. See 144.
170. Mahājaya on a gold-fish. See 158.

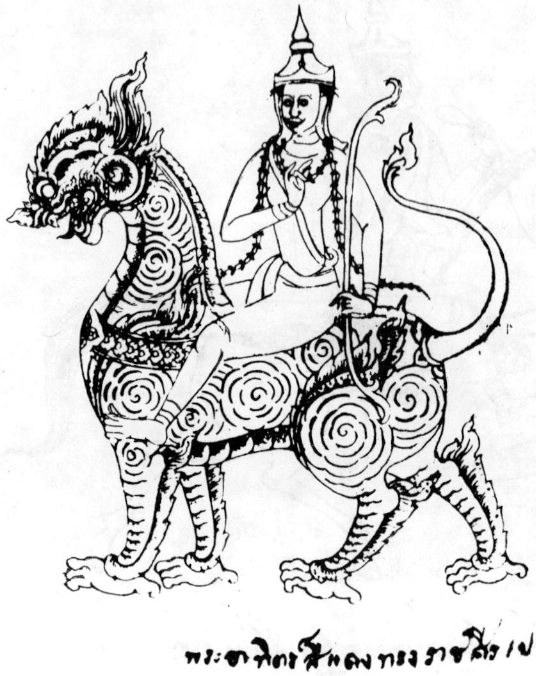

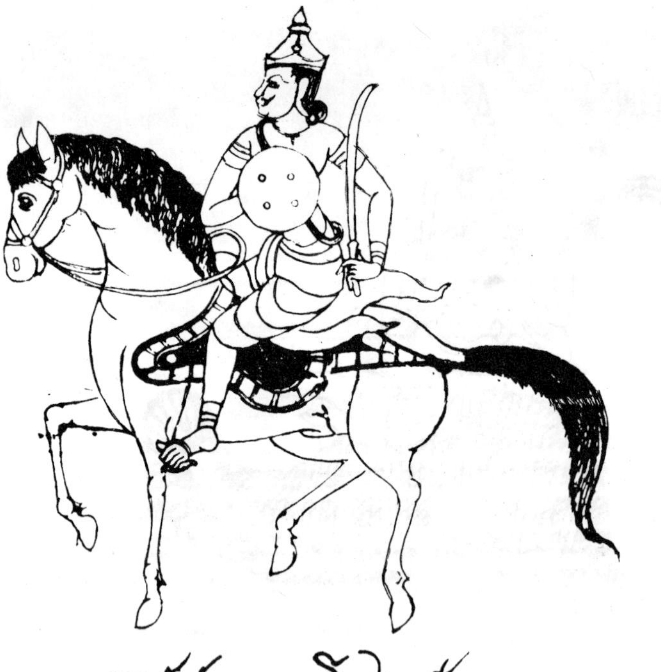

NAVA-GRAHA

171. Āditya on a lion, red colour. See 149.

172. Candra on a horse, white colour. See 150.

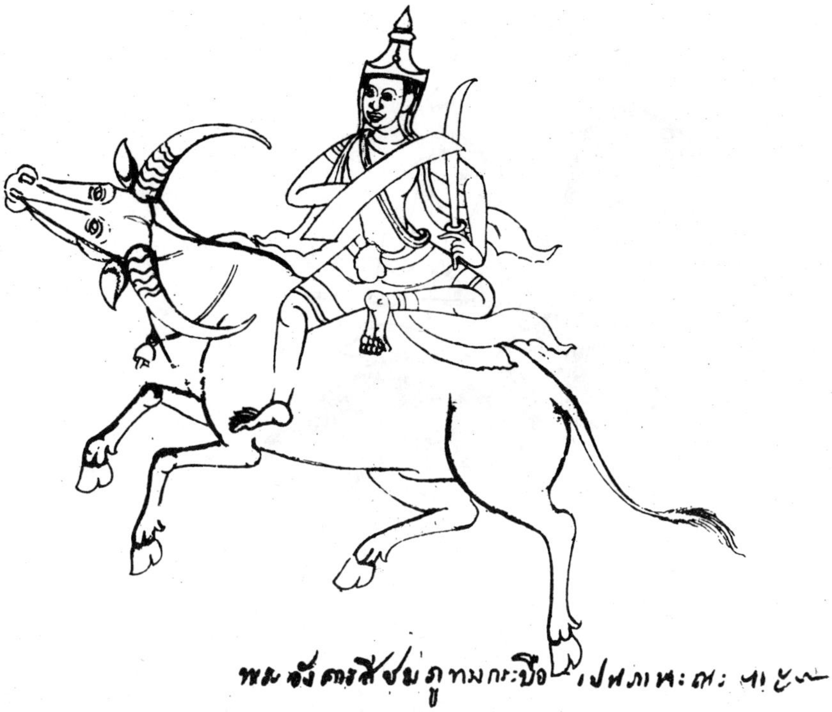

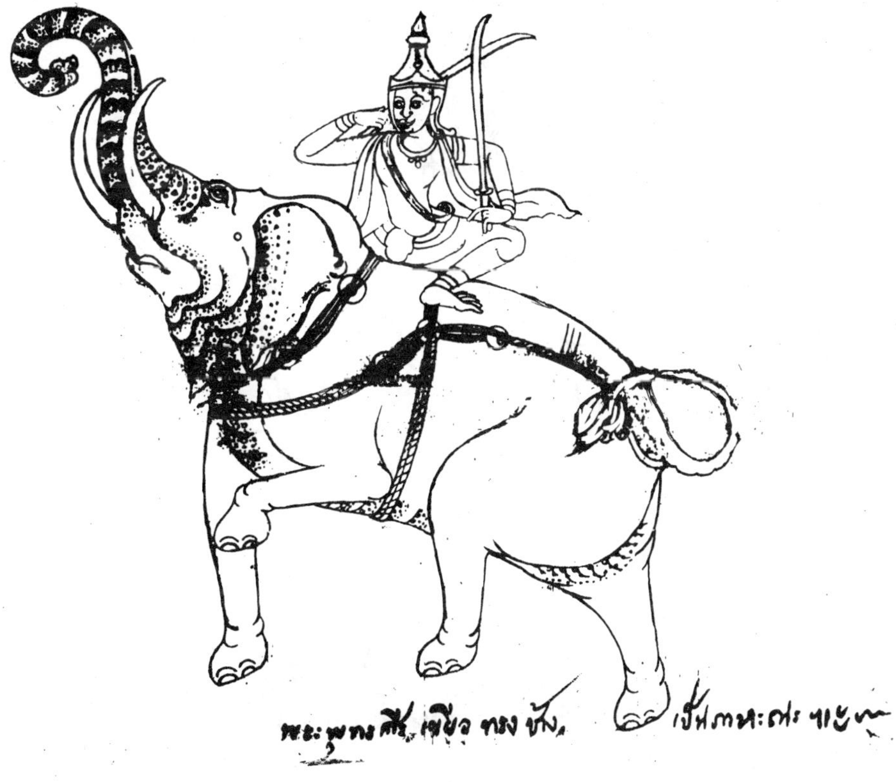

173. Aṅgāra on a buffalo, pink colour. See 151.
174. Budha on an elephant, green colour. See 152.

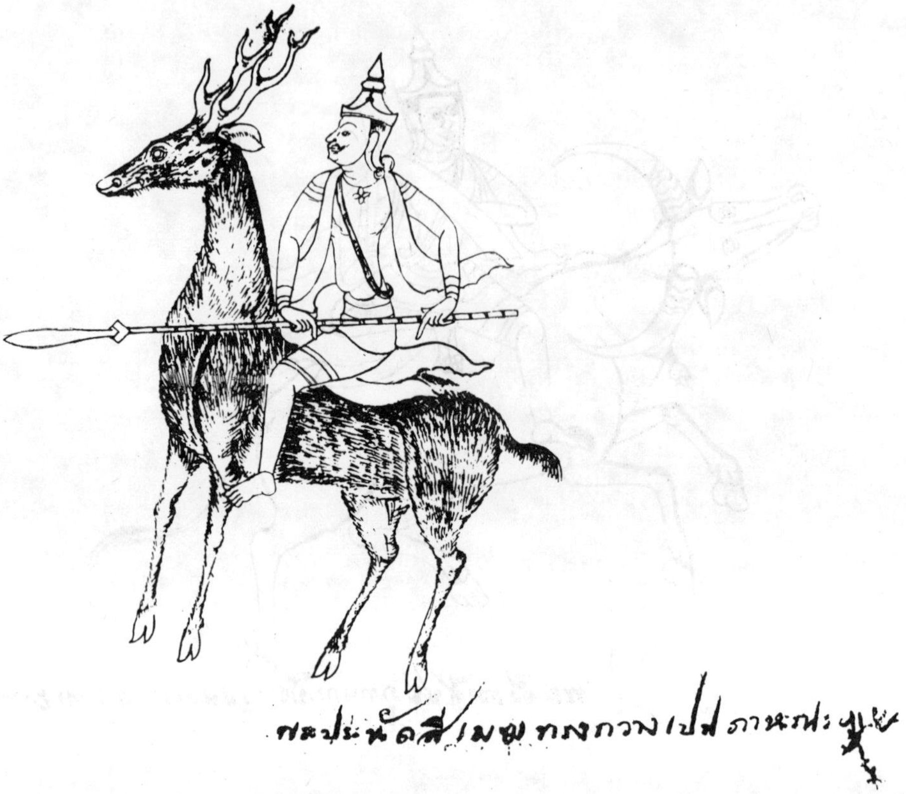

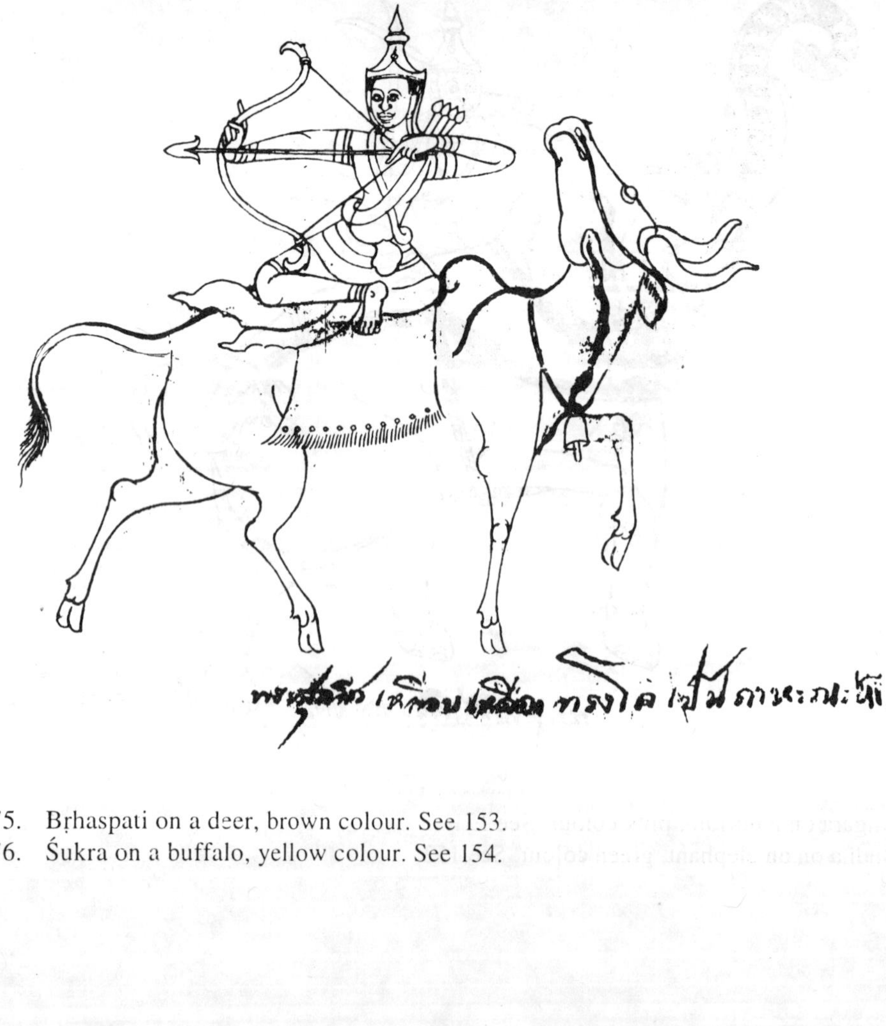

175. Bṛhaspati on a deer, brown colour. See 153.
176. Śukra on a buffalo, yellow colour. See 154.

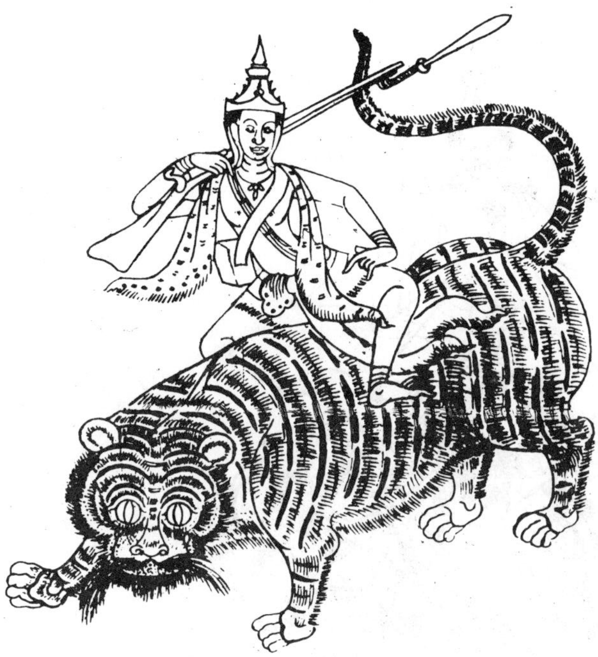

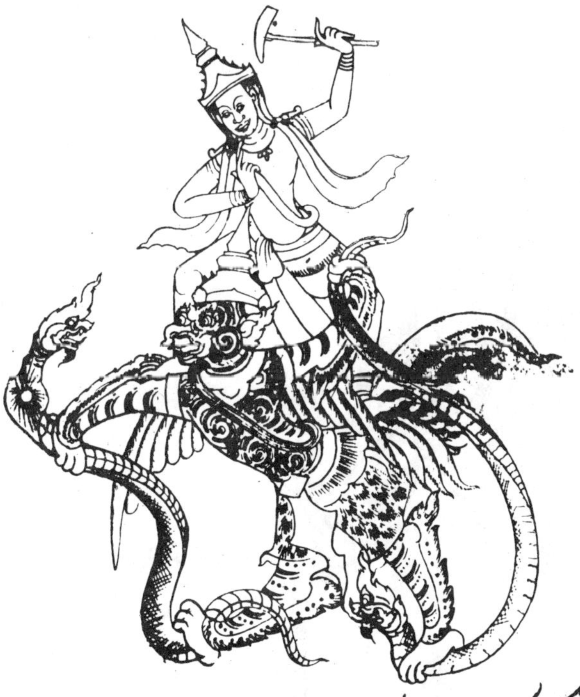

177. Śani on a tiger, black colour. See 155.
178. Rāhu on garuḍa(?), violet colour. See 156.

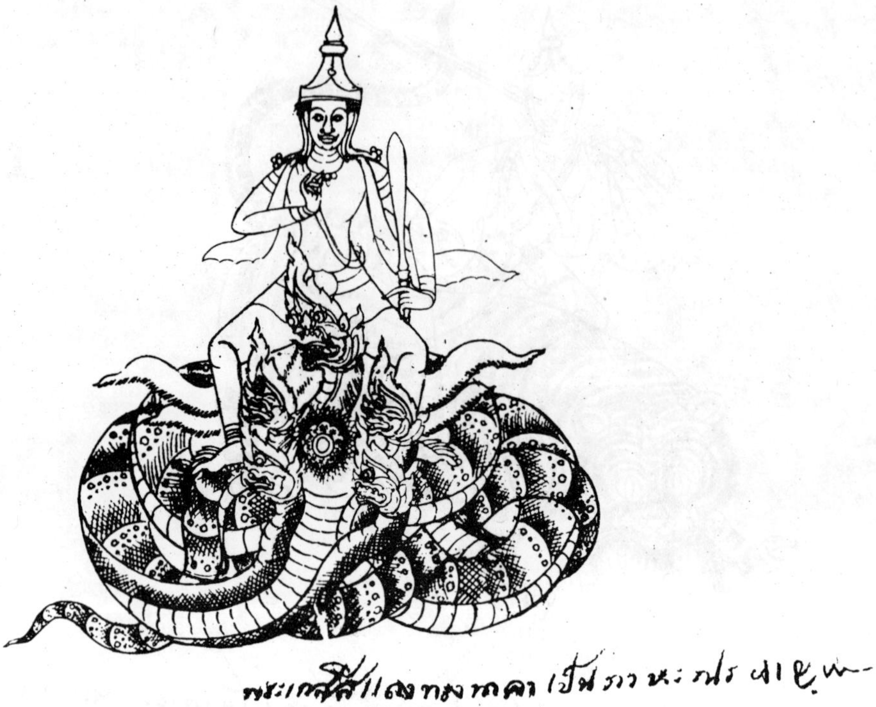

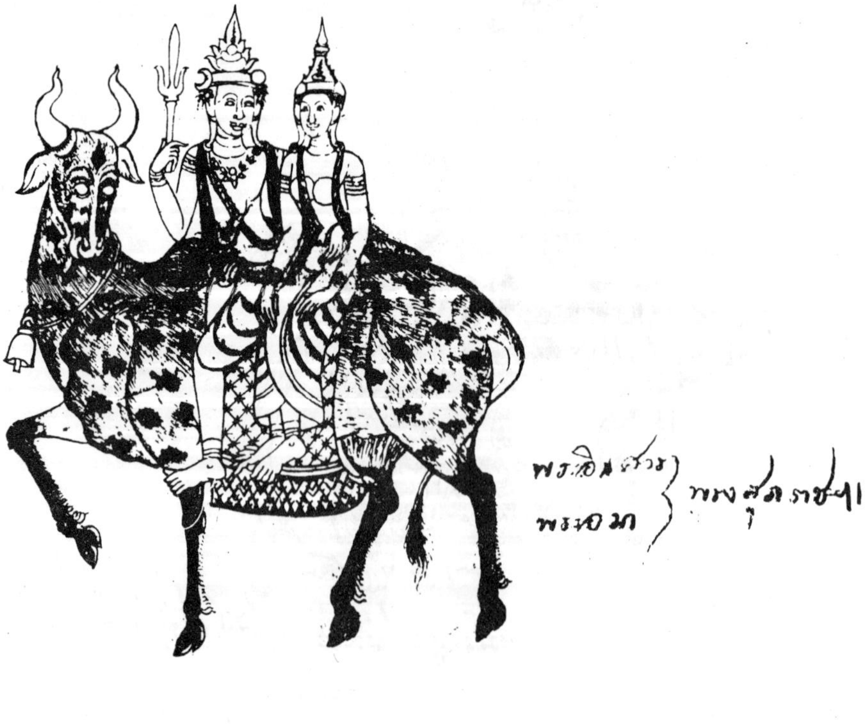

179. Ketu on a nāga, red colour. See 157.
180. Īśvara and Umā on Nandin. See 4.

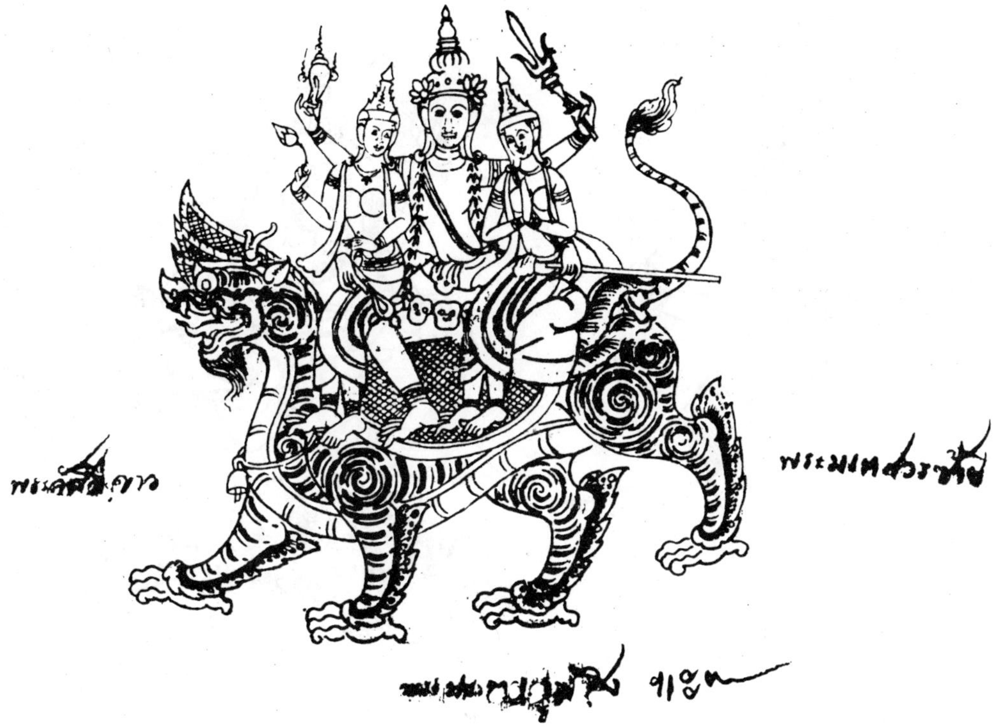

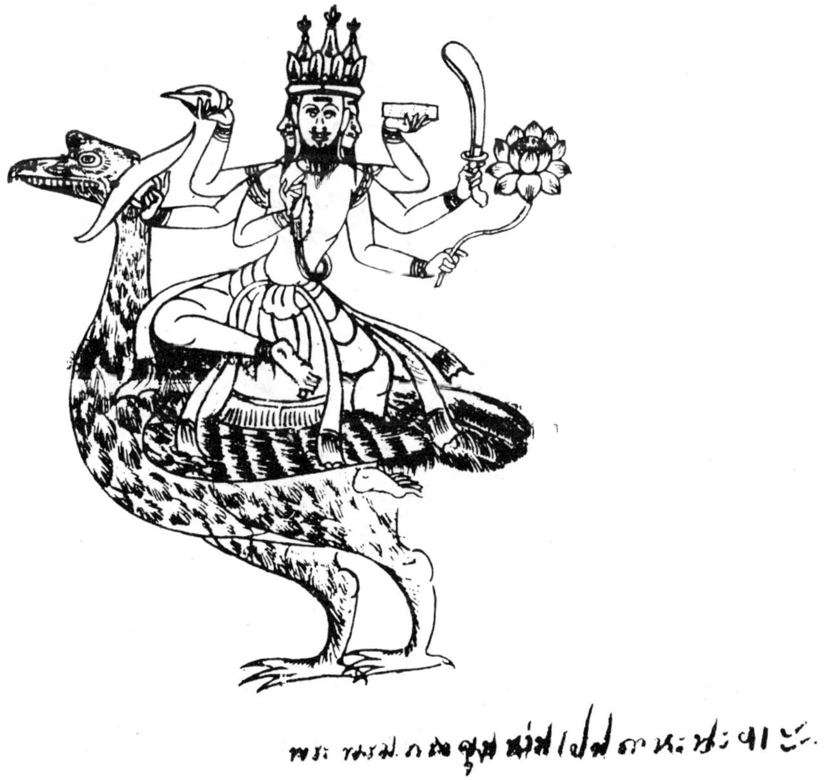

181. Nārāyaṇa flanked by Bhūdevī and Śrīdevī, all on a lion. See 28.
182. Six-armed Brahmā on a vulture.

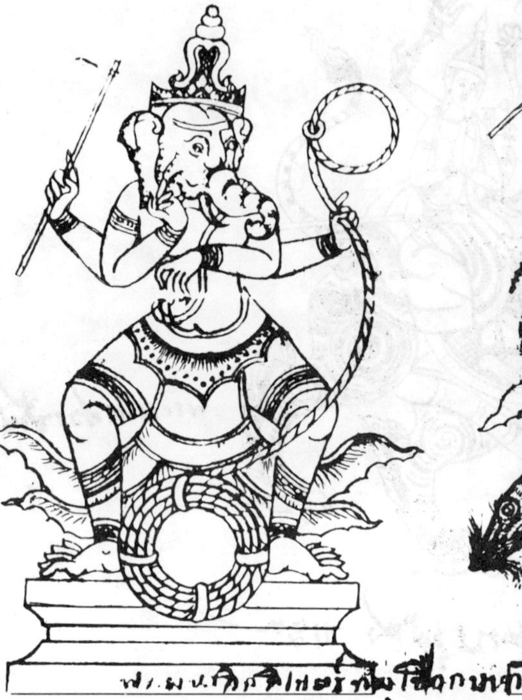

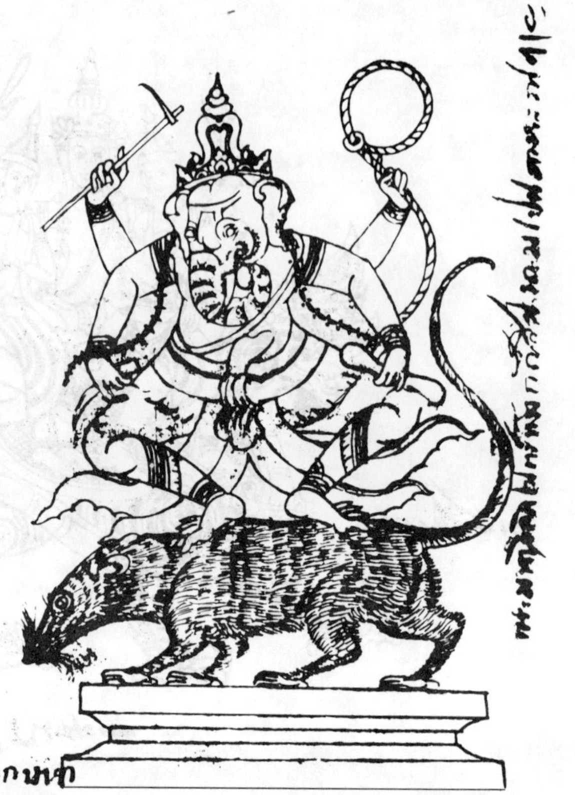

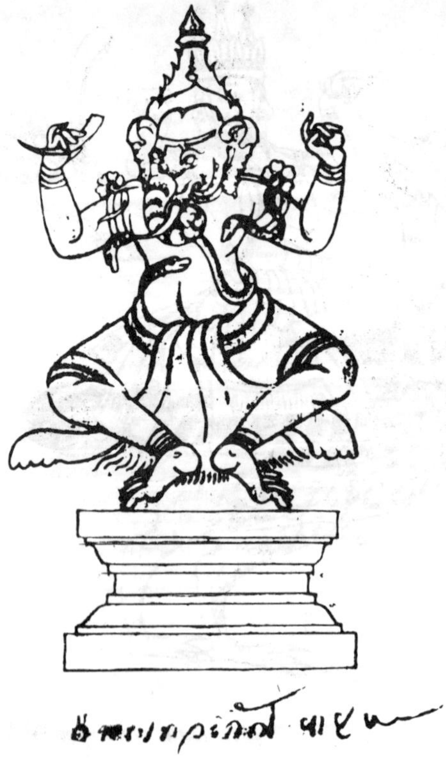

183. Four-armed Mahāvighneśvara with an awl (?) and noose. See 22.
184. Four-armed Mahāvighneśvara on his rat. See 23.
185. Devakarma Gaṇeśa. See 27.

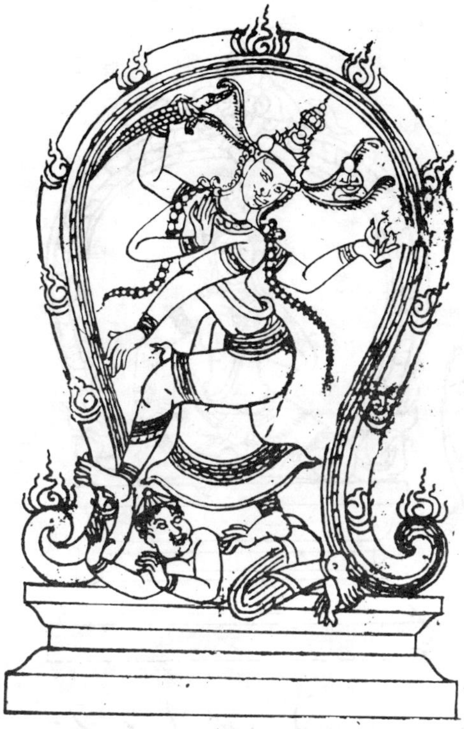

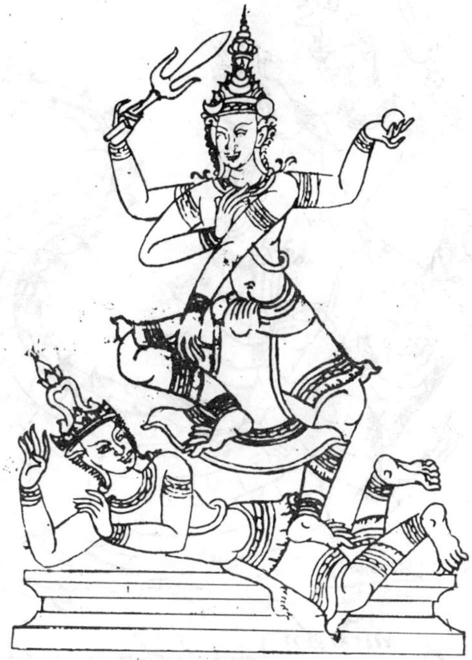

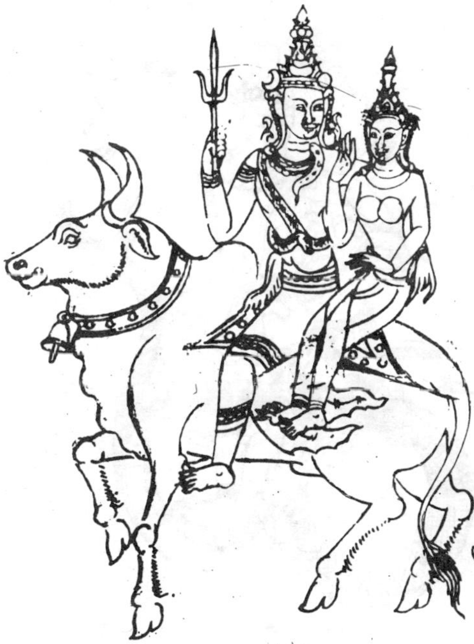

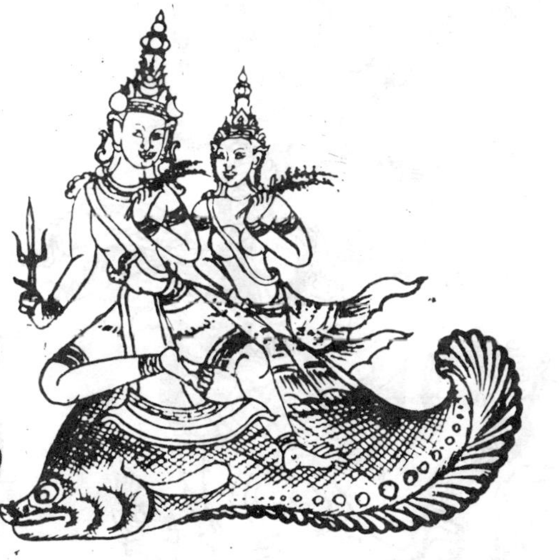

186. Four-armed Parameśvara subdues Apasmāra-puruṣa, the symbol of ignorance. See 2.
187. Four-armed Parameśvara subdues Andhaka. See 3.
188. Parameśvara and Umā on Nandin on their way to Kailāsa. See 4.
189. Parameśvara and Umā on the gold-fish Notopterus chitala. See 5.

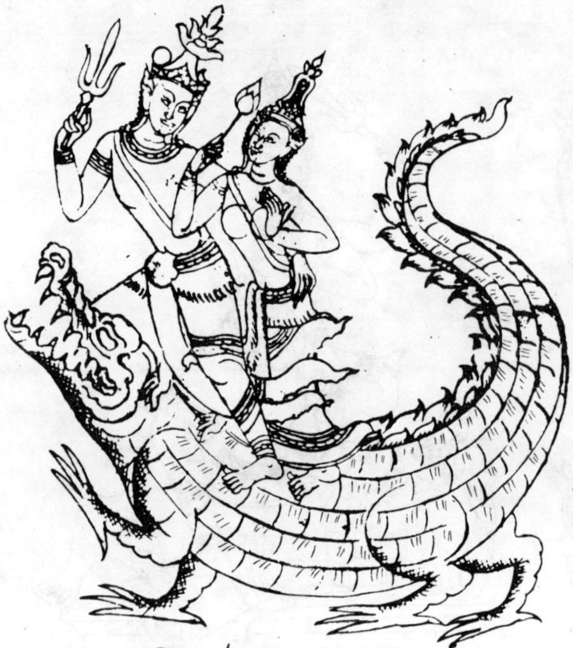

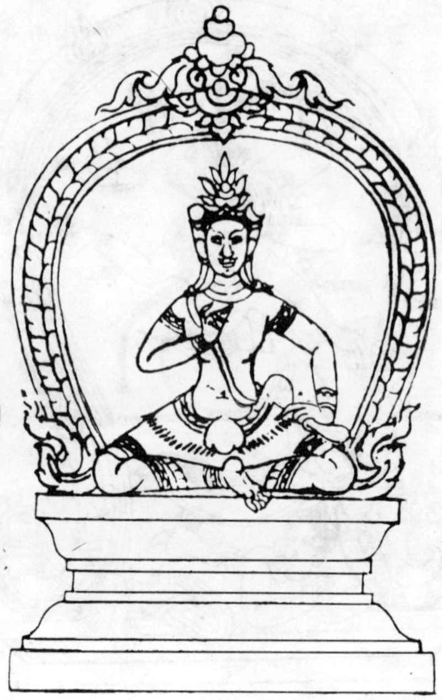

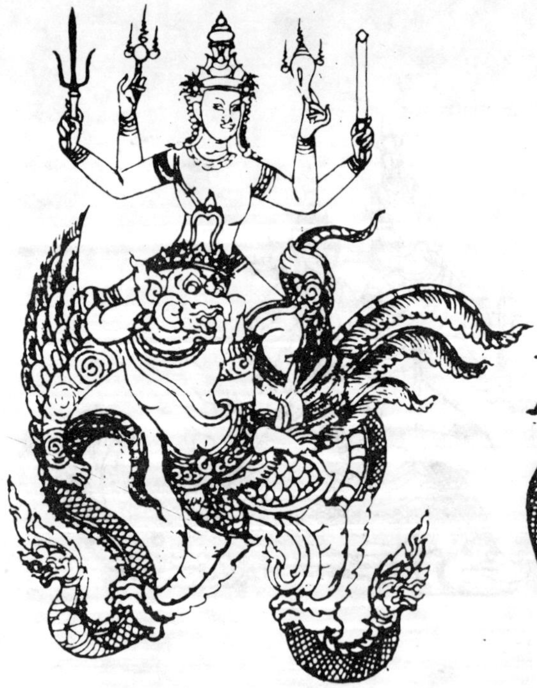

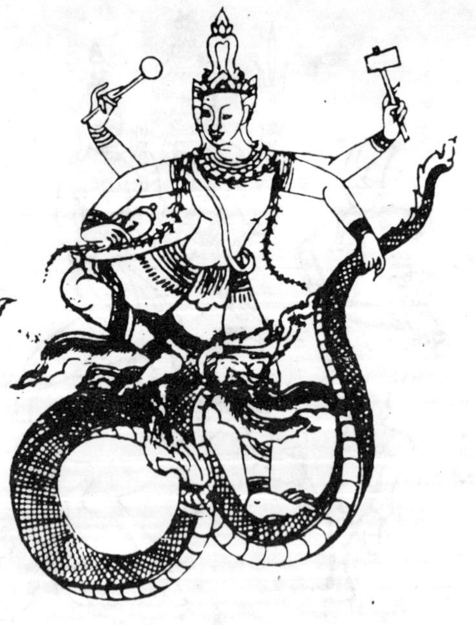

190. Īśvara and Umā on a crocodile. See 6.
191. Parameśvara sitting in the mudrā of teaching. See 7.
192. Four-armed Nārāyaṇa going to Vaikuṇṭha on garuḍa. See 8.
193. Four-armed Nārāyaṇa subduing the nāga. See 9.

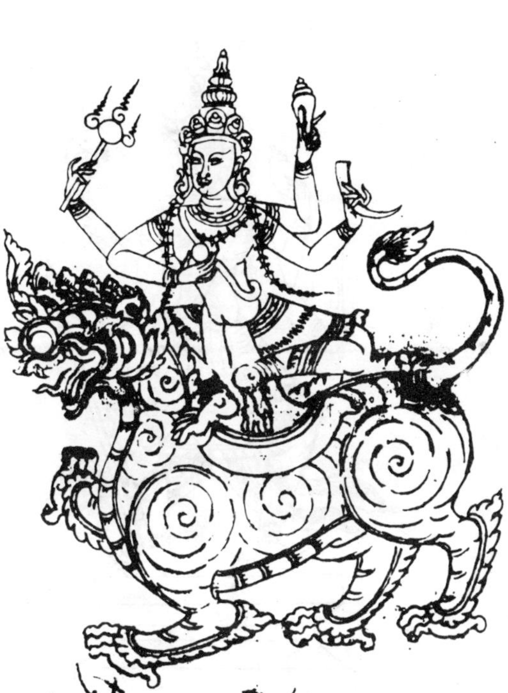

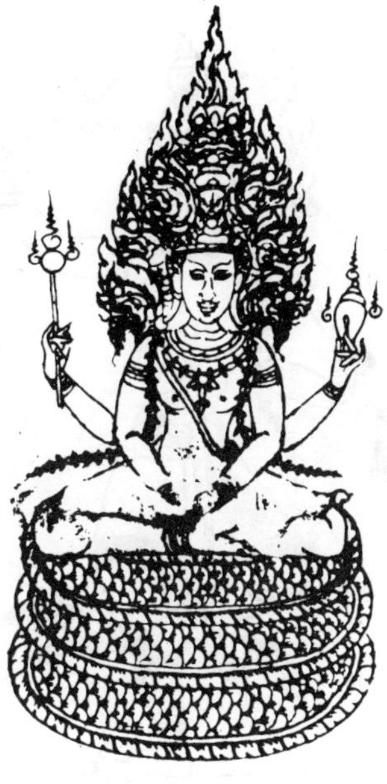

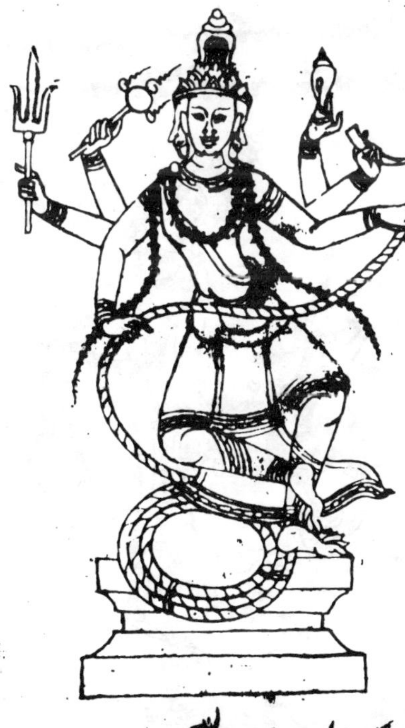

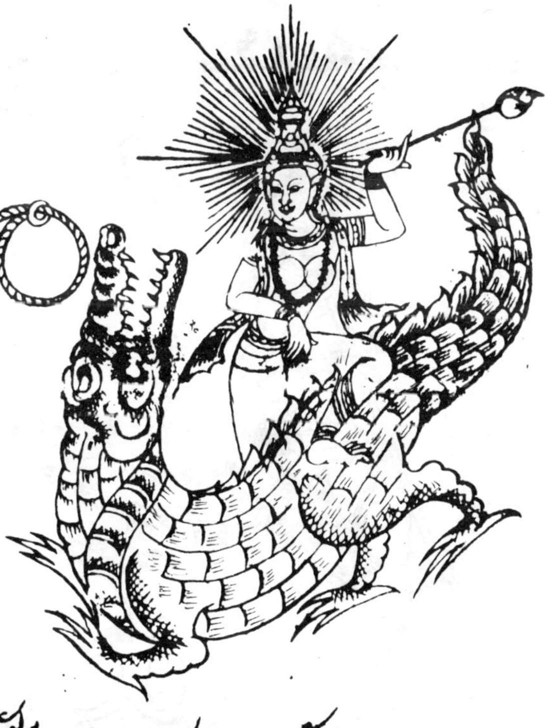

194. Four-armed Nārāyaṇa on his way to Kailāsa on a lion. See 10.
195. Four-armed Nārāyaṇa meditating on a nāga. See 11.
196. Six-armed Nārāyaṇa with a rope to subdue Ekadanta. See 12.
197. Umā subdues a crocodile. See 13.

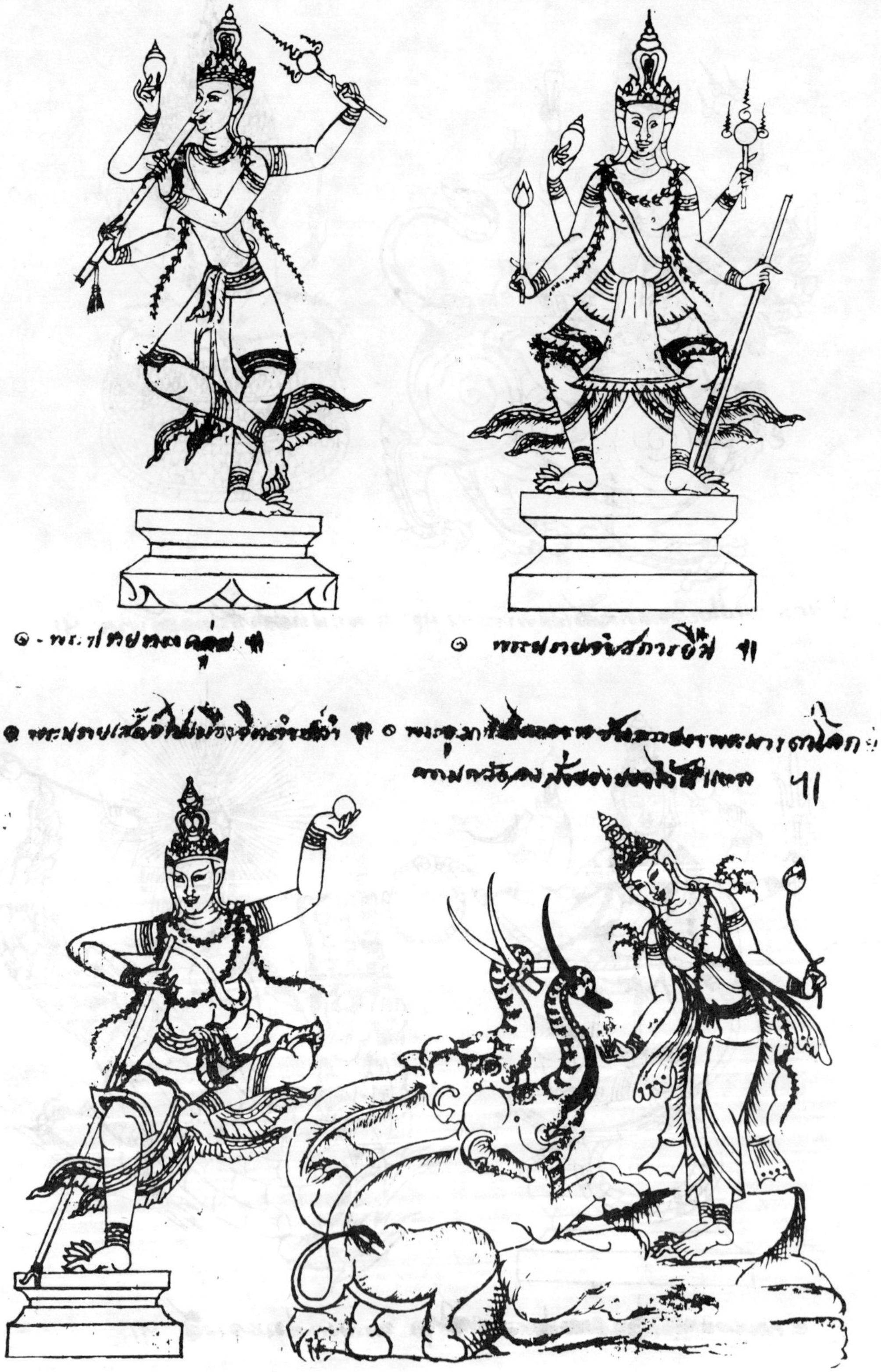

198. Four-armed Nārāyaṇa playing the flute. See 14.
199. Four-armed Nārāyaṇa standing upright. See 15.
200. Two-armed Nārāyaṇa going to Citramalā: See 16.
201. Elephants offering their tongues to Umā. See 17.

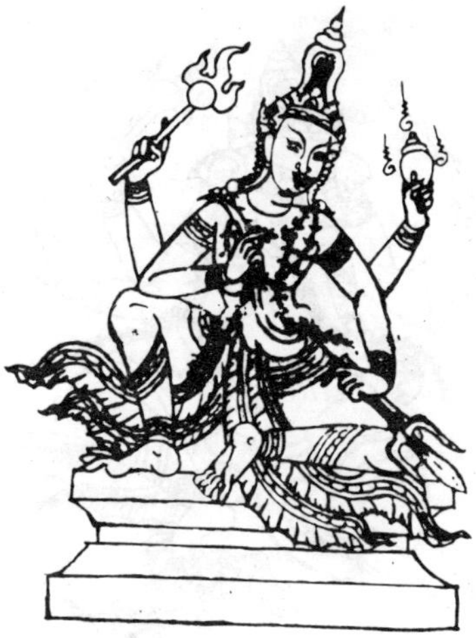

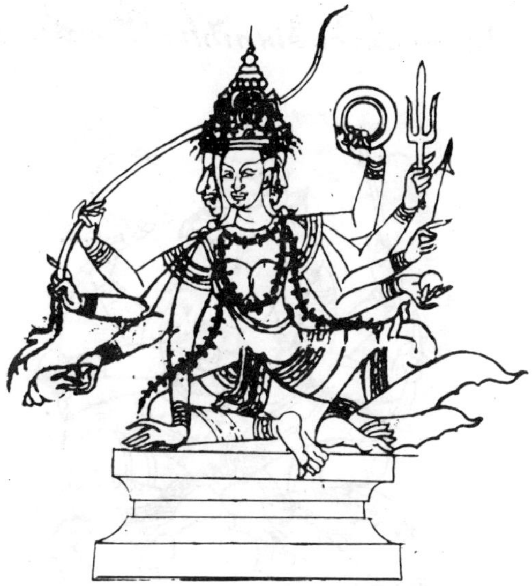

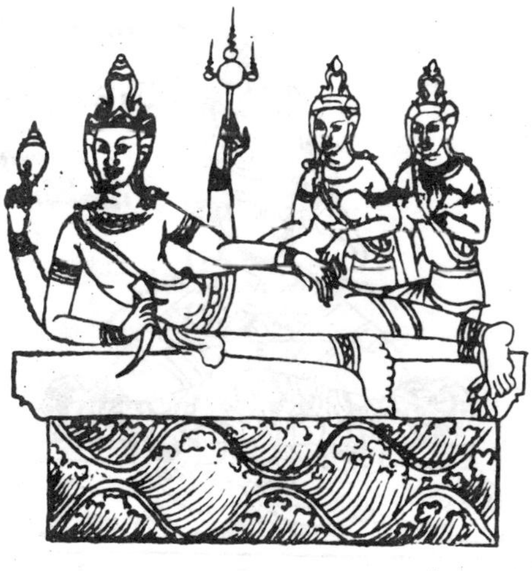

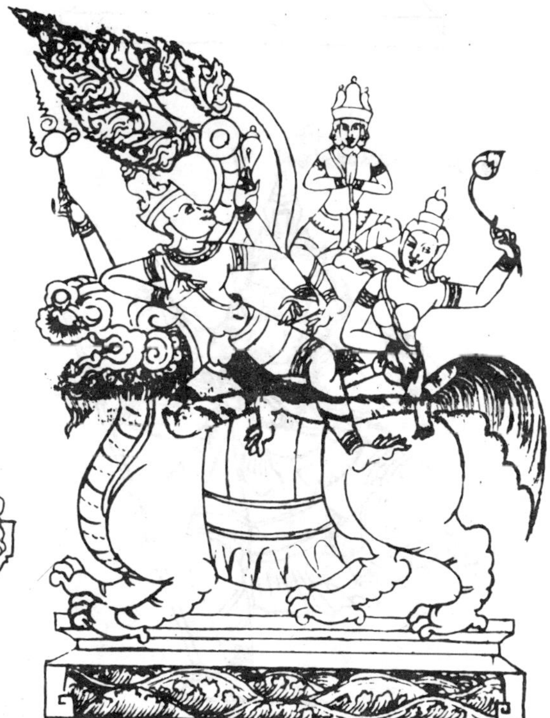

202. Four-armed Nārāyaṇa seated. See 18.
203. Eight-armed Devakarma Nārāyaṇī, with three visible faces. See 19.
204. Four-armed Nārāyaṇa meditating afloat on the ocean, accompanied by Bhūdevī and Śrīdevī. See 20.
205. Four-armed Nārāyaṇa lying on the nāga, accompanied by Brahmā and Śrīdevī. See 21.

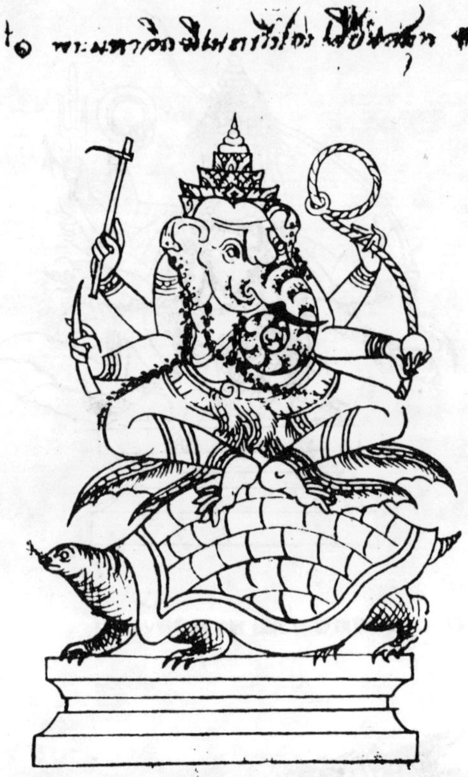

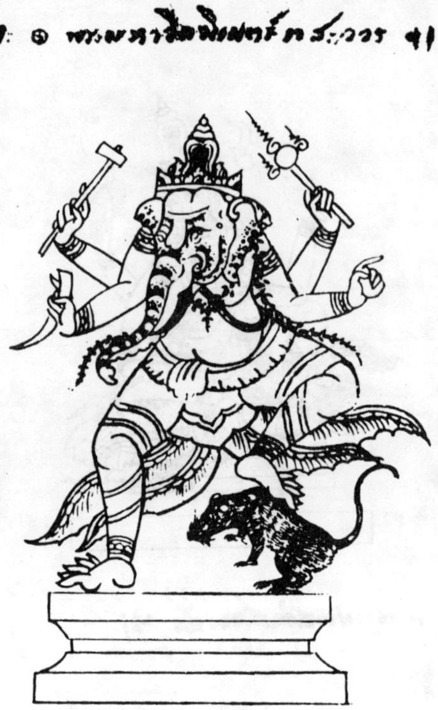

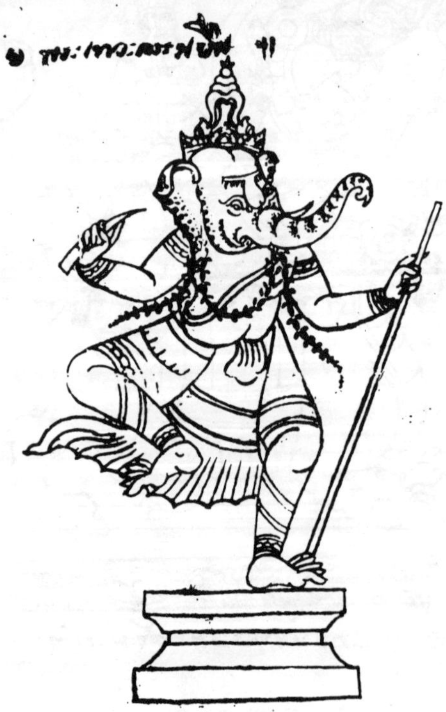

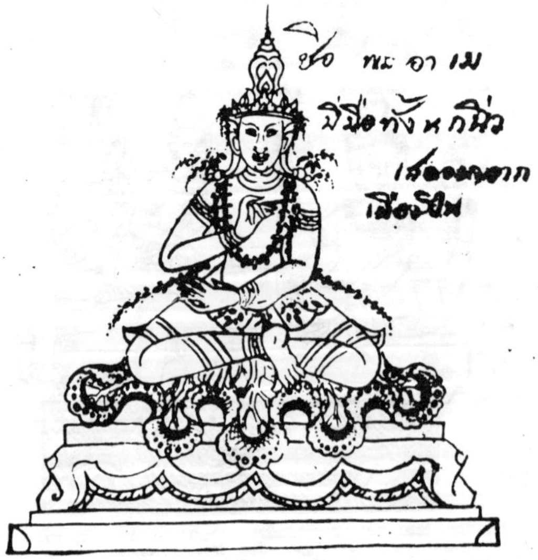

206. Four-armed Mahāvighneśvara on a tortoise. See 24.
207. Four-armed Mahāvighneśvara on his rat. See 23.
208. Devakarma. See 26.
209. Six-finger deity. See 39.

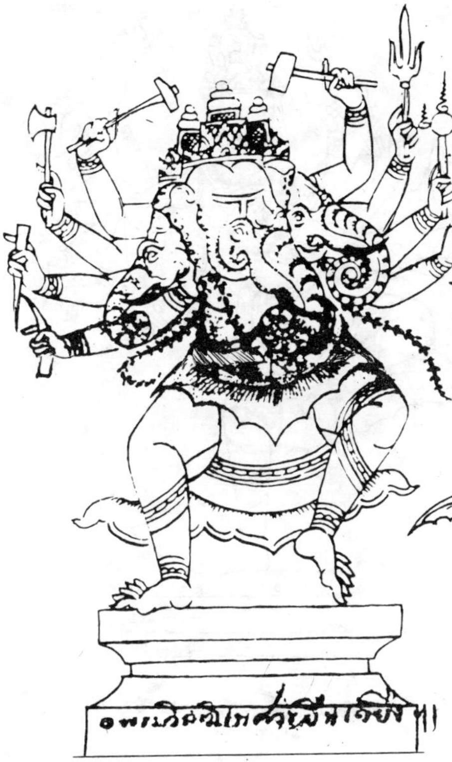

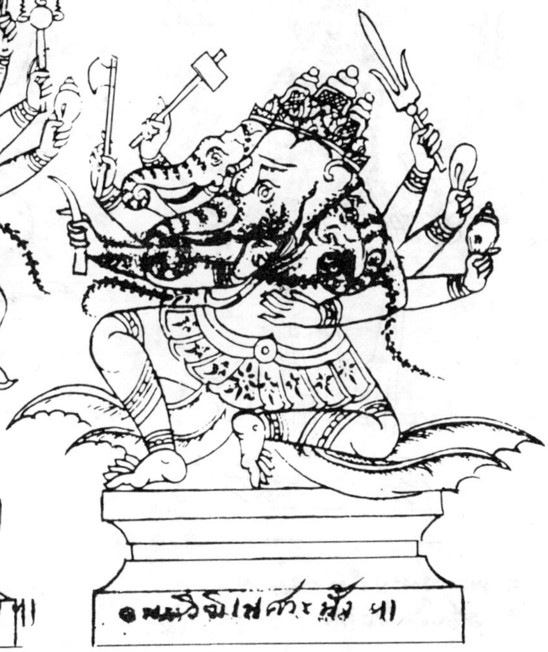

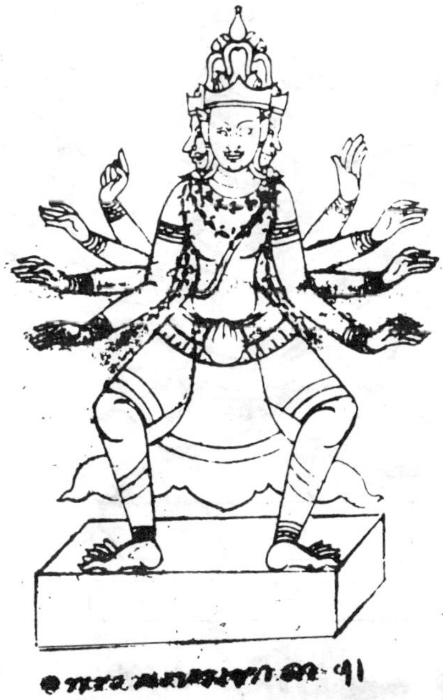

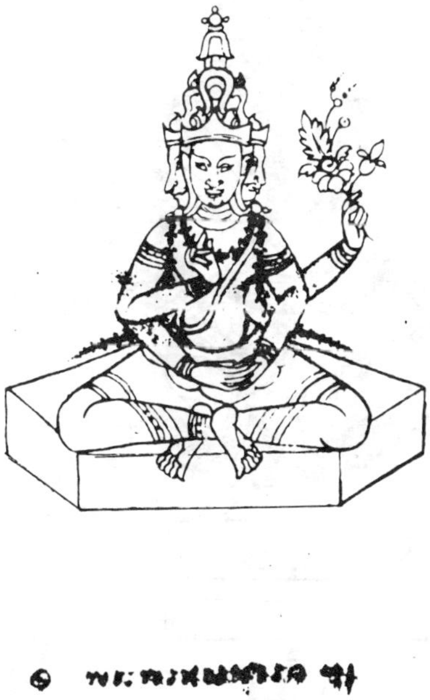

210. Eight-armed Vighneśvara standing. See 28.
211. Eight-armed Vighneśvara sitting. See 98.
212. Eight-armed four-faced Brahmā Dhātā (attributes have not been drawn). See 30.
213. Brahmanātha. Sarma 26a.

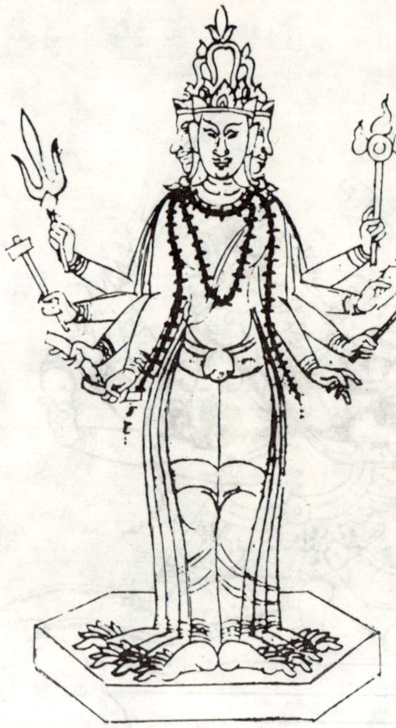

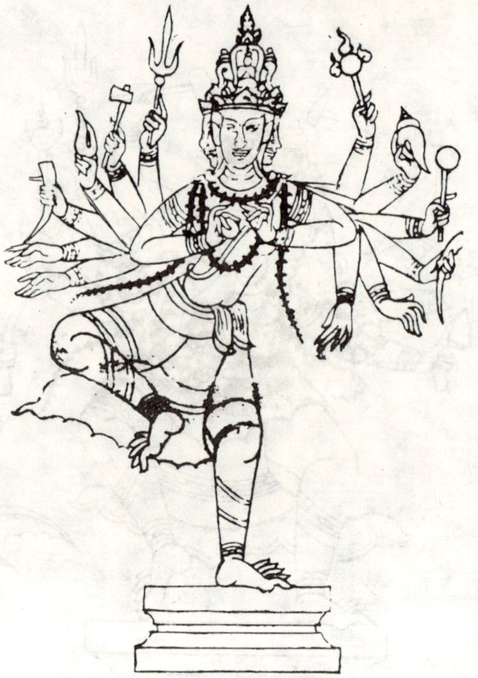

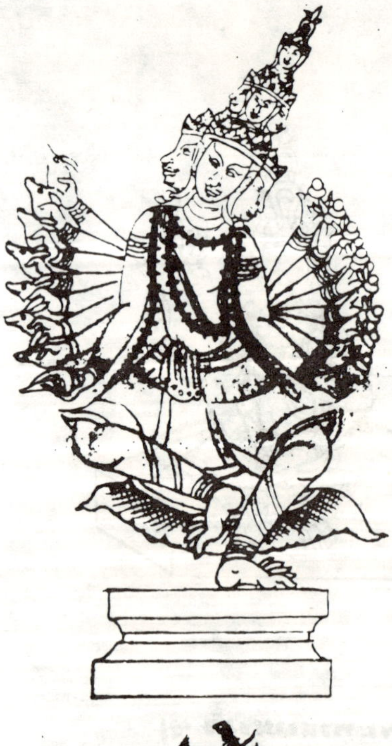

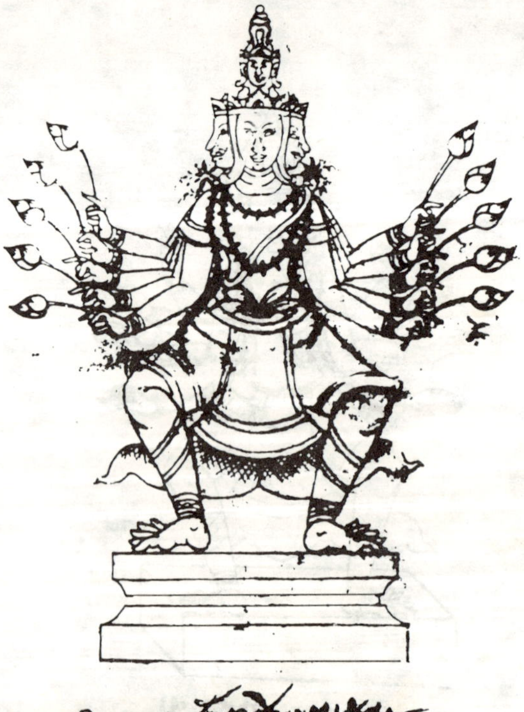

214. Eight-armed four-faced Sahāṁpati Brahmā. See 32.
215. Fourteen-armed four-faced Brahmā-Maheśvara. See 33.
216. Sixteen-armed eight-faced Śraddhāsiddha. See 34.
217. Ten-armed four-faced Śraddhāsiddha. See 35.

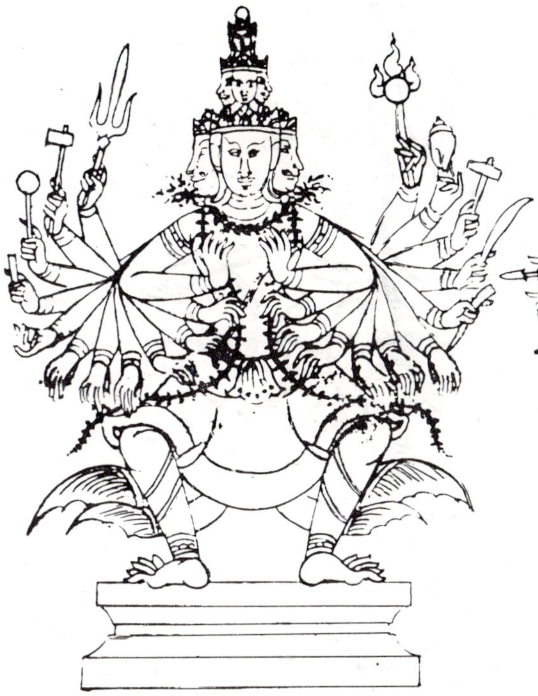

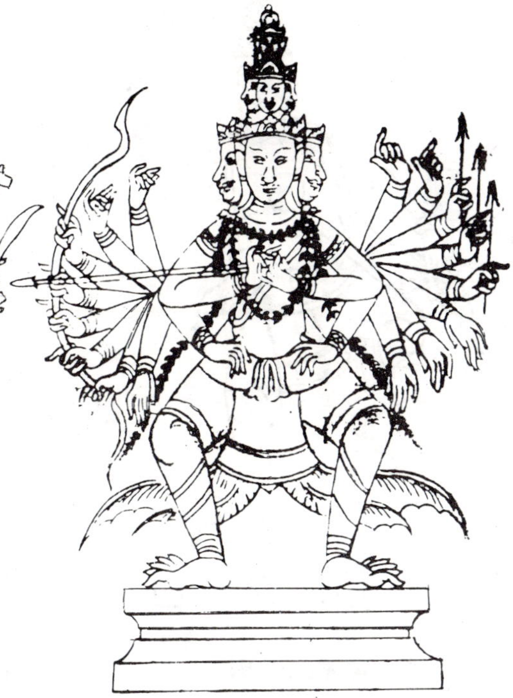

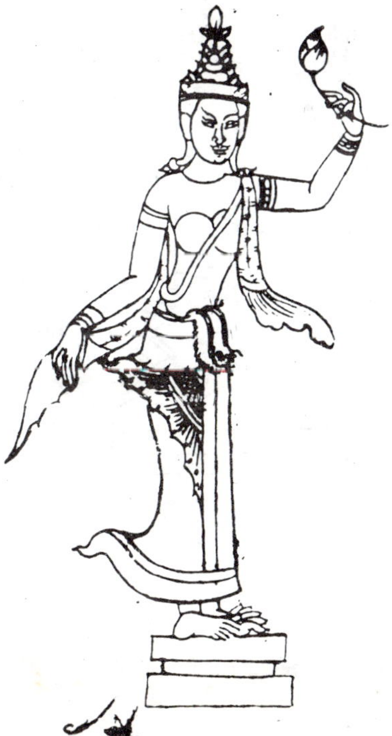

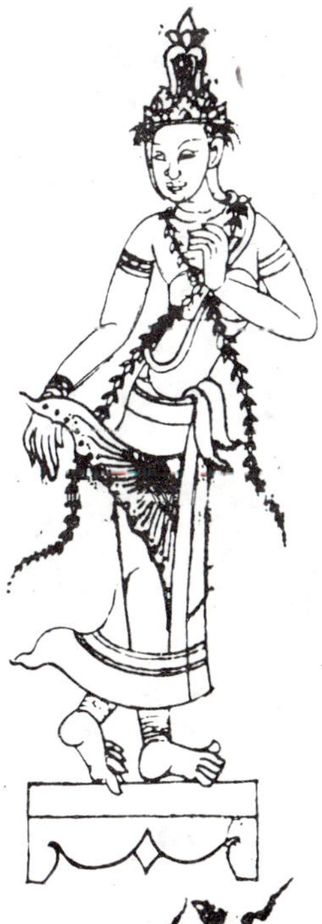

218. Twentyfour-armed eight-faced Śraddhādeva. See 36.
219. Twenty-armed eight-faced Śraddhādeva. See 37.
220. Lakṣmī. See 40.
221. Maheśvarī. See 41.

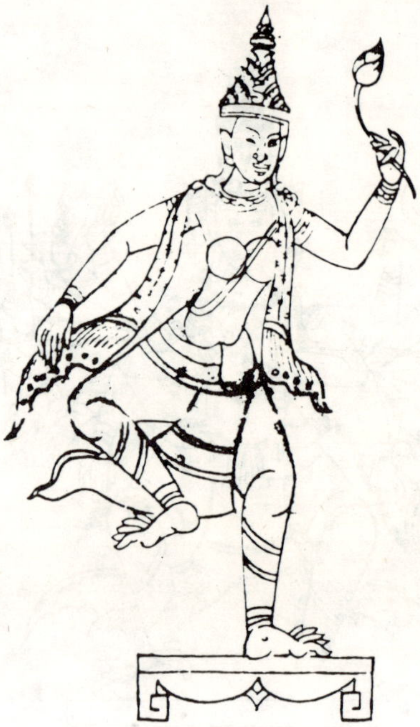

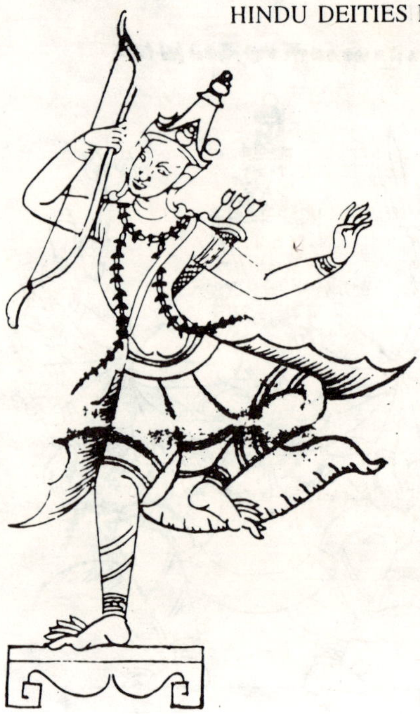

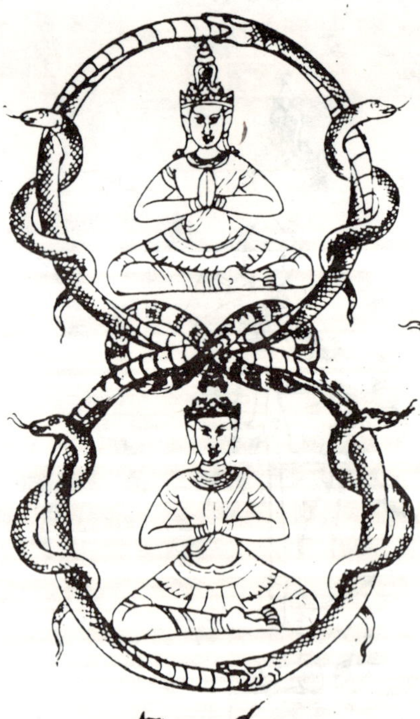

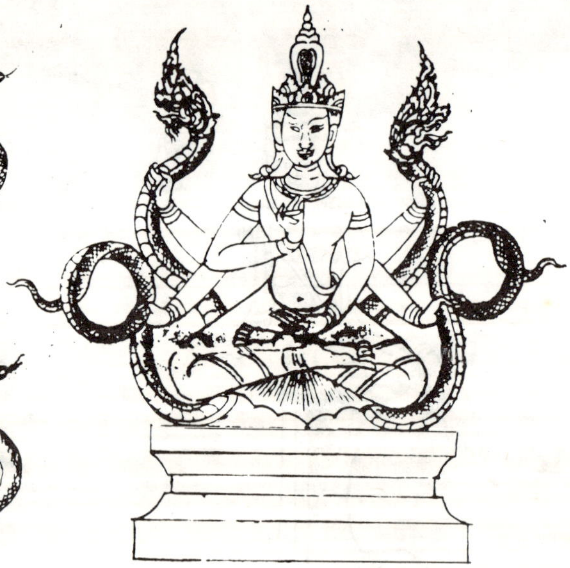

222. Umā bhagavatī. See 42.
223. Īśvara.
Sarma 41a braḥ Praḥmeśvar dr̥ṅ dhnū mōlī | « B. Parameśvara holding bow and quiver». R.h. free, l.h. bow.
224. Karmasiddhi-deva. See 44.
225. Six-armed Nārāyaṇa tames Nandukkha. See 45.

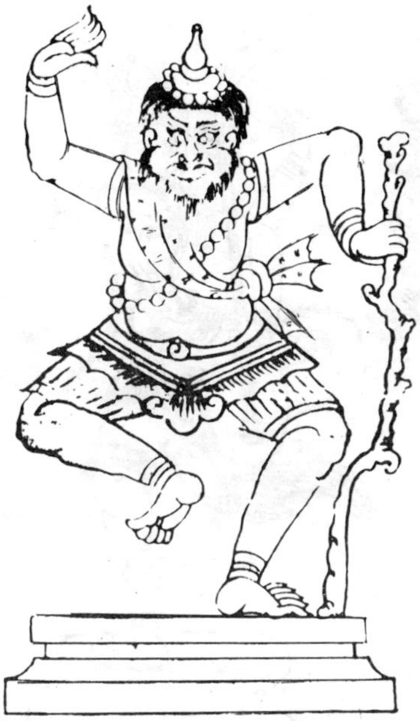

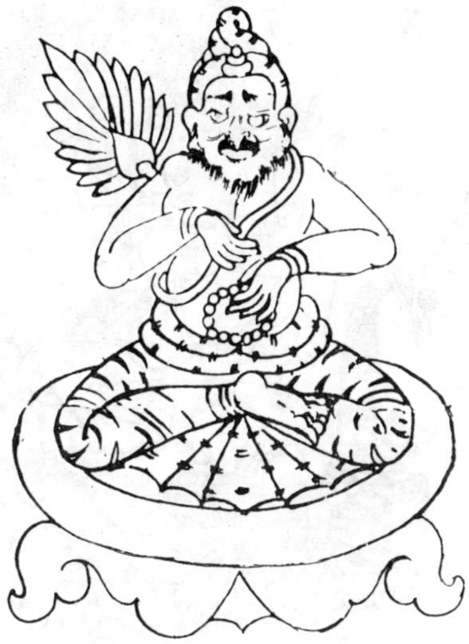

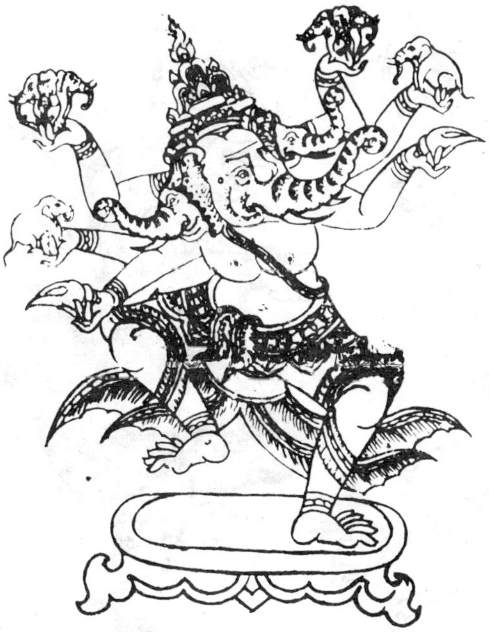

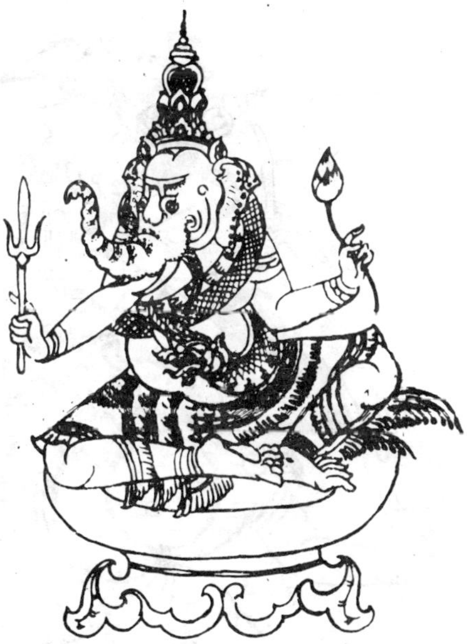

226. Deva Paśusakha. See 46.
227. Ṛṣi with a fan. See 49.
228. Six-armed Kuñjarānaneśvara, with three visible heads. See 50.
229. Śivaputra. See 51.

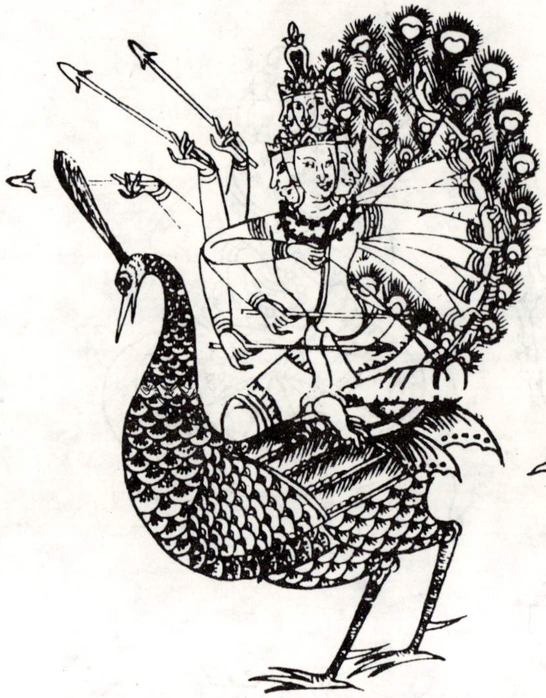

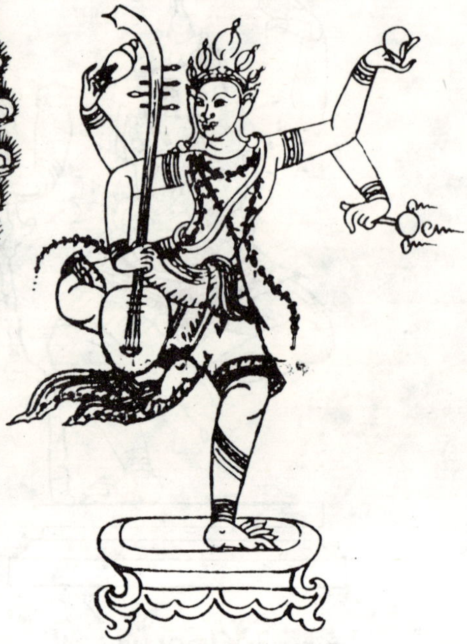

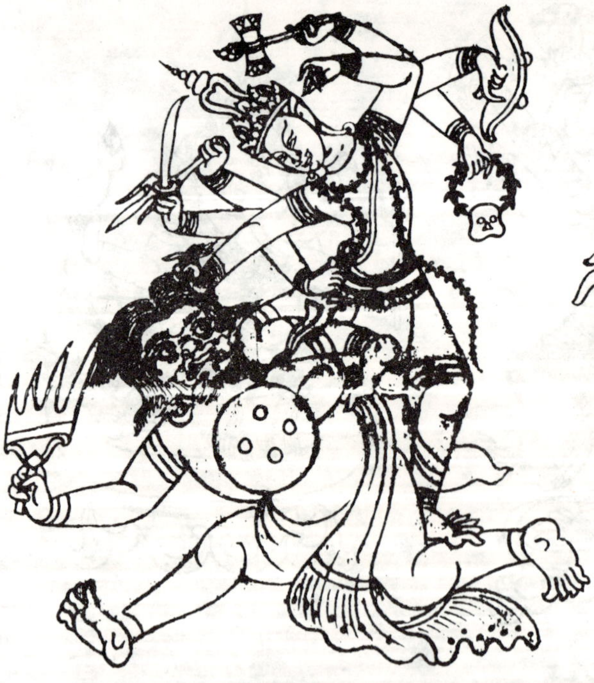

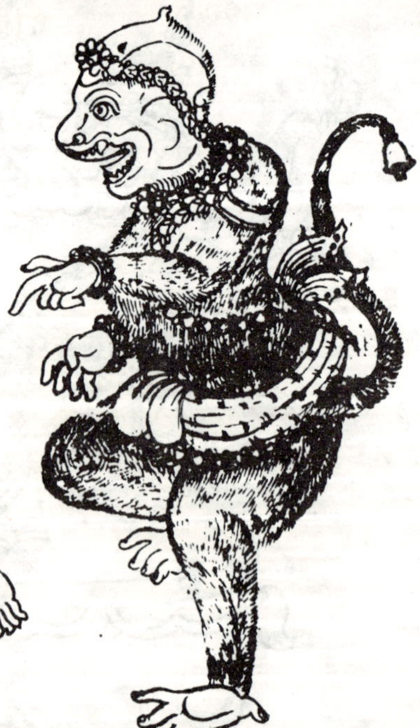

230. Twelve-armed Skanda-kumāra on peacock. See 48.
231. Four-armed Pañcaśikha playing vīṇā. See 49.
232. Eight-armed Īśvara on Kumbha yakṣa. See 50.
233. Vānararāja Jāmbavant. See 51.

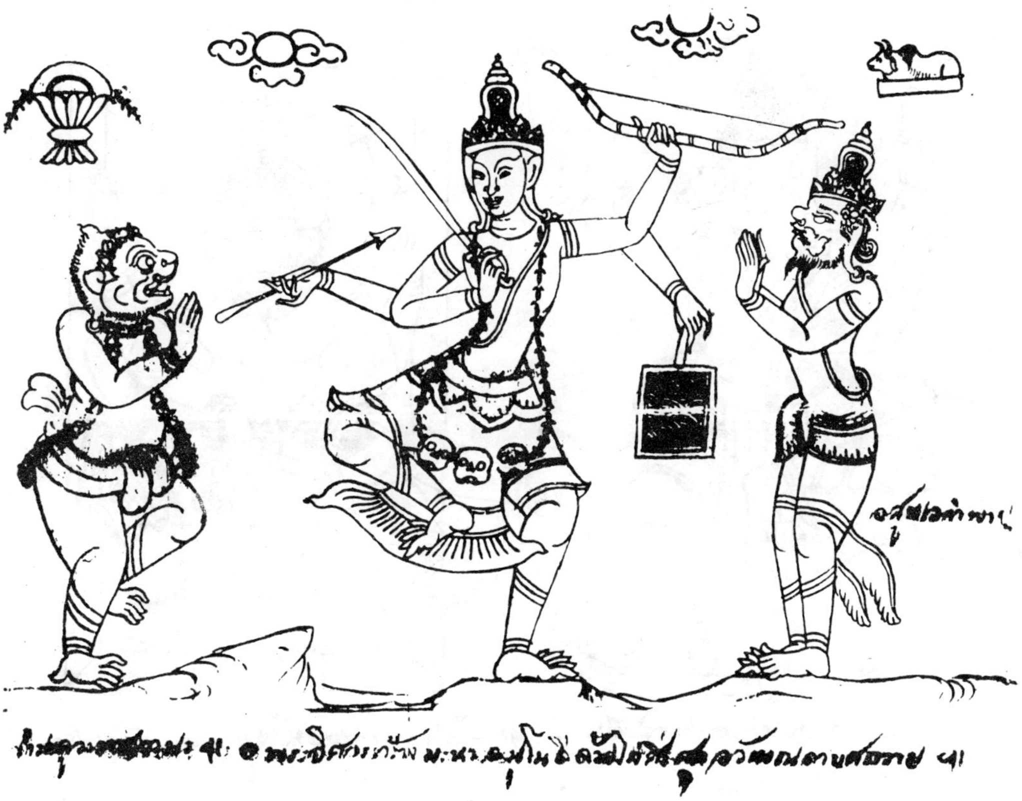

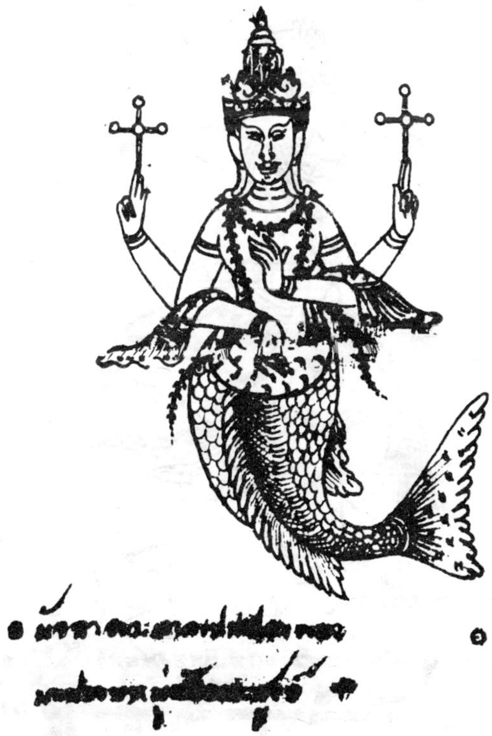

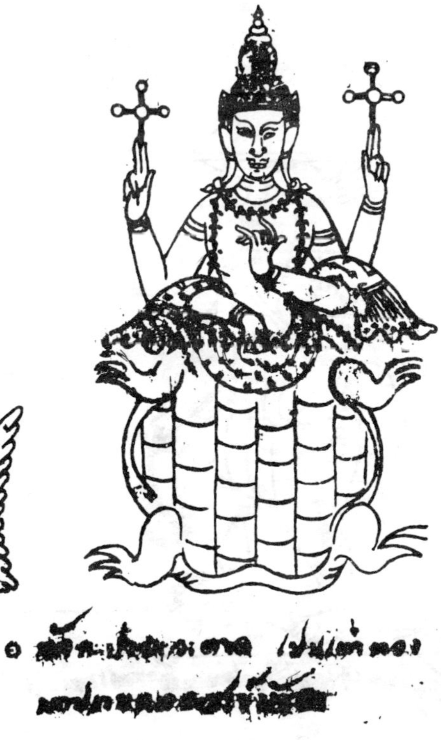

234. Four-armed Īśvara. See 52.
235. Matsyāvatāra. See 53.
236. Kūrmāvatāra. See 54.

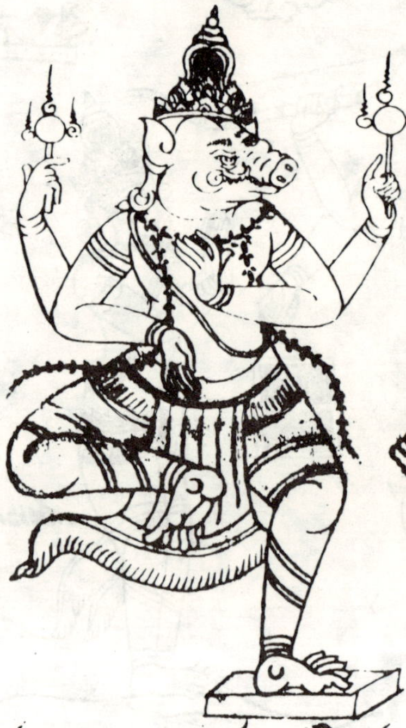

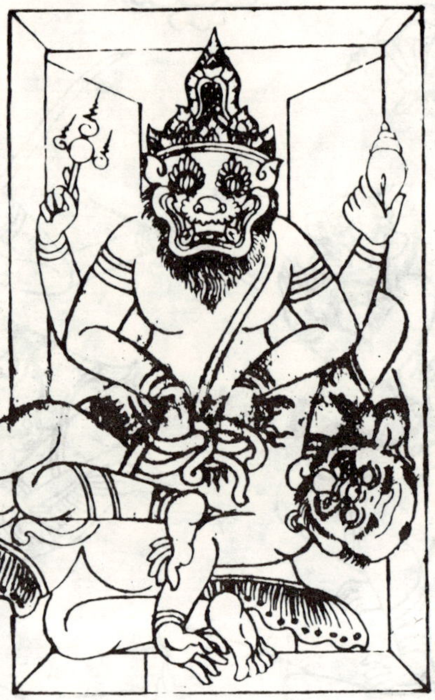

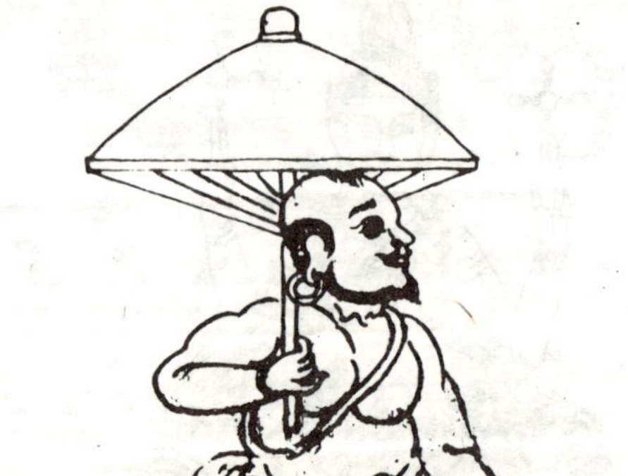

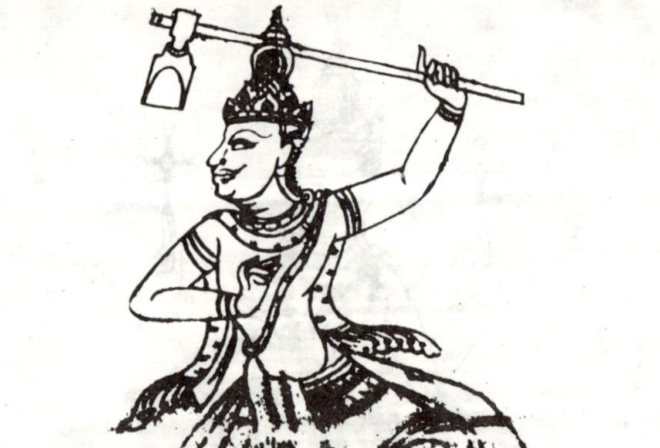

237. ŚvetaVarāhāvatāra. See 55.
238. Siṁhāvatāra. See 56.
239. Kubjāvatāra (= Vāmanāvatāra). See 57.
240. Paraśurāmāvatāra. See 58.

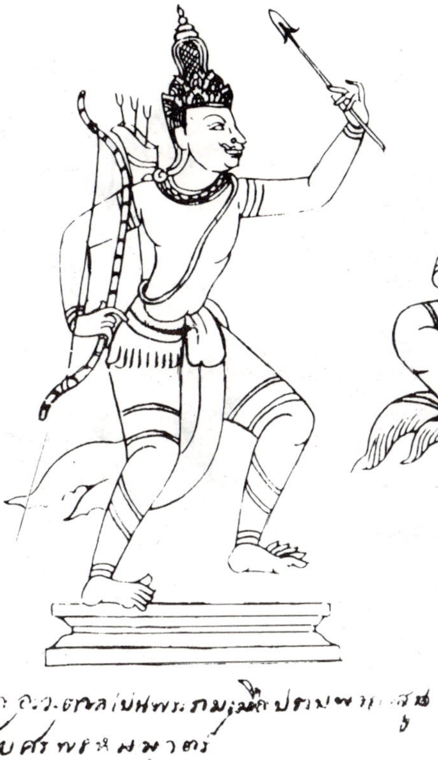

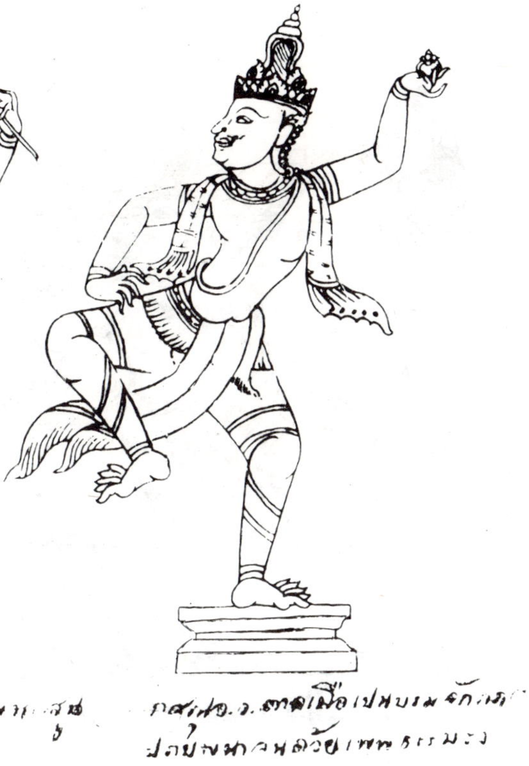

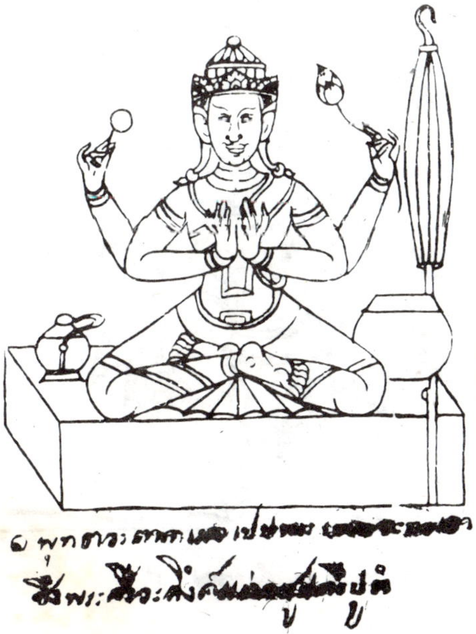

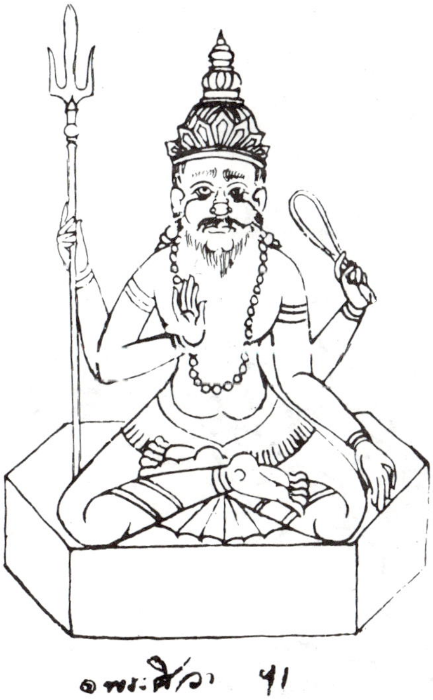

241. Rāmāvatāra. See 59.
242. Viṣṇu conquers with cakra (?).
243. Buddhāvatāra. See 61.
244. Four-armed Śiva. See 62.

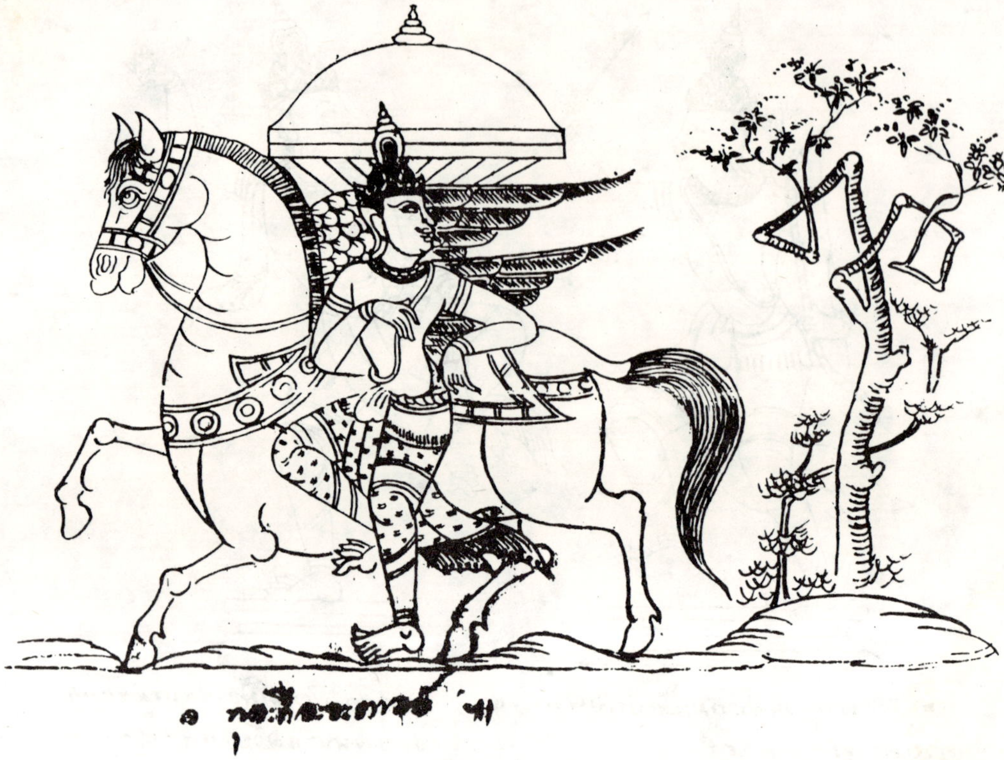

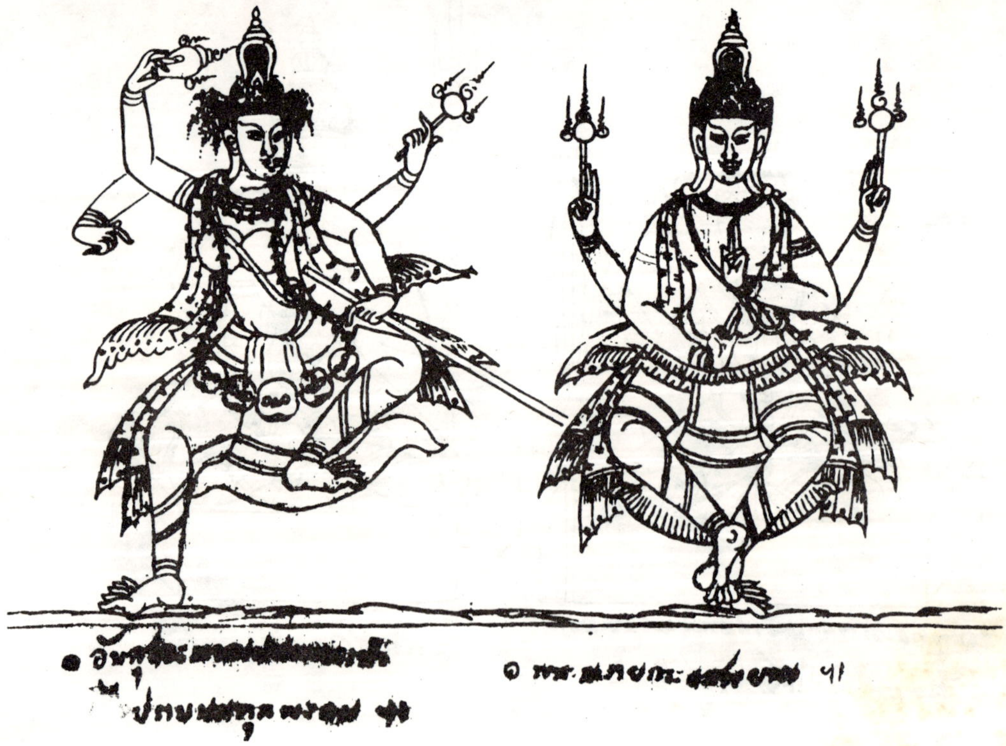

245. Uttarī avatāra=Kalkin. See 63.
246. Four-armed Īśvara vanquishes Andhaka. cf.3 who is different.
247. Four-armed Nārāyaṇa in a dancing posture. See 65.

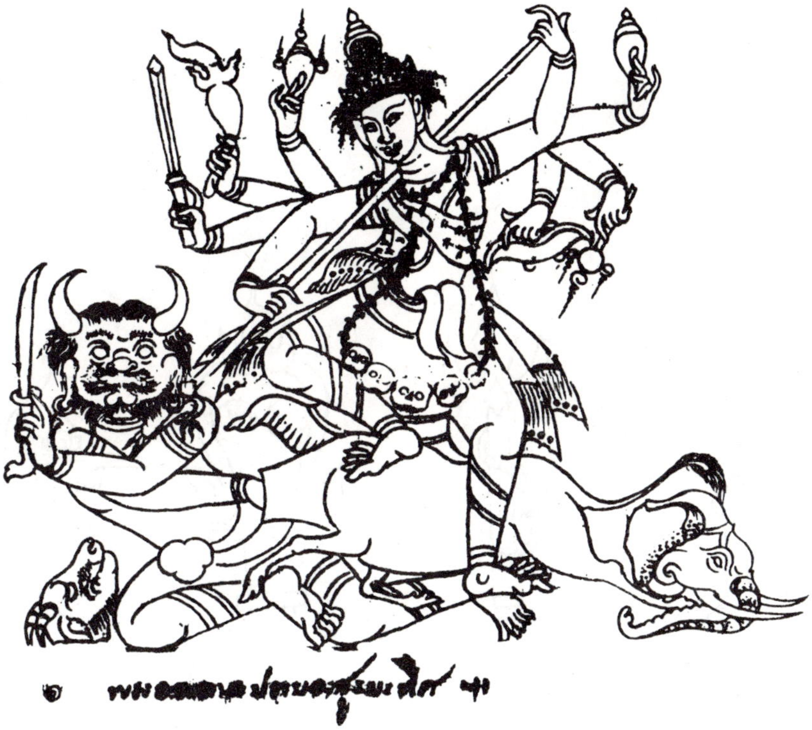

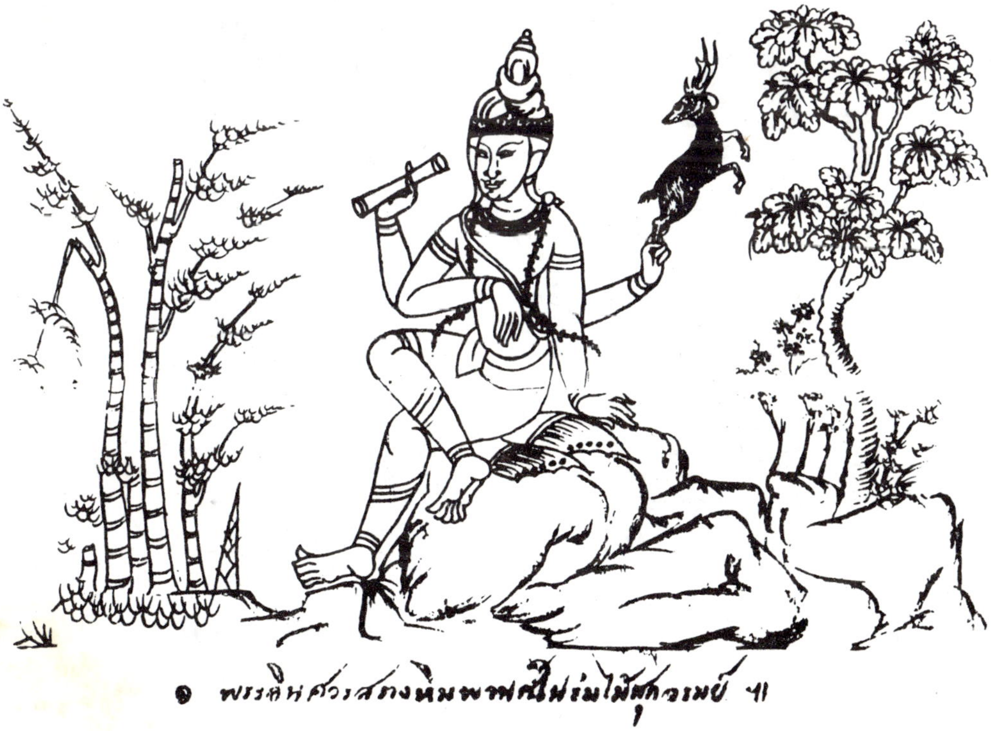

248. Eight-armed Nārāyaṇa vanquishes Mahiṣāsura. See 66.
249. Four-armed Īśvara creates Himavat under the shade of the sukrom tree. See 67.

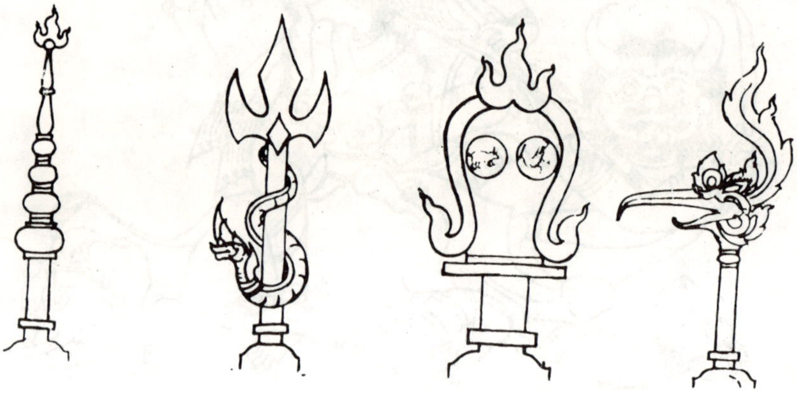

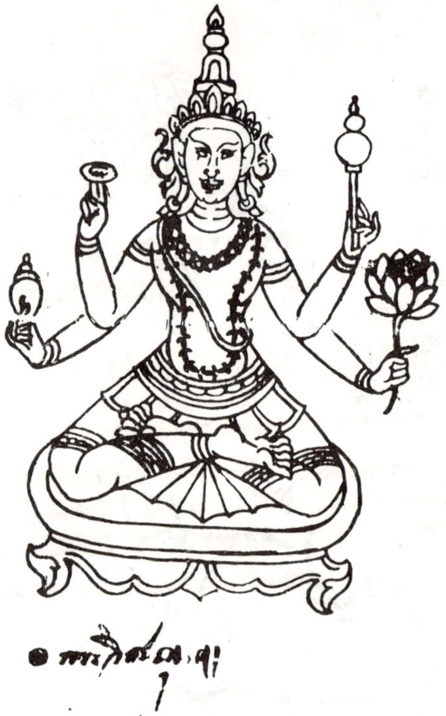

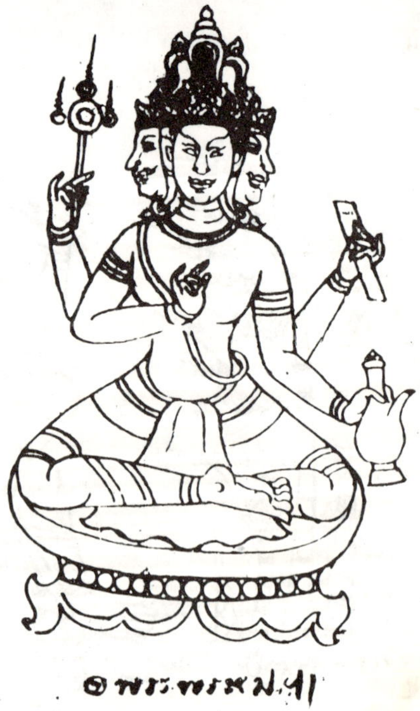

250. Symbols.
251. Four-armed Viṣṇu. See 68.
252. Four-armed four-faced Brahmā Dhātā. See 69.

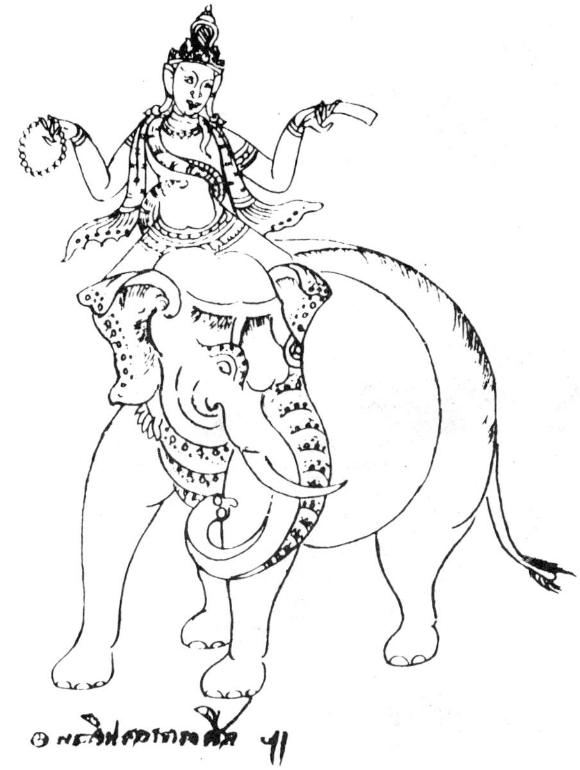

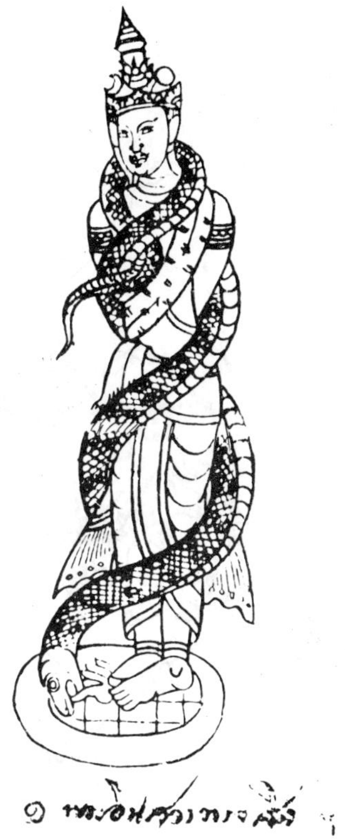

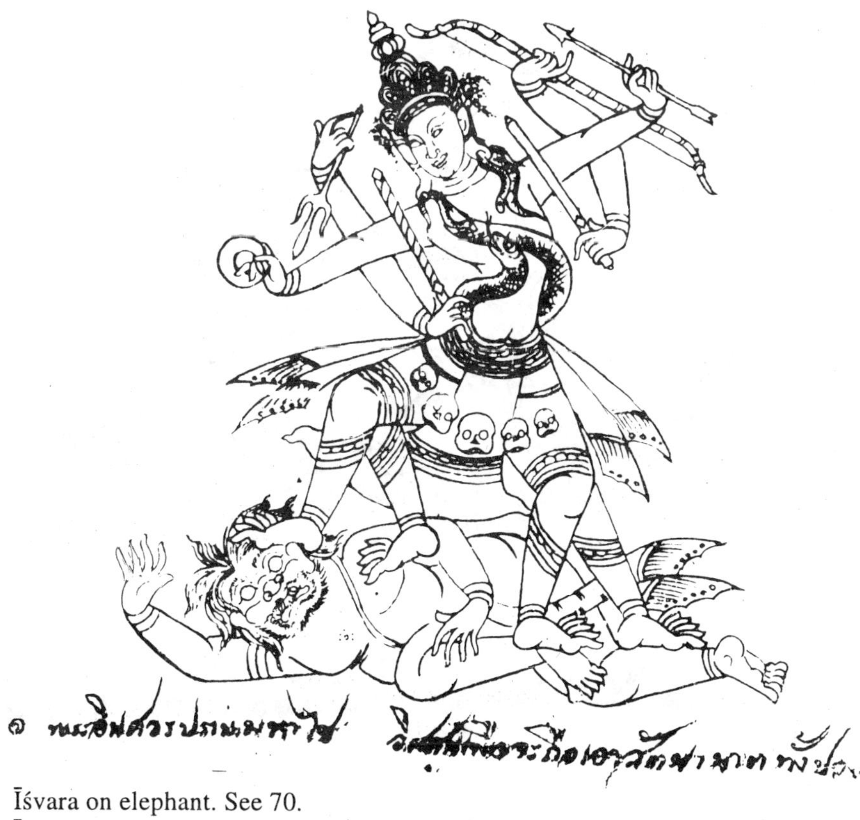

253. Īśvara on elephant. See 70.
254. Īśvara entwined by a serpent. See 71.
255. Īśvara vanquishes Mahiṣāsura (?). See 72.

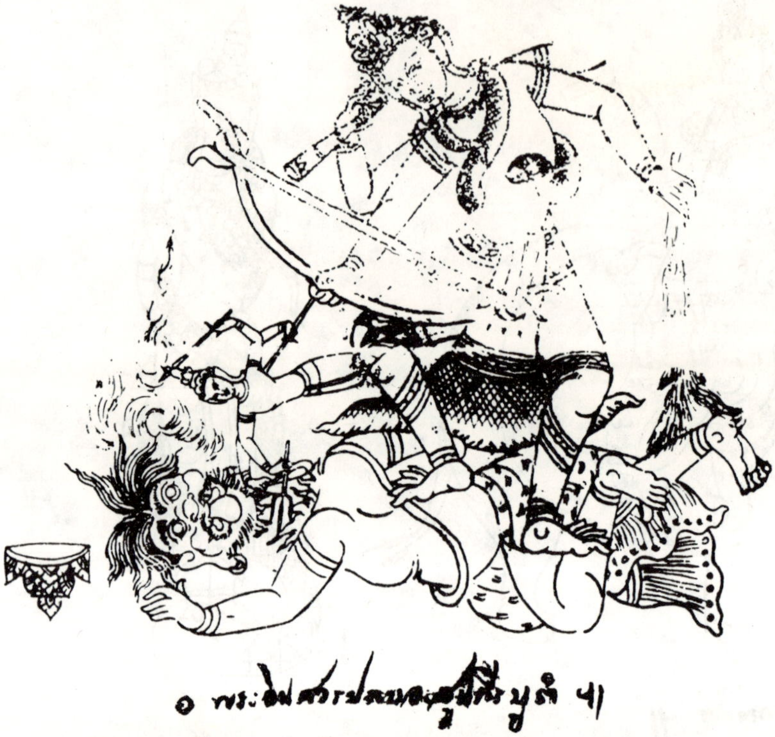

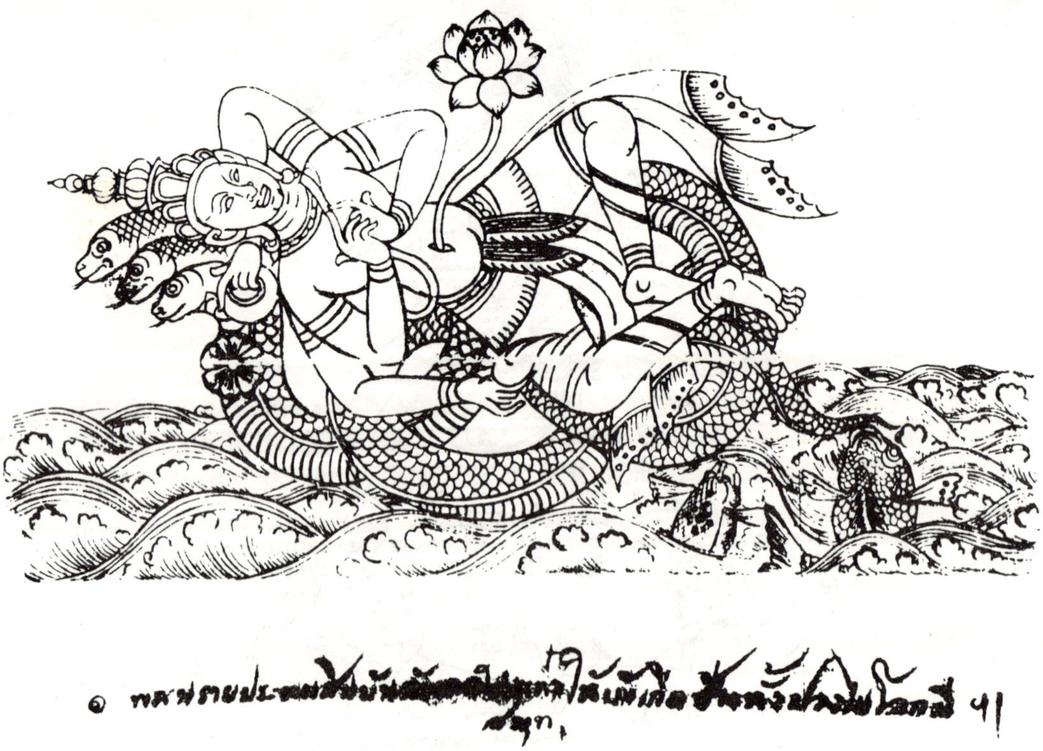

256. Four-armed Īśvara slays Tripura asura. See 73.
257. Four-armed Nārāyaṇa dormant on Śeṣa-nāga. See 74.

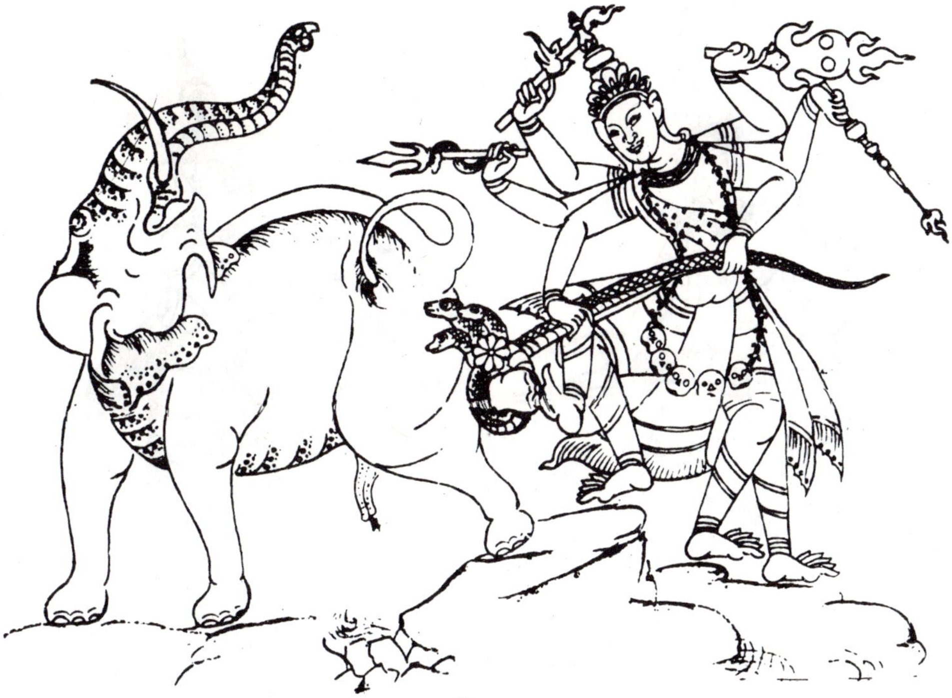

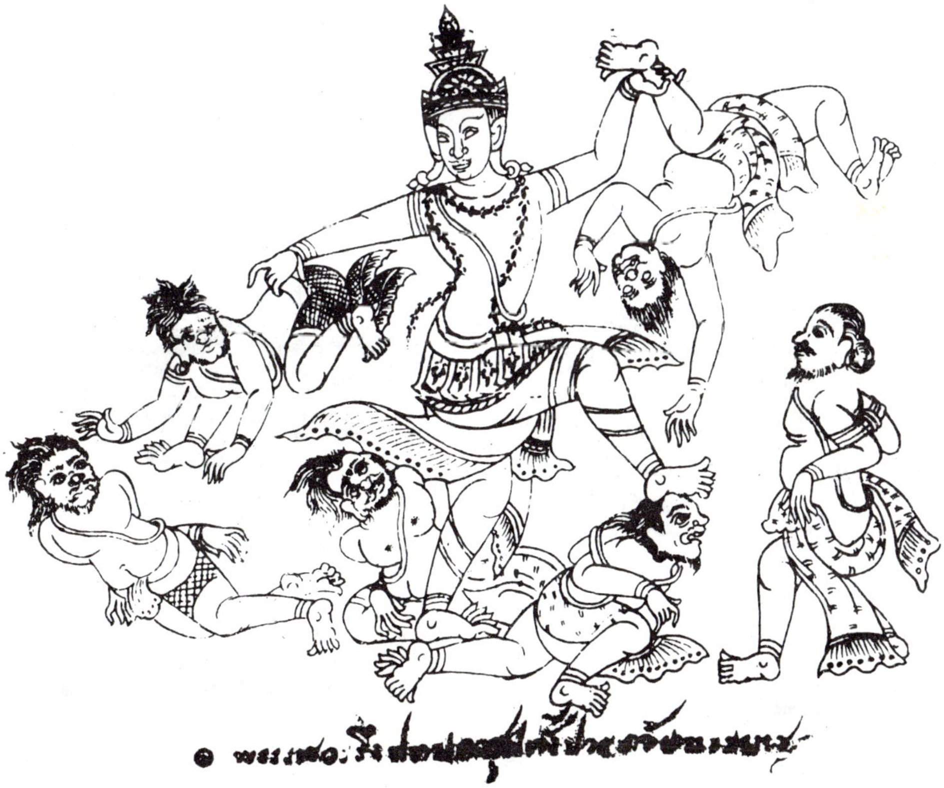

258. Six-armed Nārāyaṇa subdues the elephant Ekadanta. See 75.
259. Draḥ riṅ. See 76.

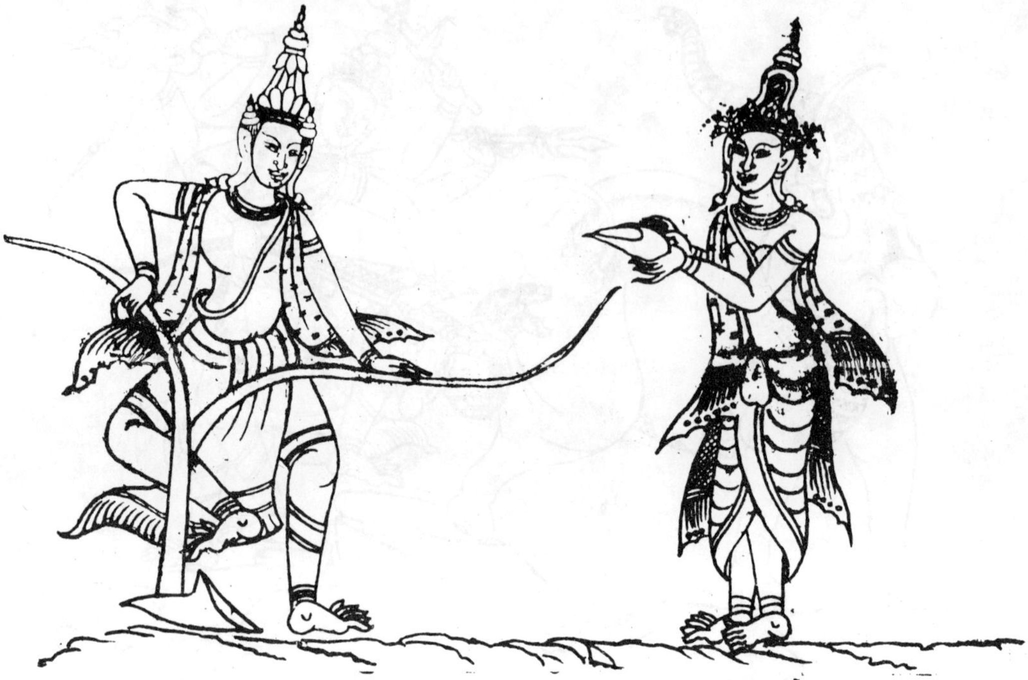

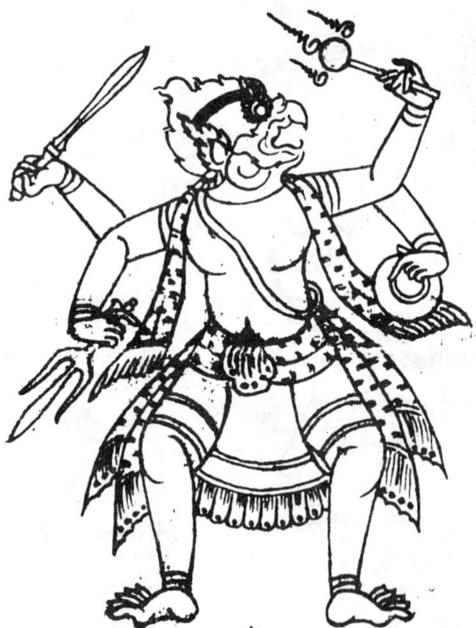

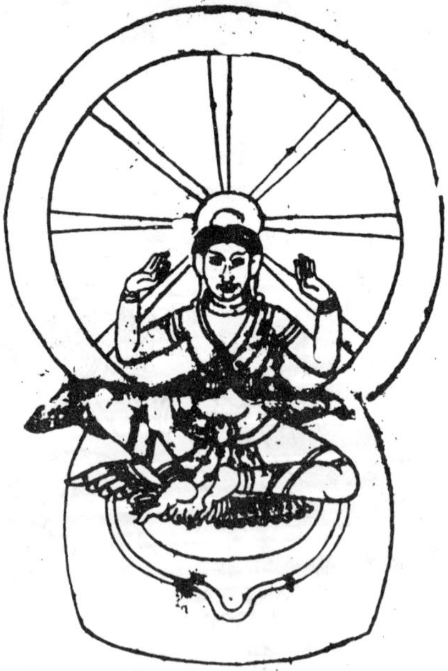

260. Baladeva. See 77.
261. Nang Devī. See 78.
262. Konchai (?). See 79.
263. Mahāmeṣa (?). See 80.

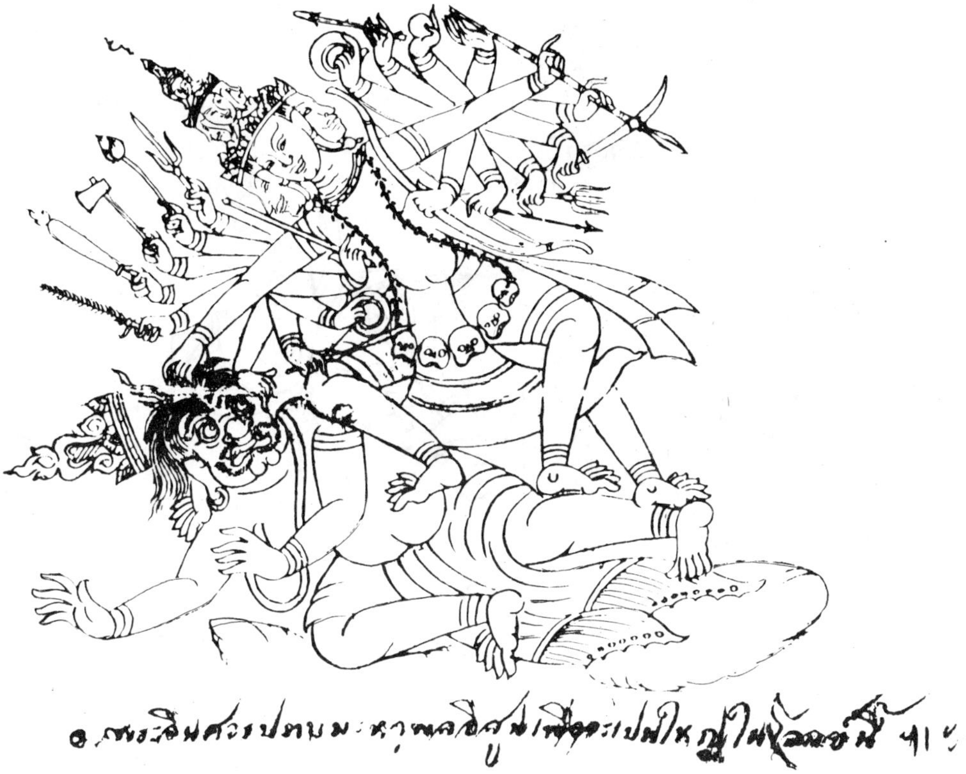

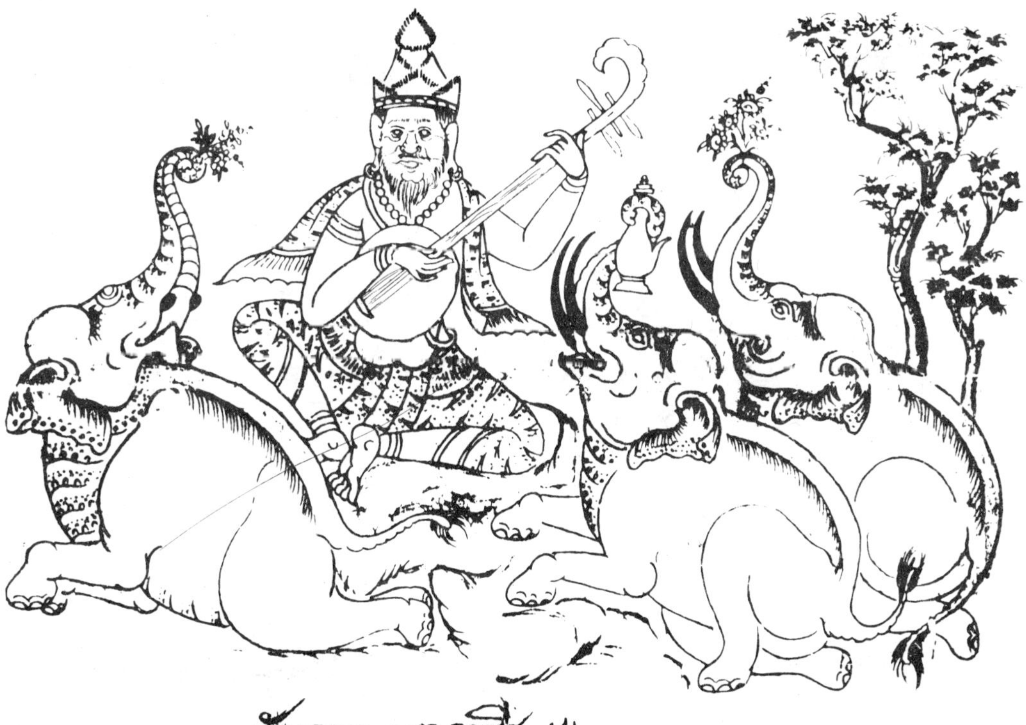

264. Twenty-armed Īśvara annihilating an asura. See 81.
265. Elephants come to listen to maharṣi. See 82.

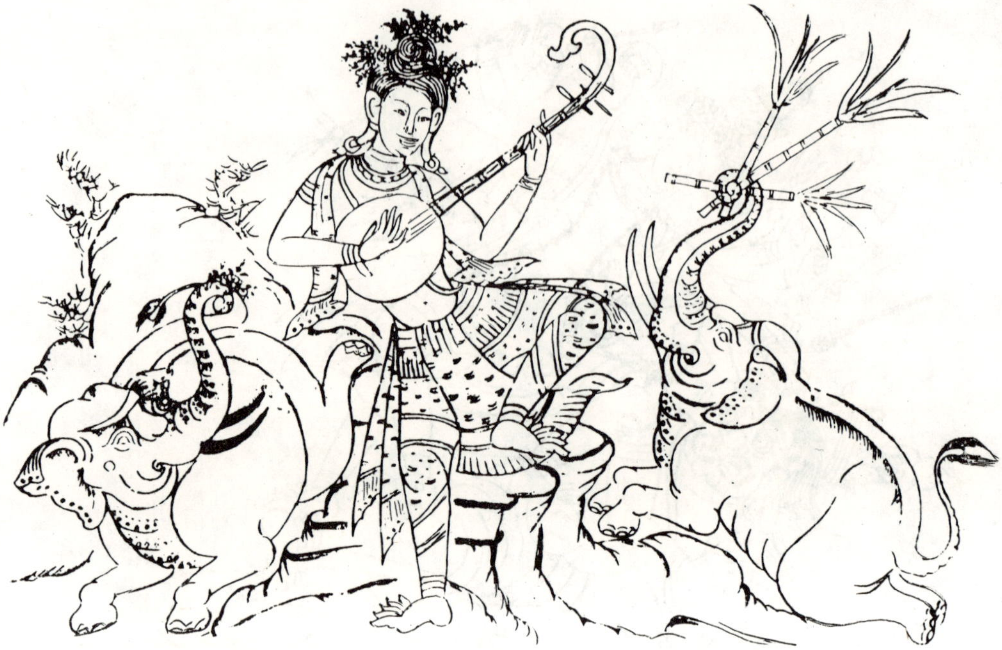

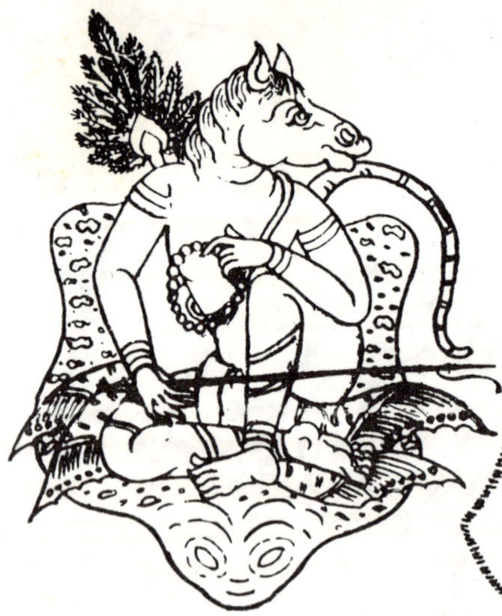

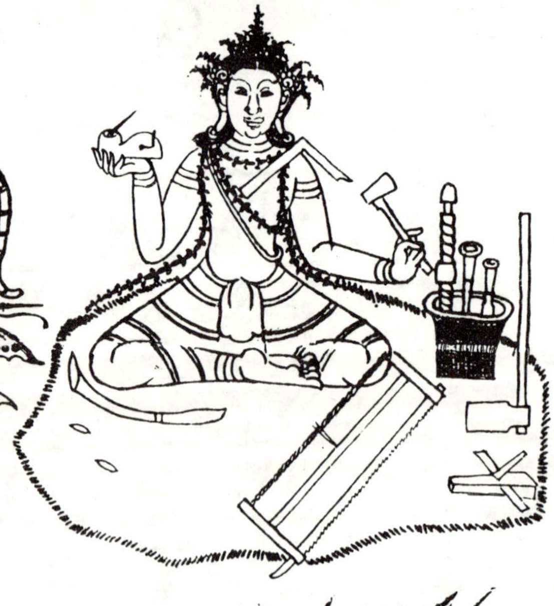

266. Uthyenurāja playing vīṇā, surrounded by elephants. See 83.
267. Guru of horses (is he Hayagrīva?). See 84.
268. Viśvakarmā. See 85.

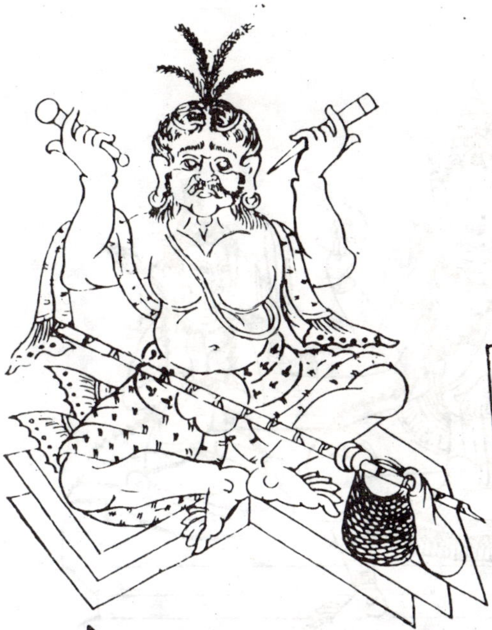

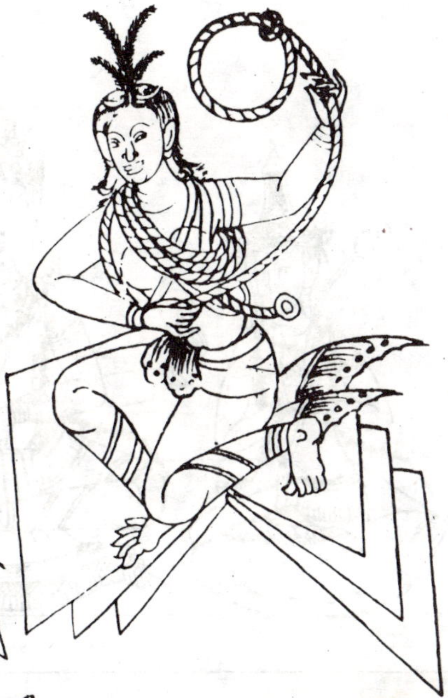

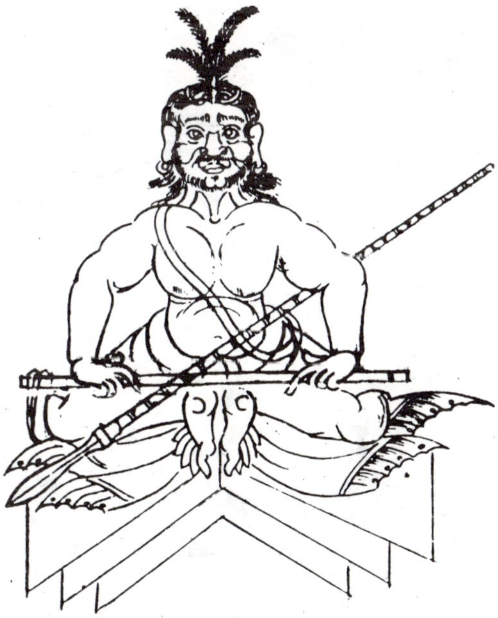

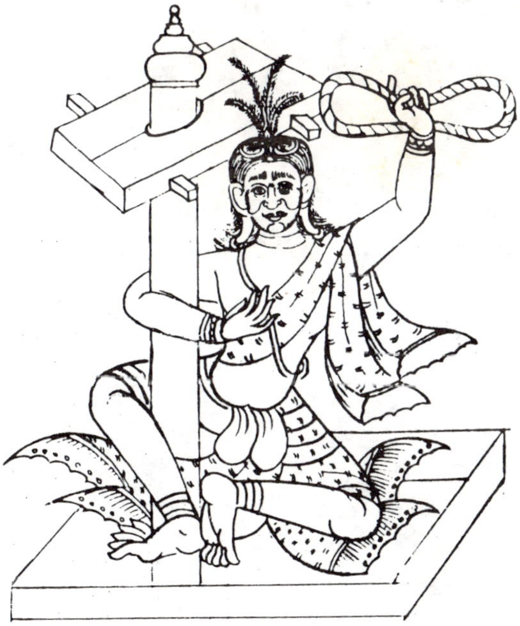

269. Trainer of elephants who lives in Leksong(?). See 86.
270. Goddess of elephants who lives in Siravang(?). See 87.
271. Trainer of elephants. See 88.
272. Trainer of elephants. See 89.

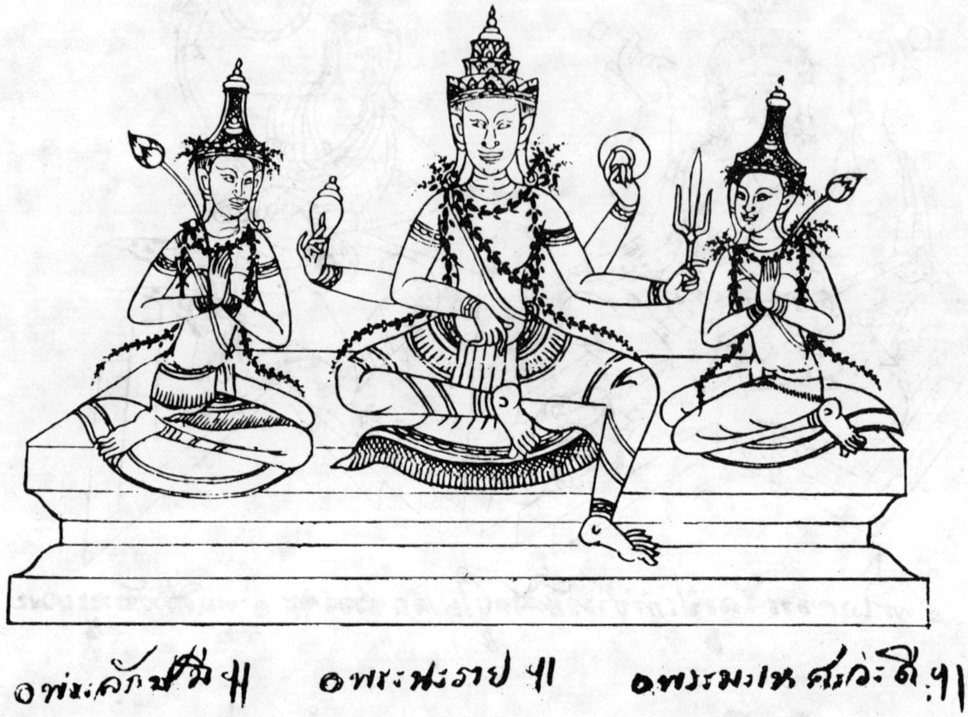

273. Nārāyaṇa flanked by Lakṣmī and Maheśvarī. See 90.

SANSKRIT AND TAMIL TEXTS

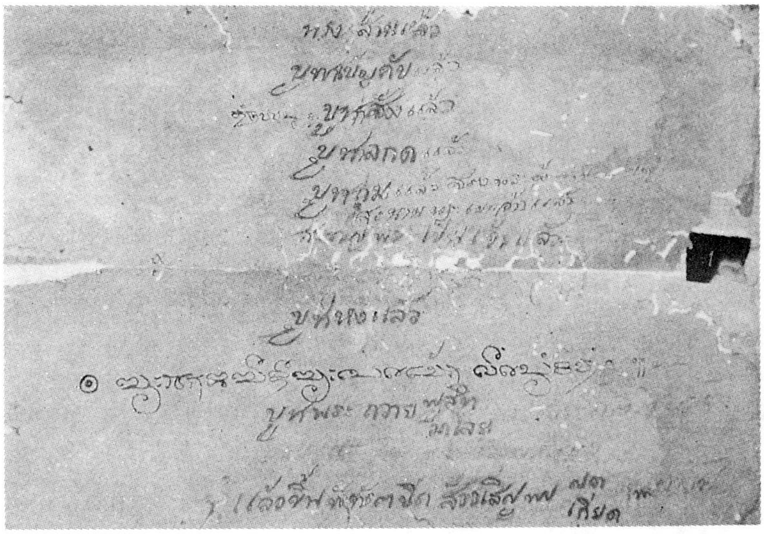

1

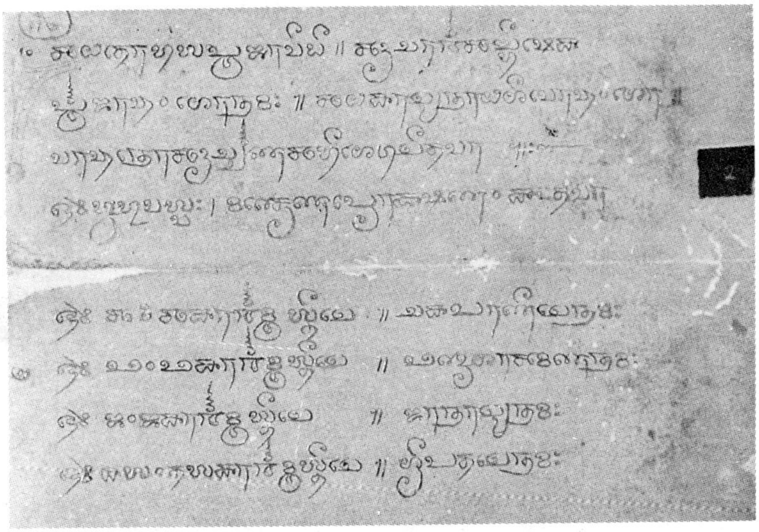

2

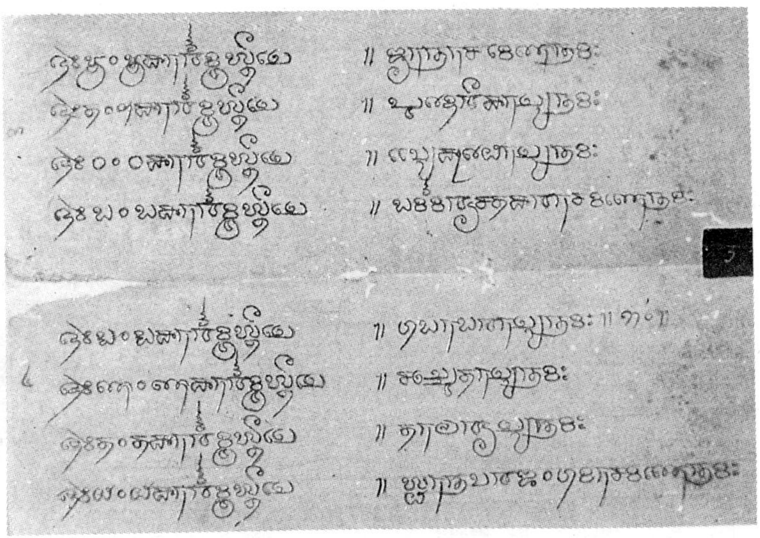

3

4

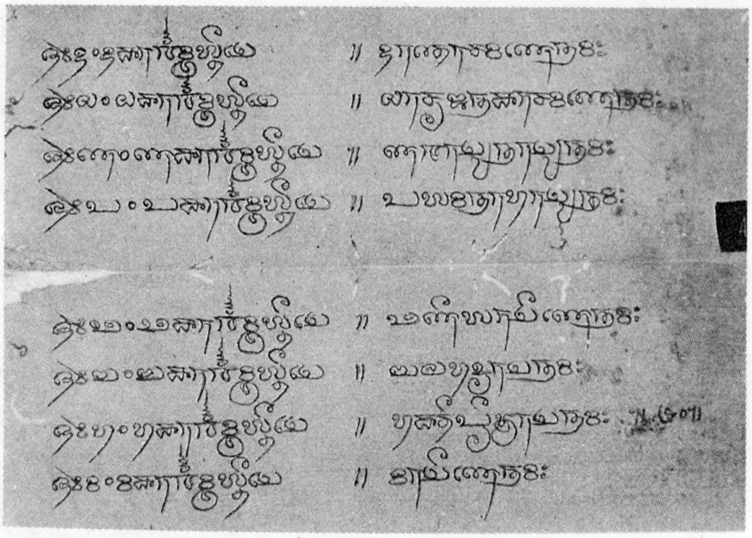

5

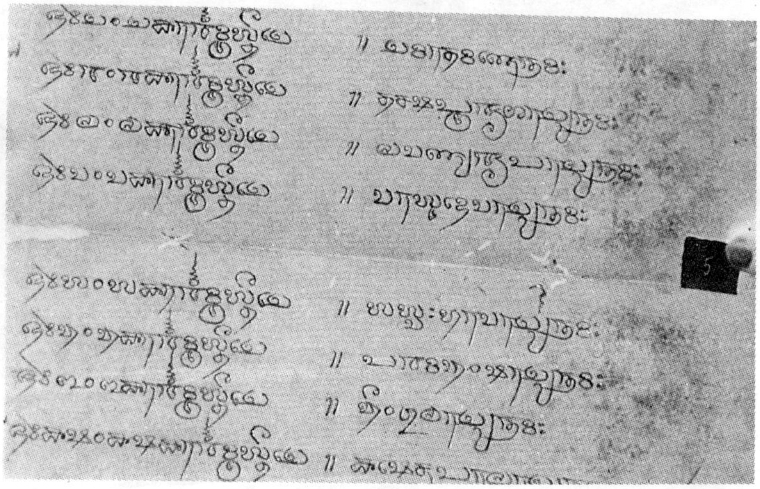

6

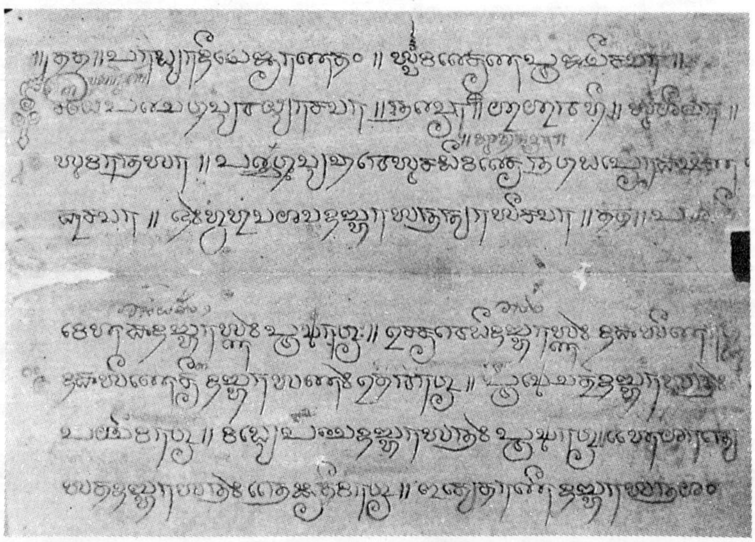

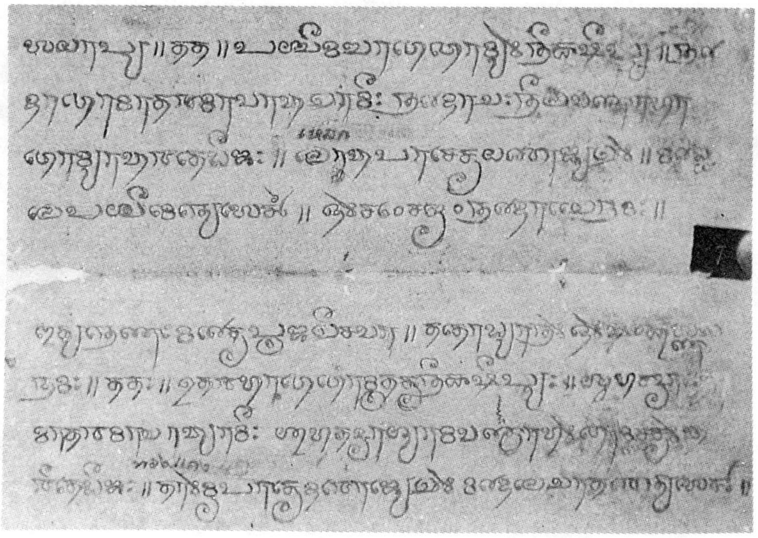

7

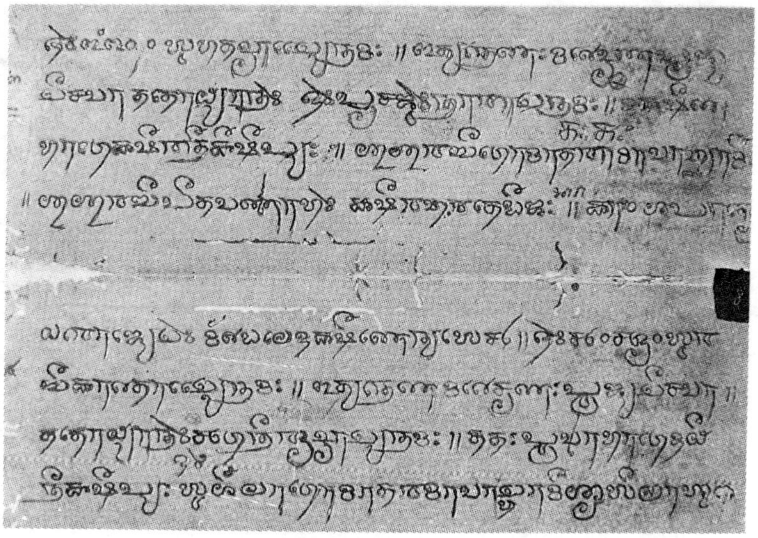

8

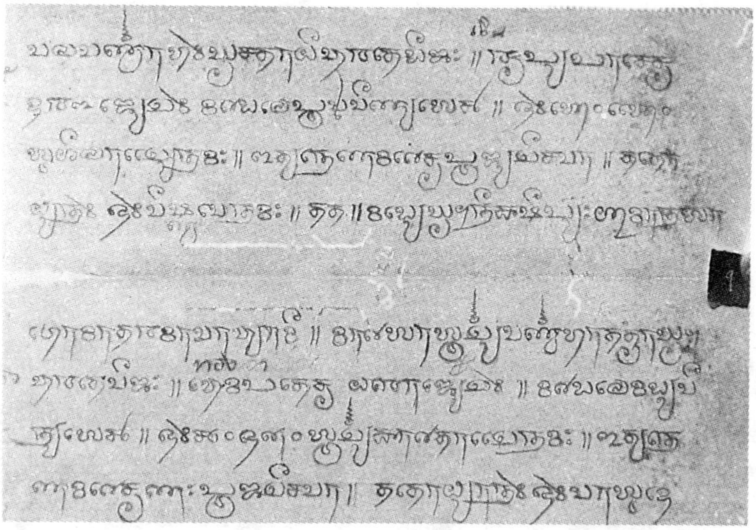

9

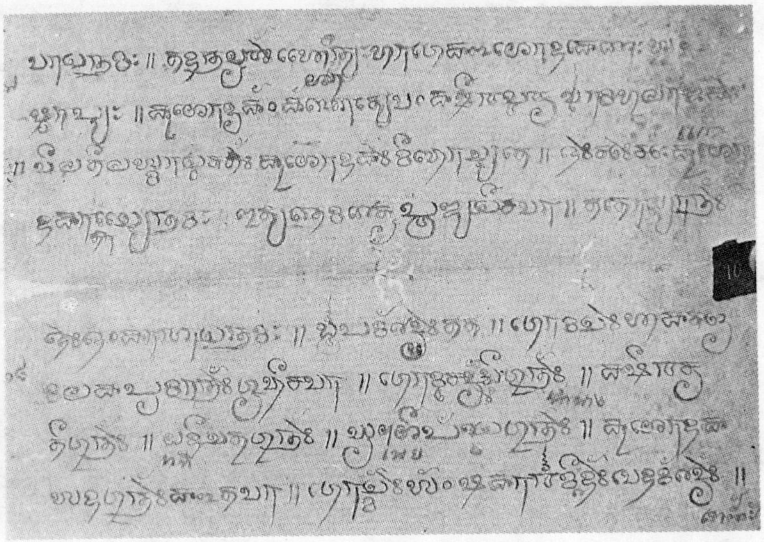

10

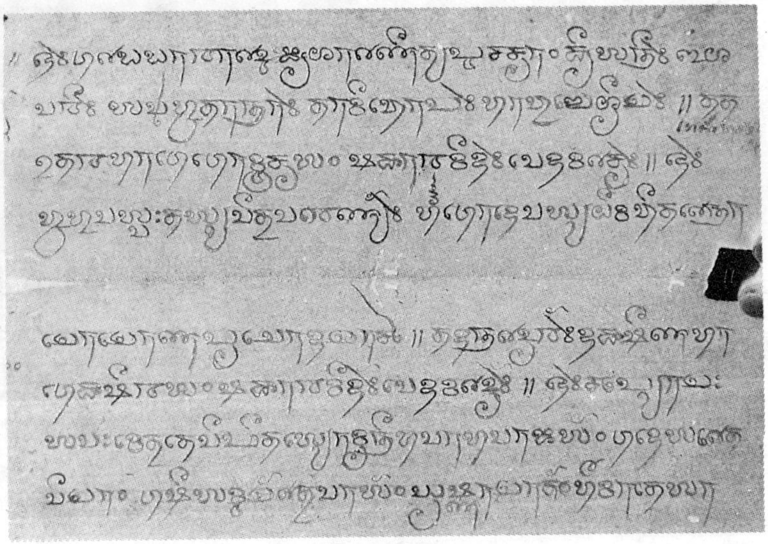

11

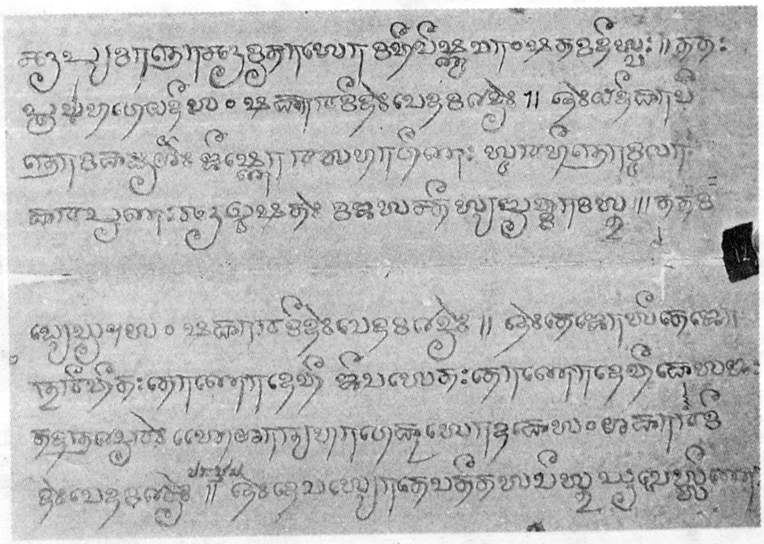

12

13

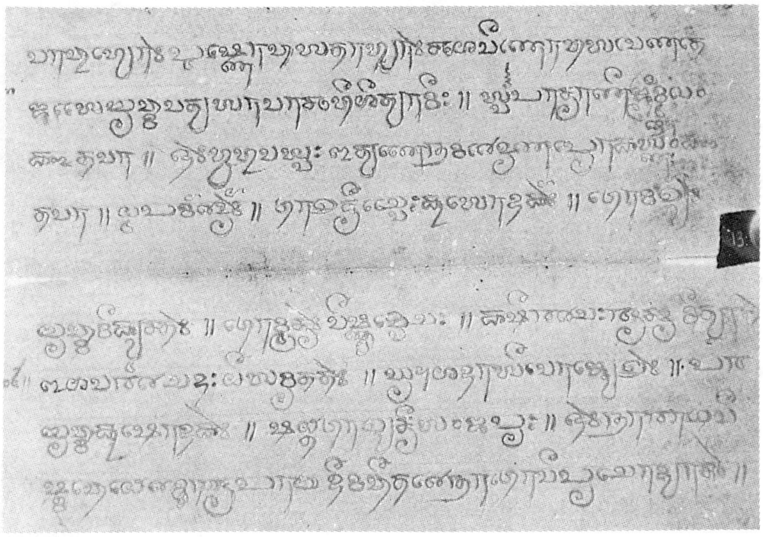

14

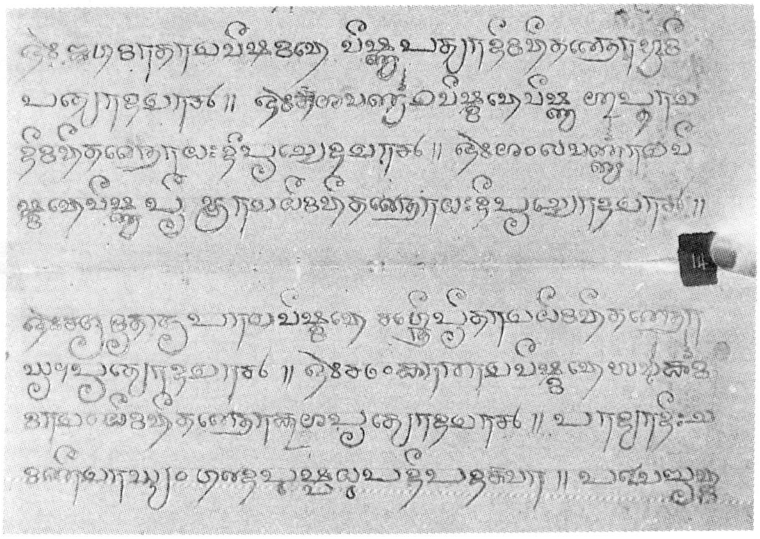

15

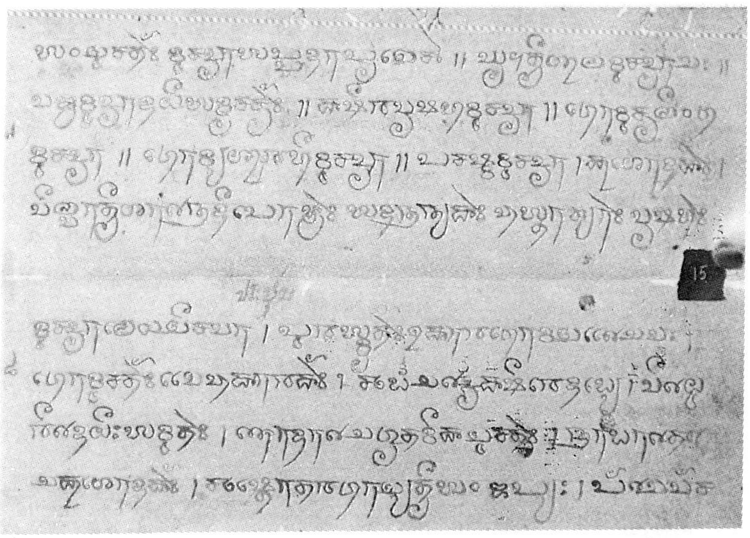

16

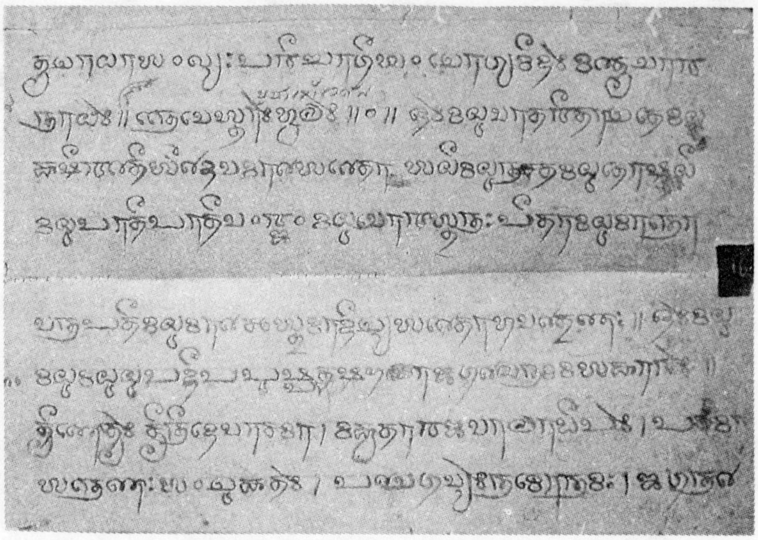

17

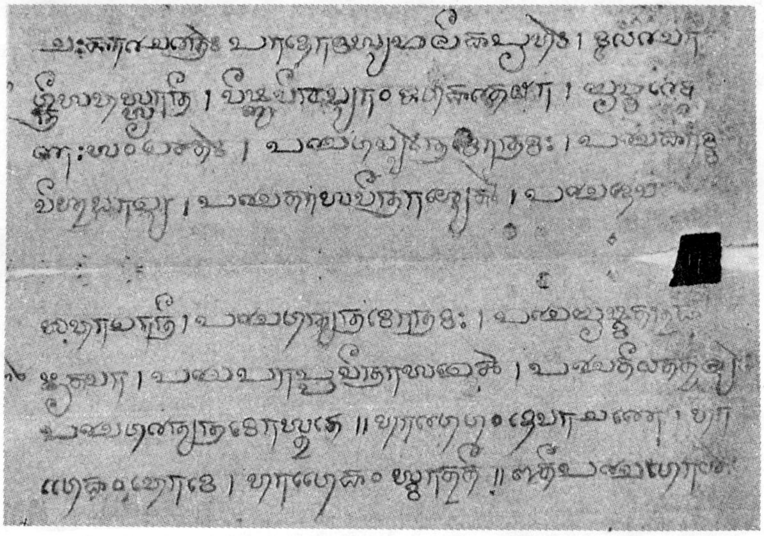

18

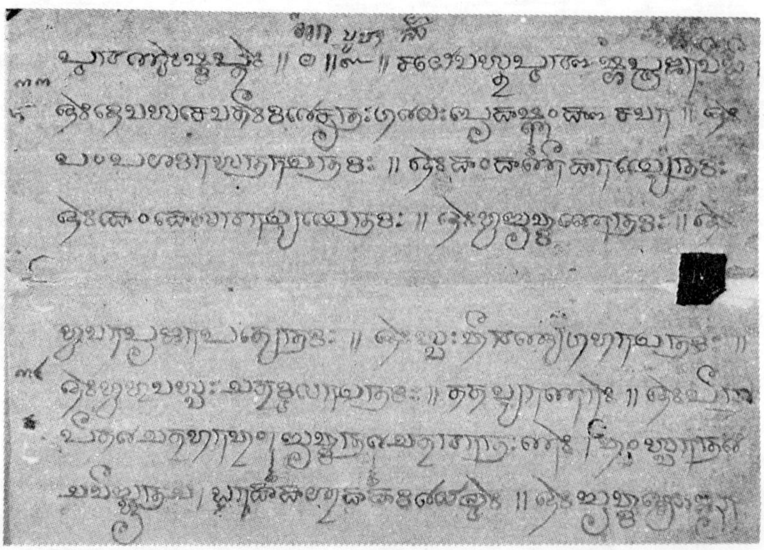

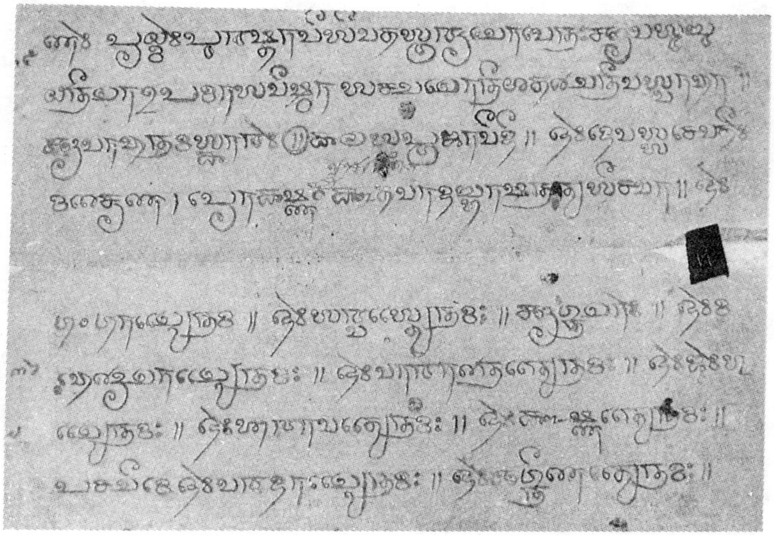

19

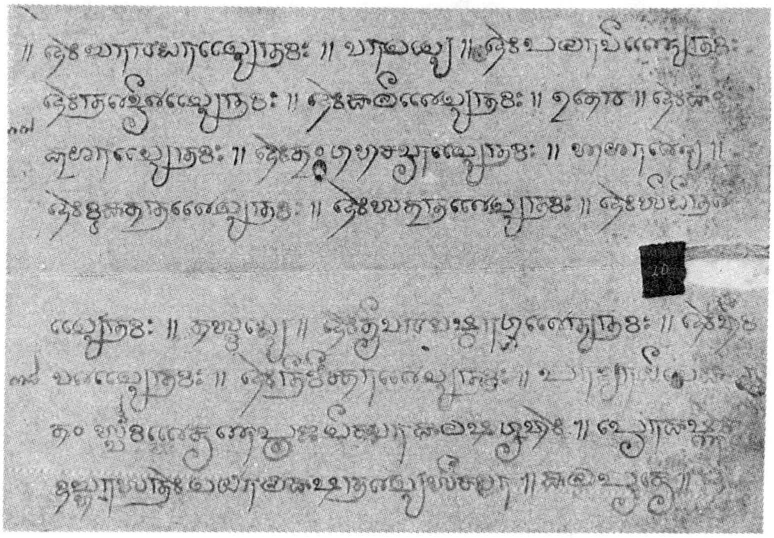

20

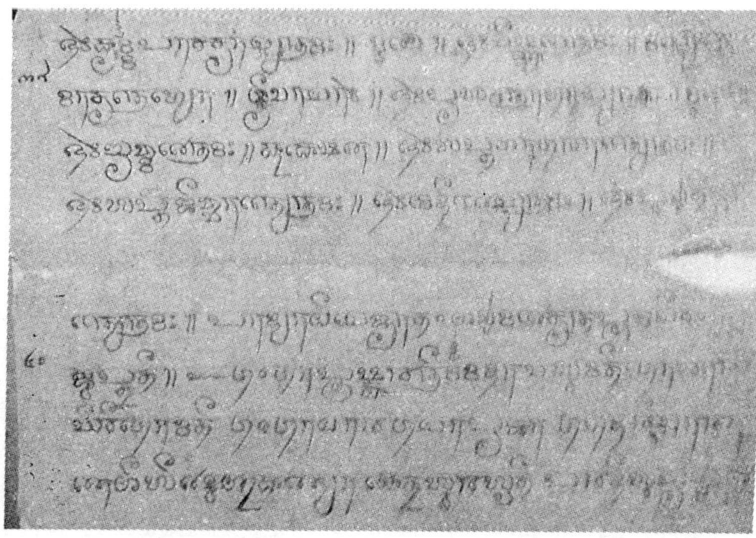

21

22

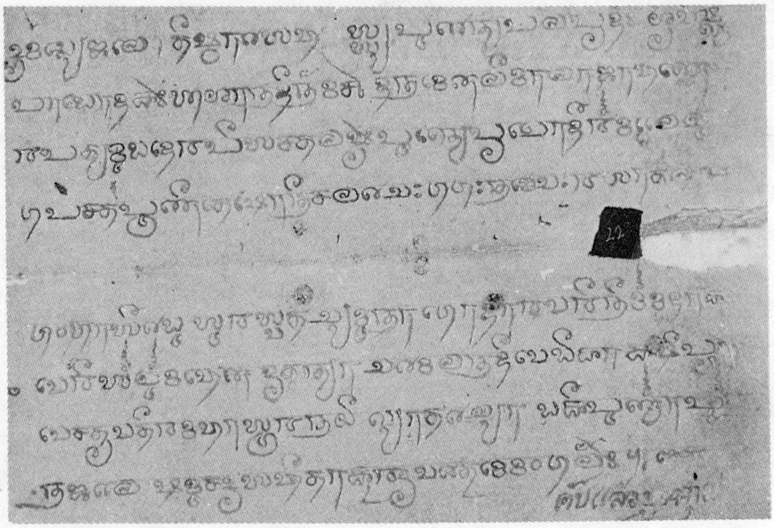

23

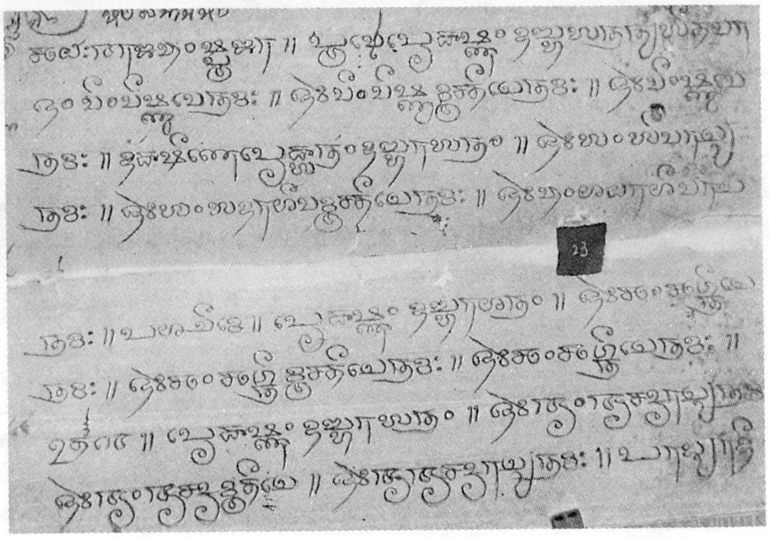

24

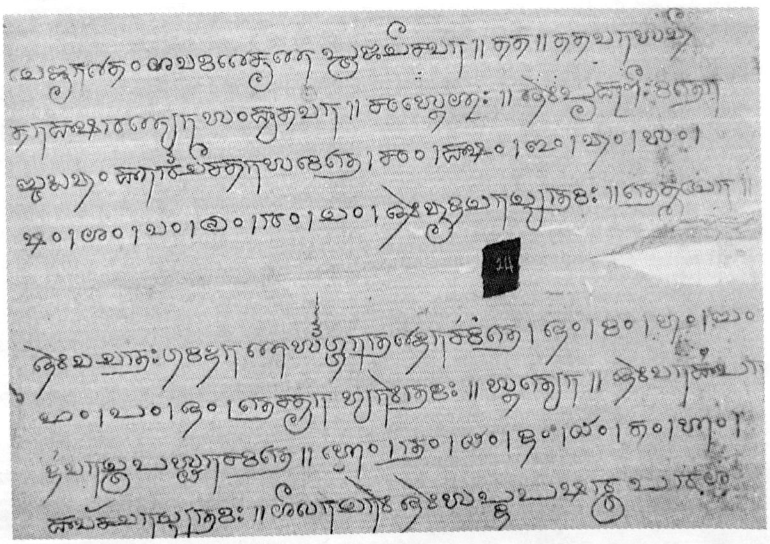

25

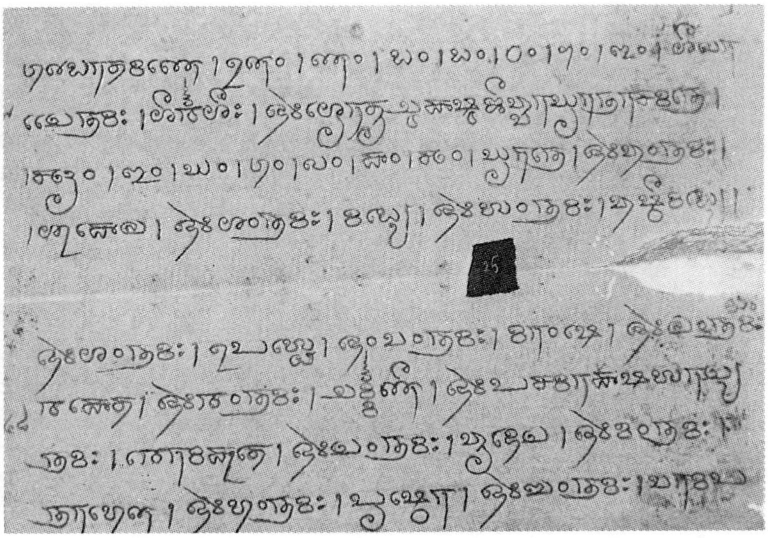

26

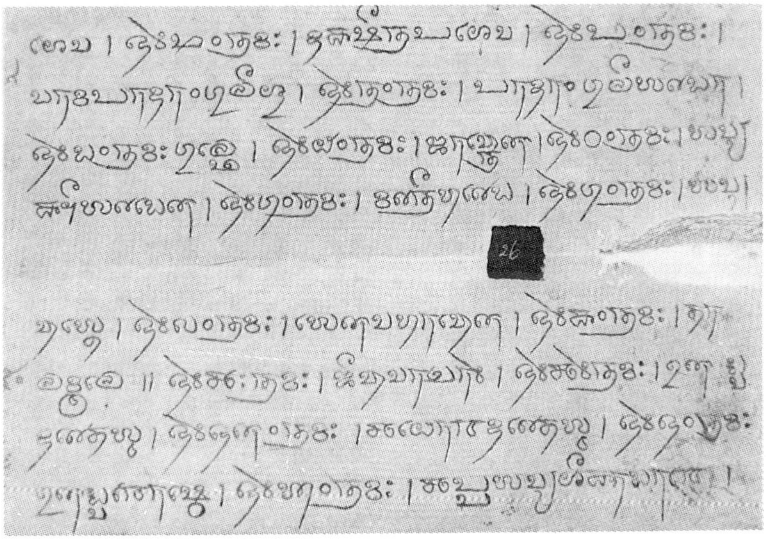

27

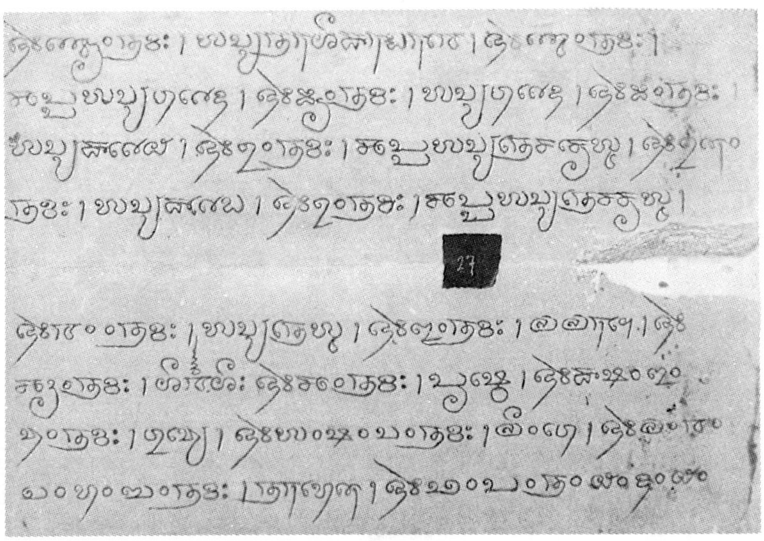

28

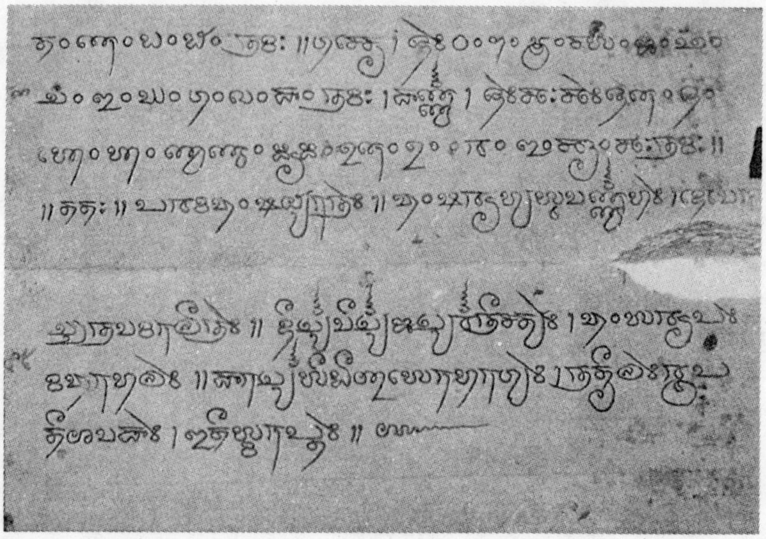

29

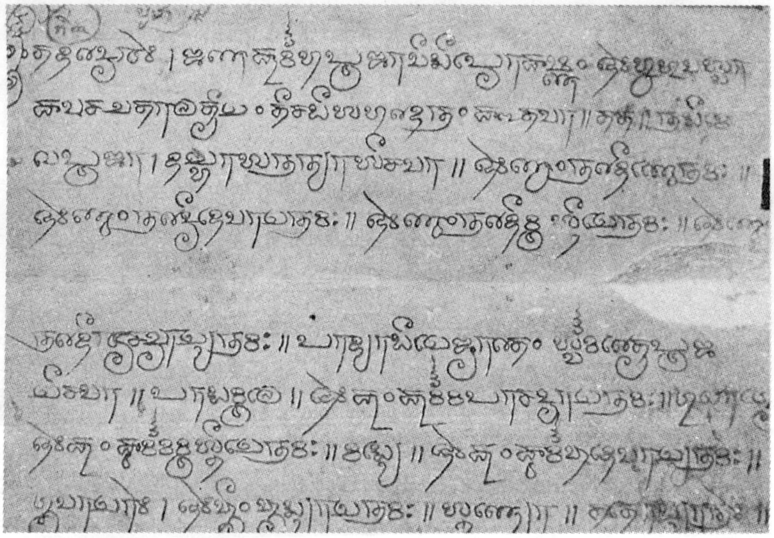

30

31

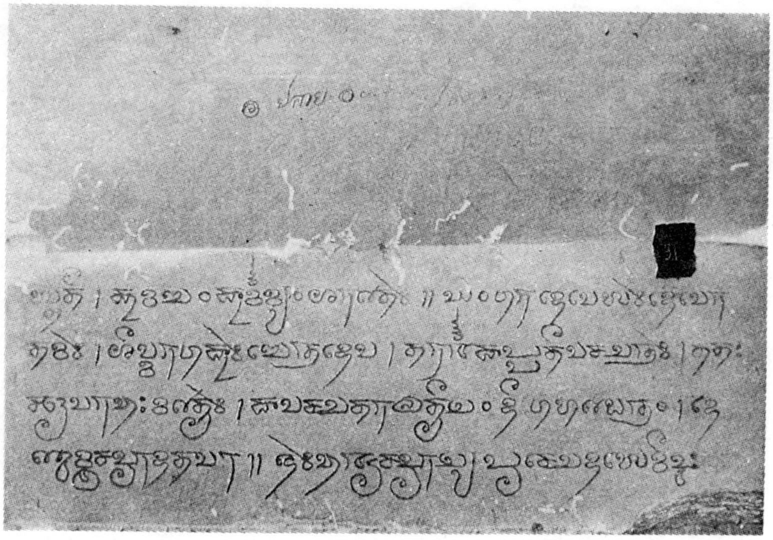

32

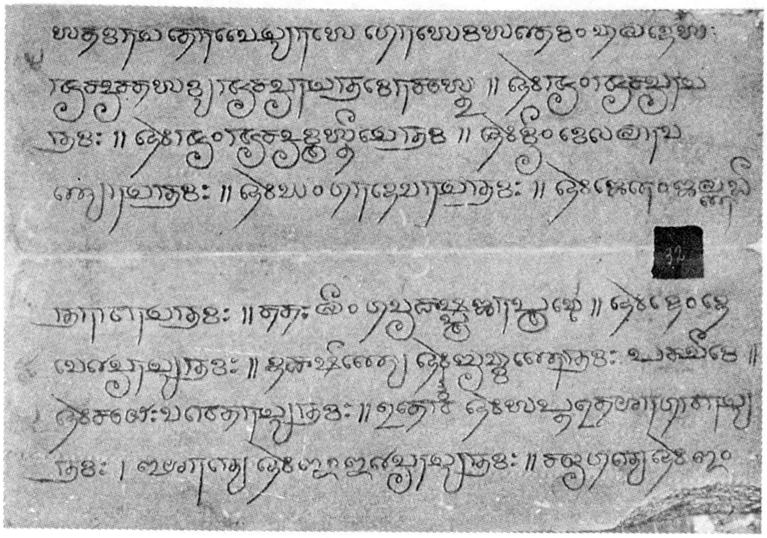

33

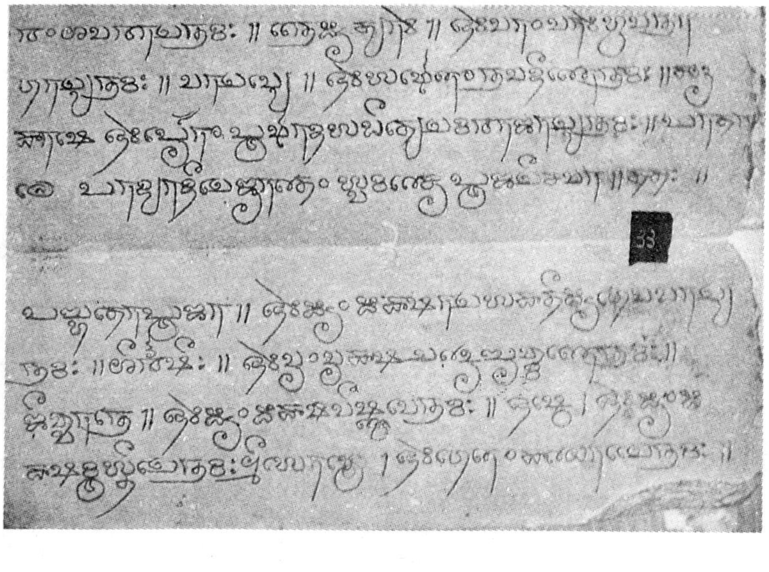

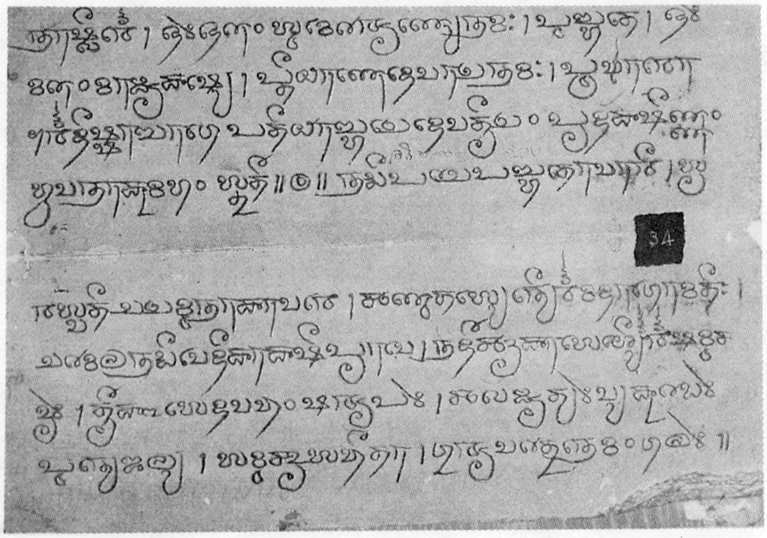

34

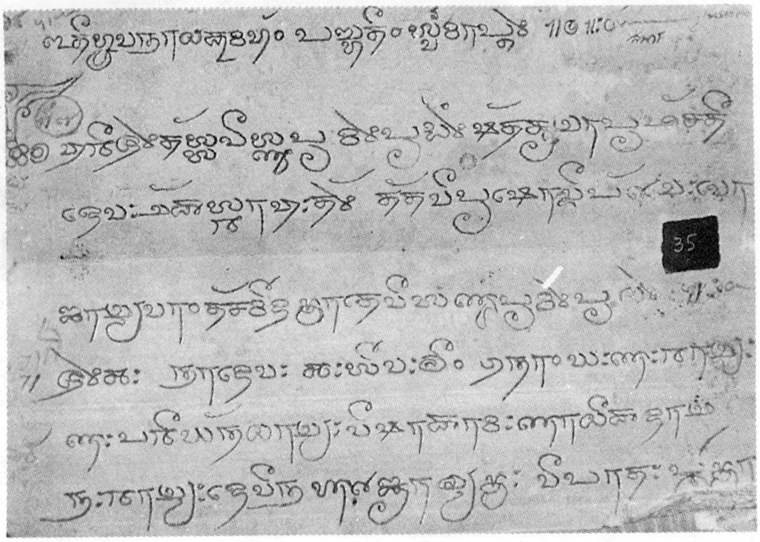

35

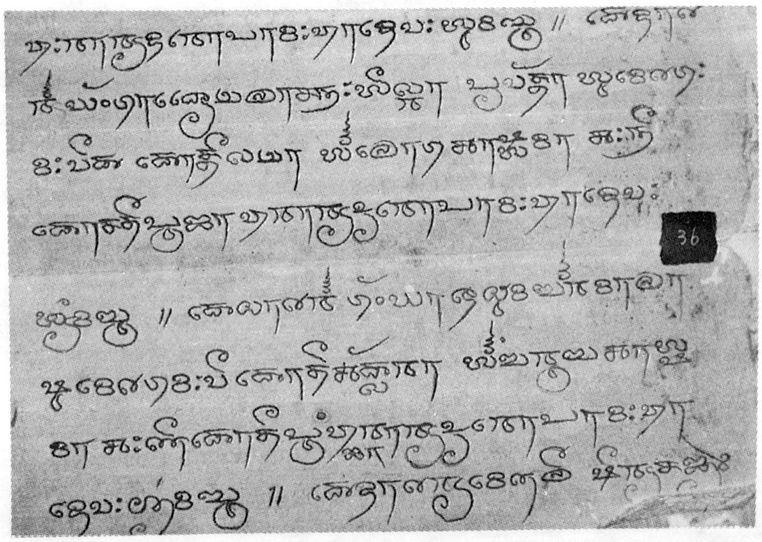

36

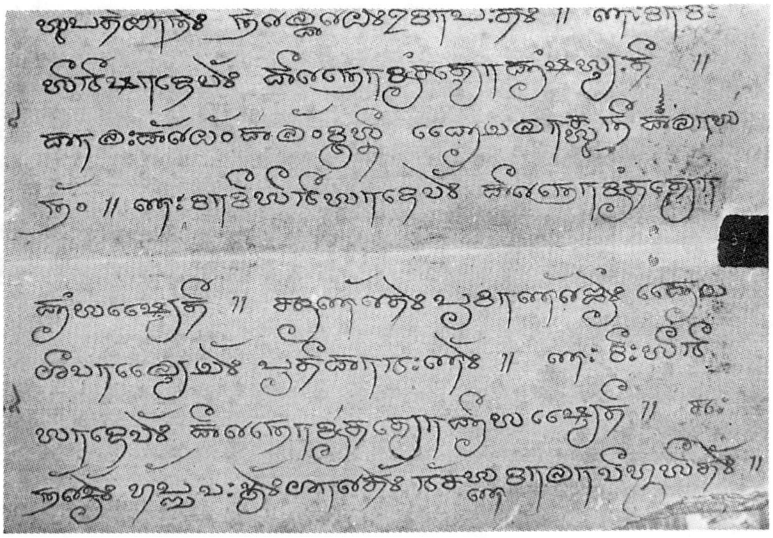

37

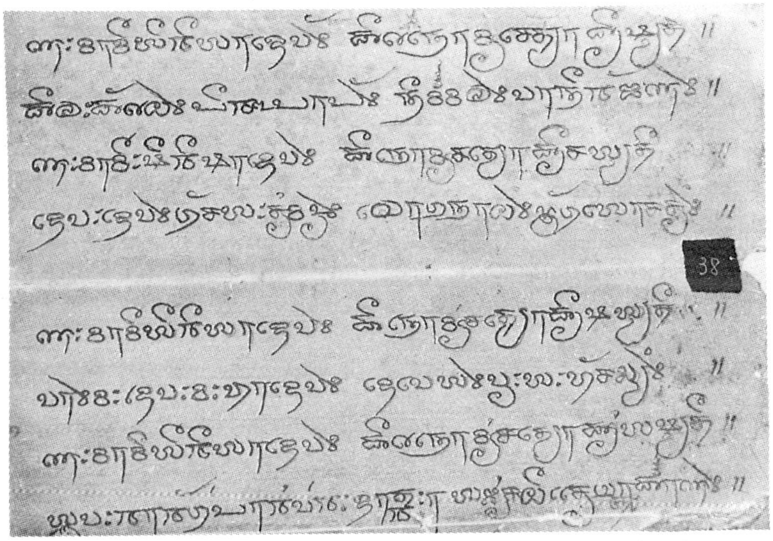

38

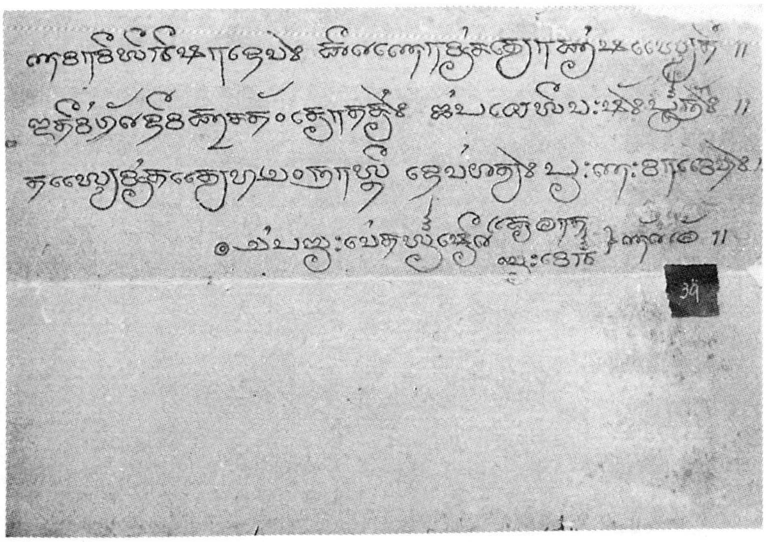

39

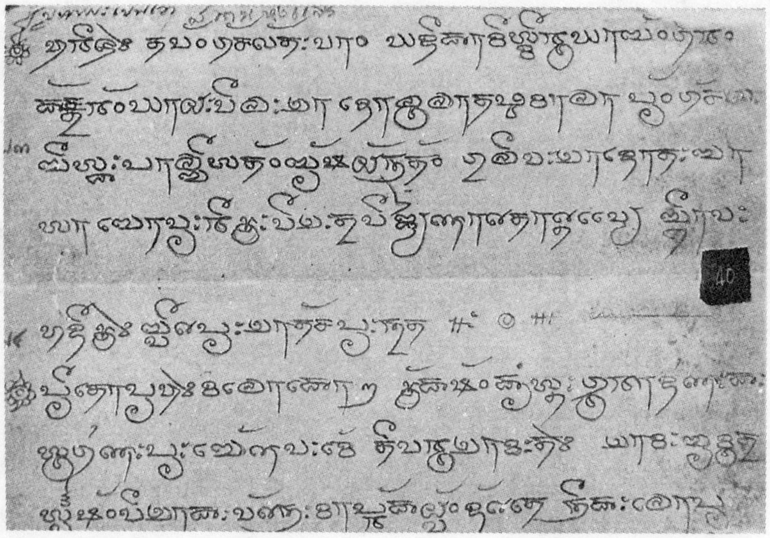

40

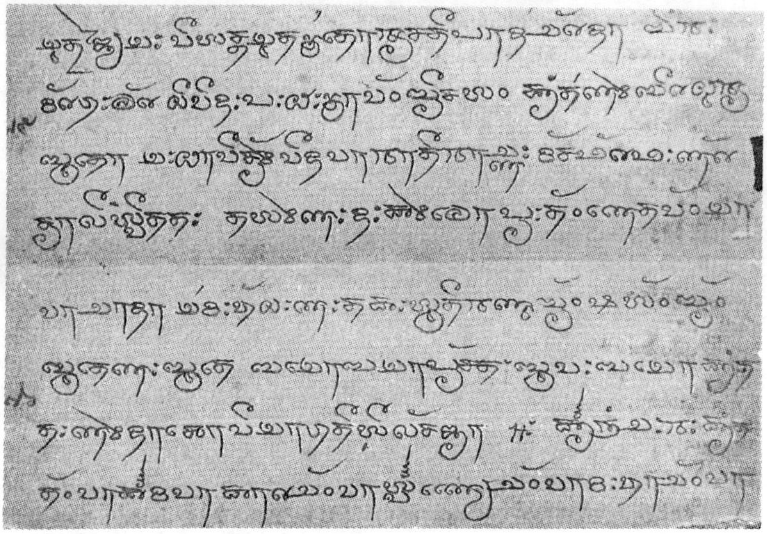

41

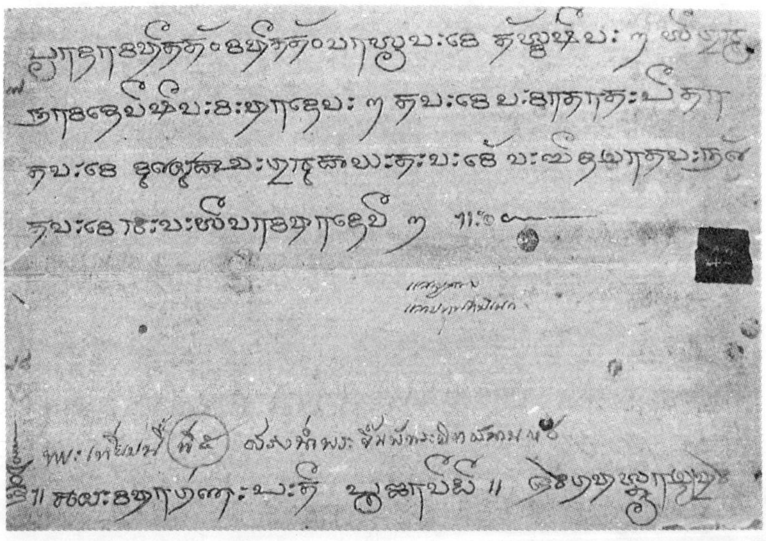

42

43

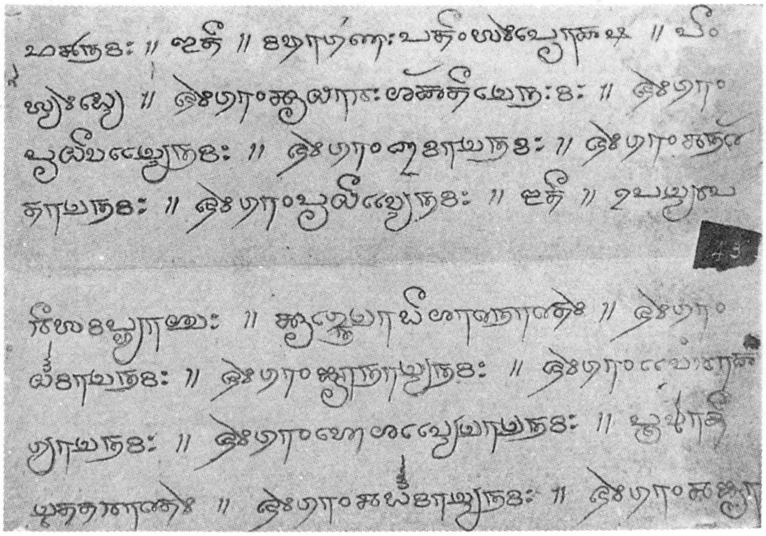

44

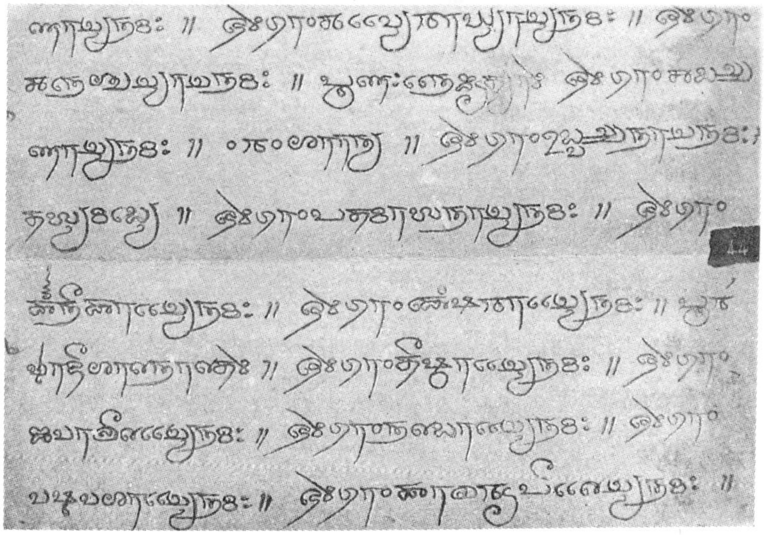

45

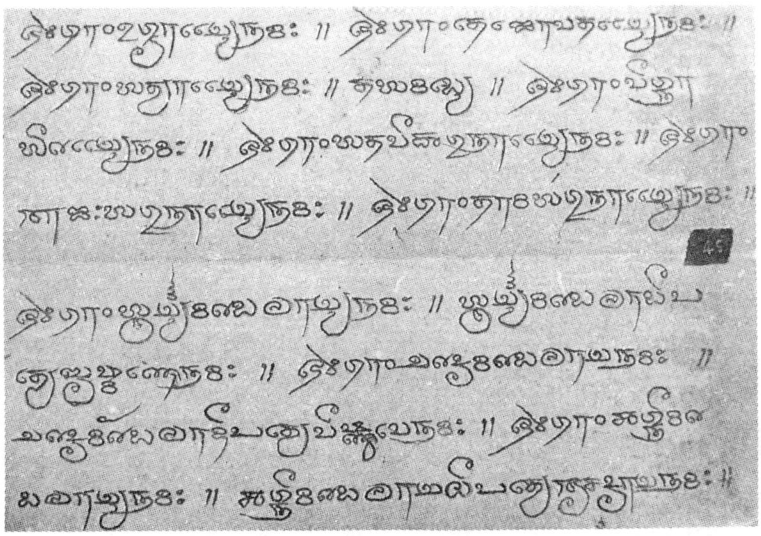

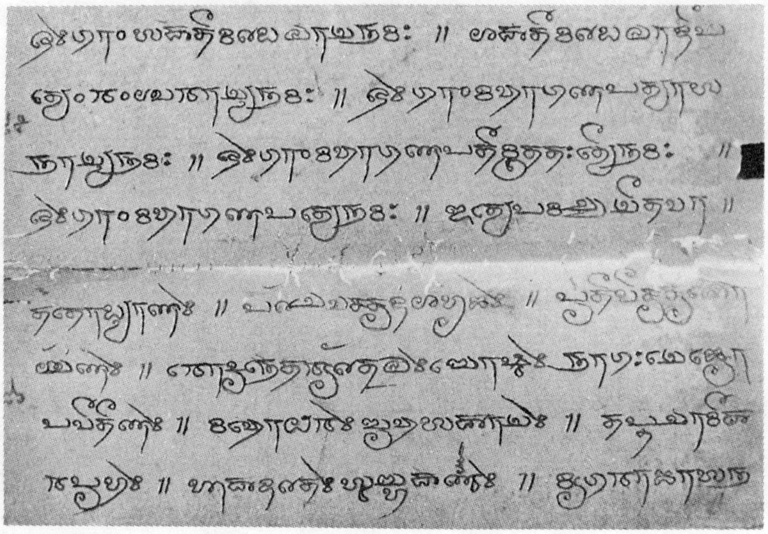

46

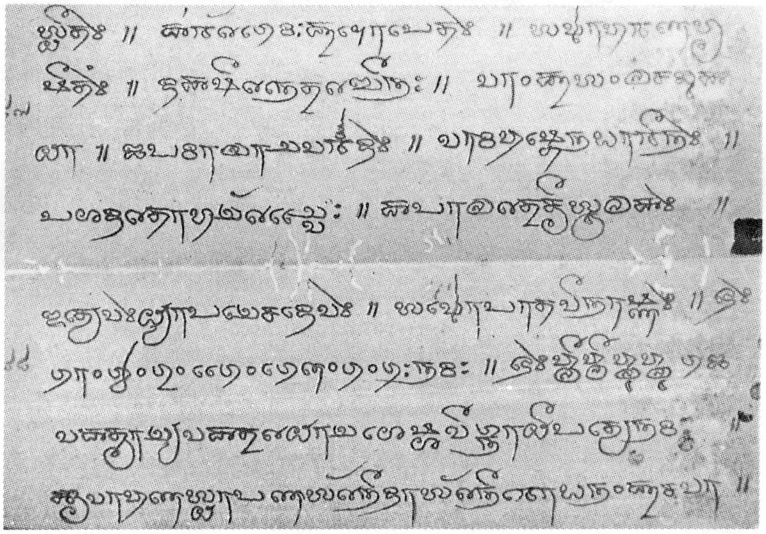

47

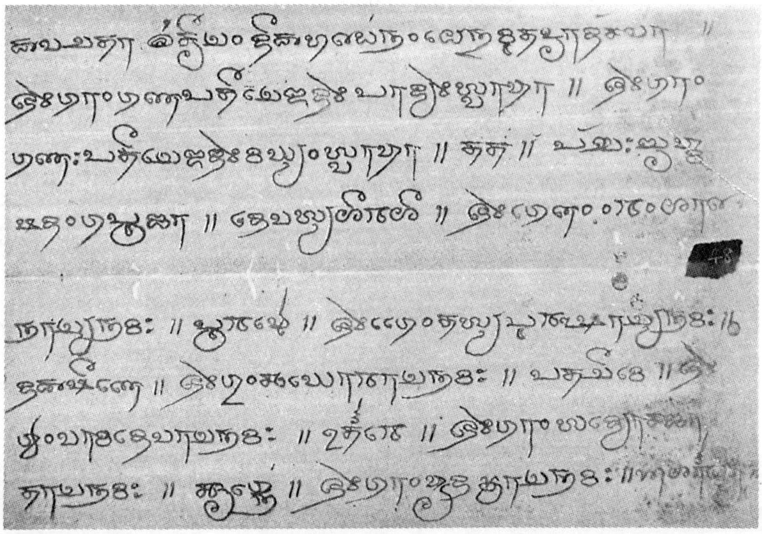

48

49

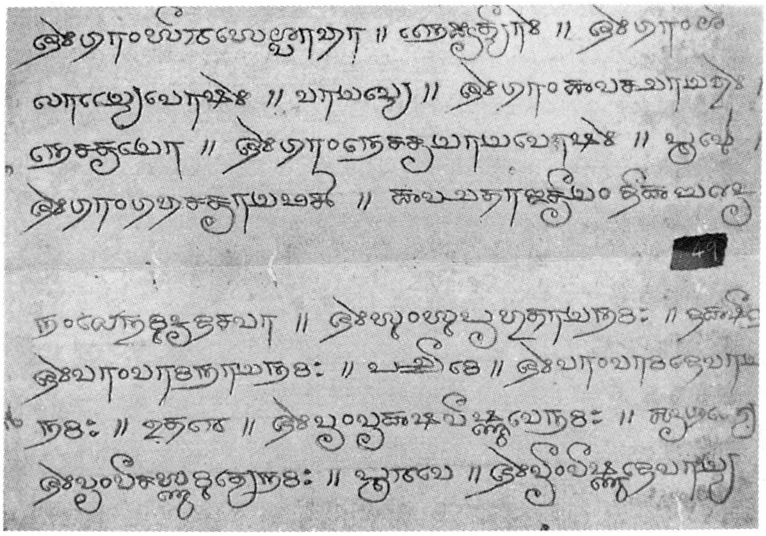

50

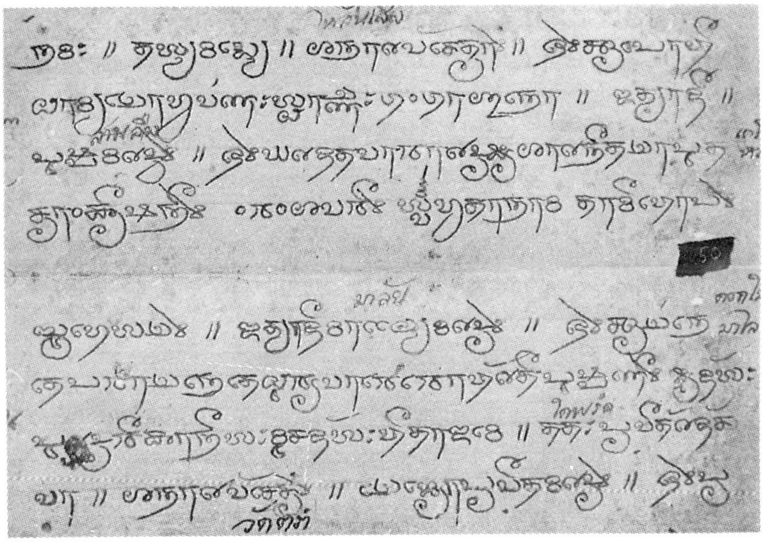

51

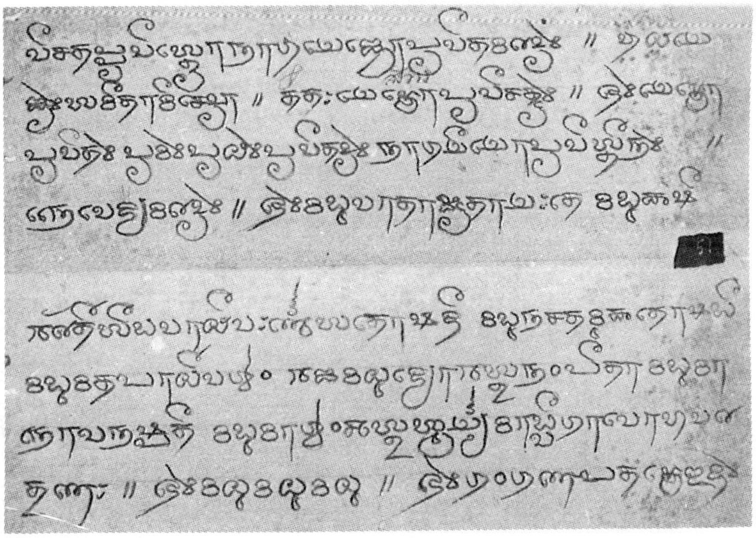

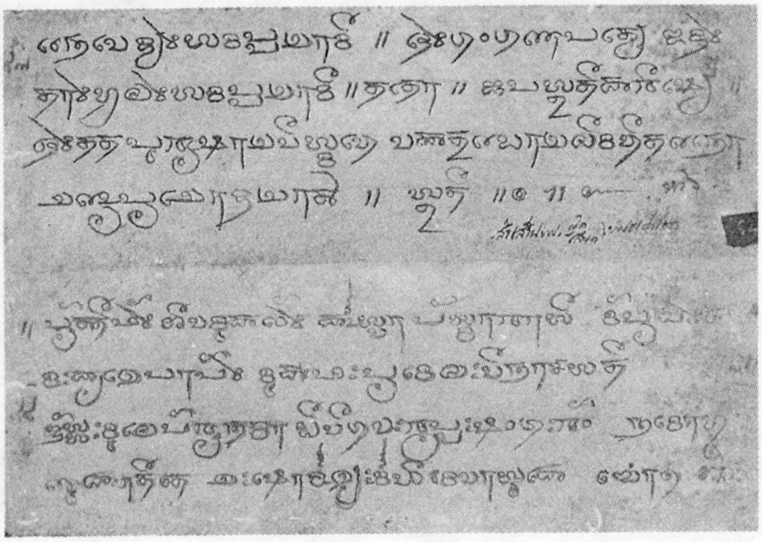

52

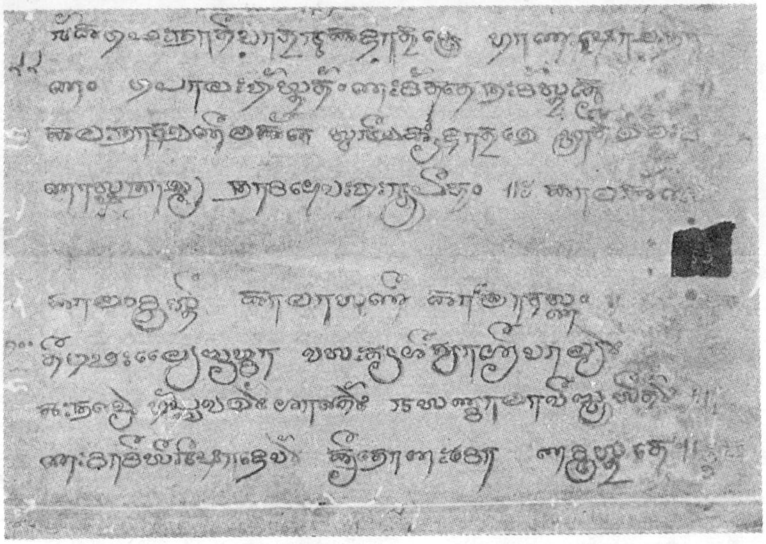

53

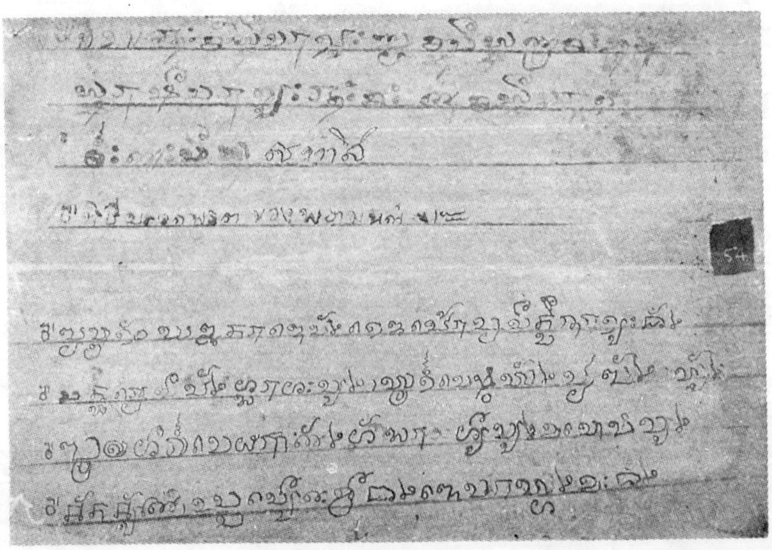

54

55

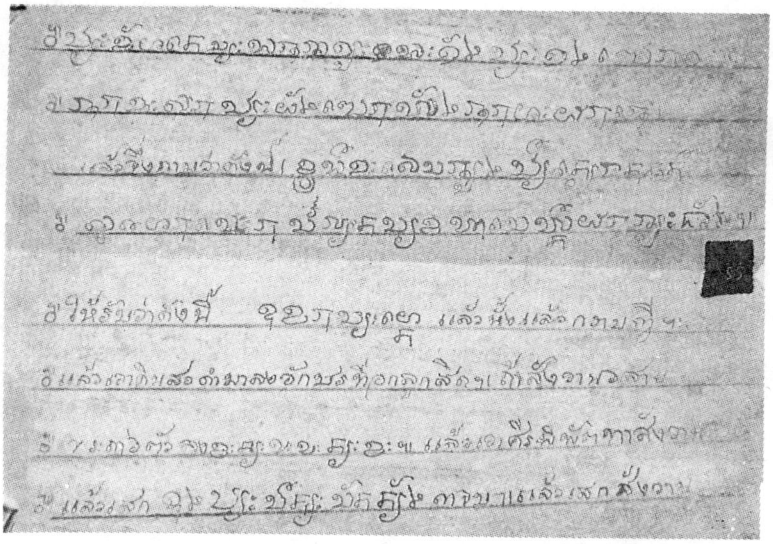

56

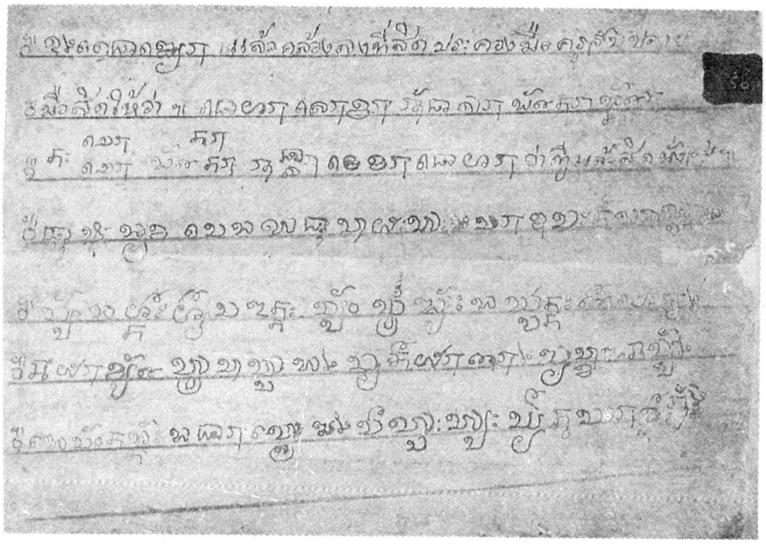

57

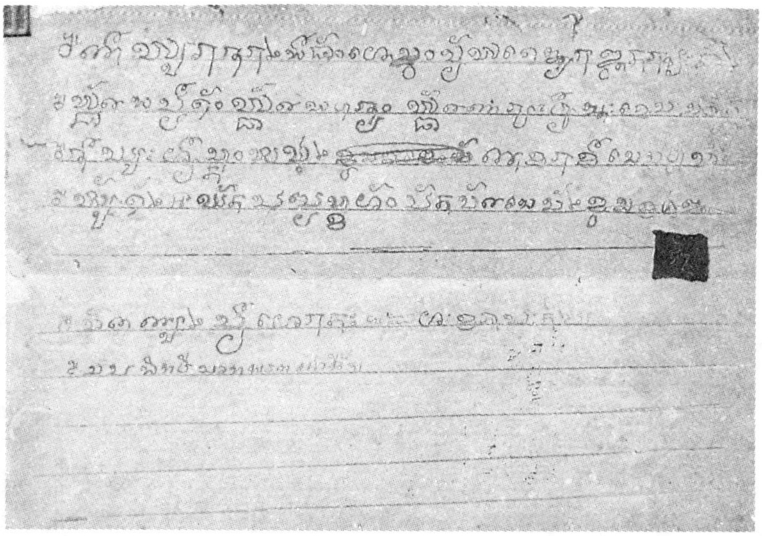

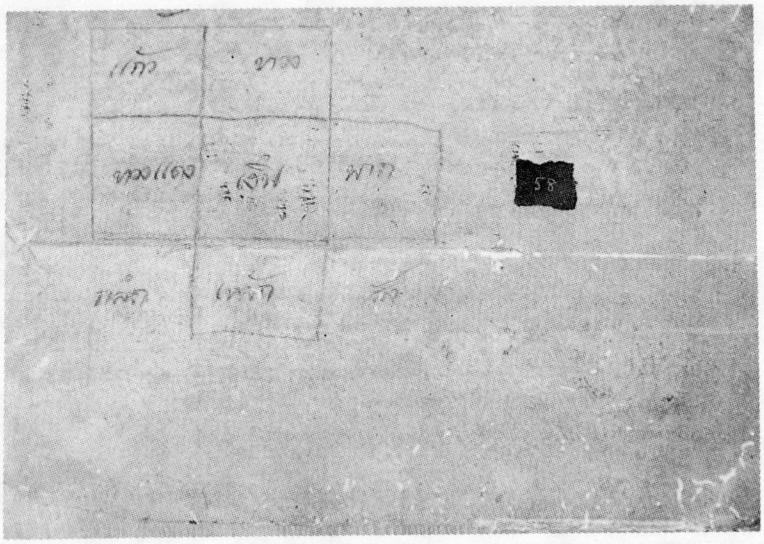

58

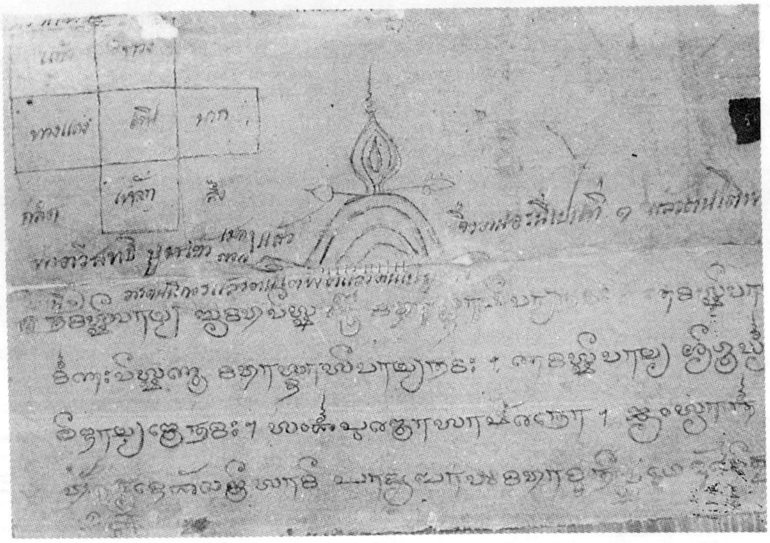

59

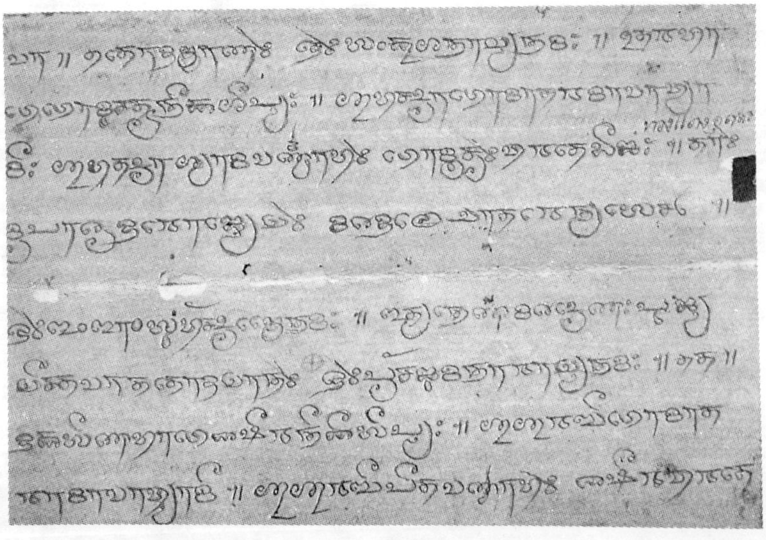

60

61

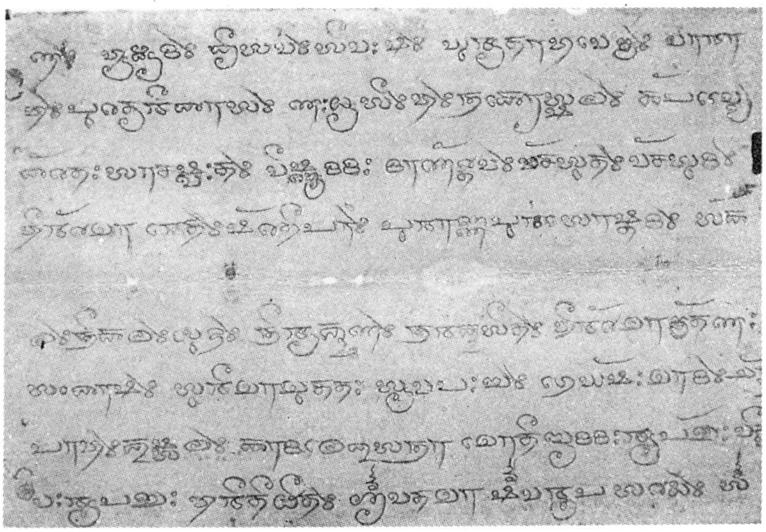

62

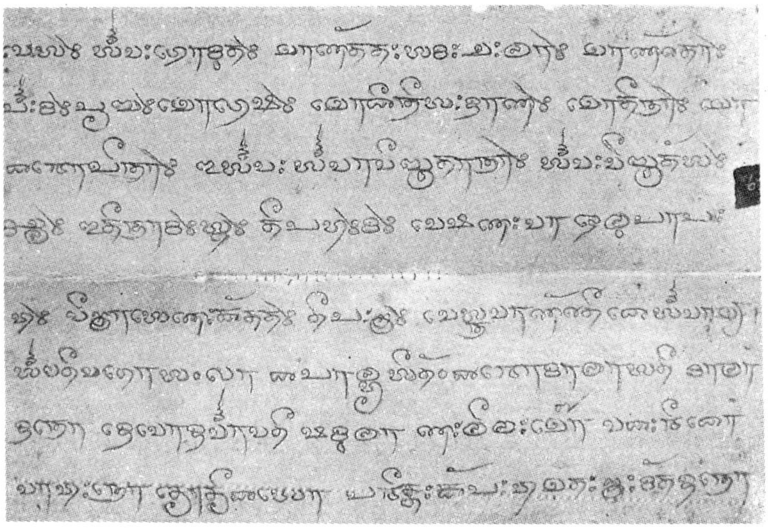

63

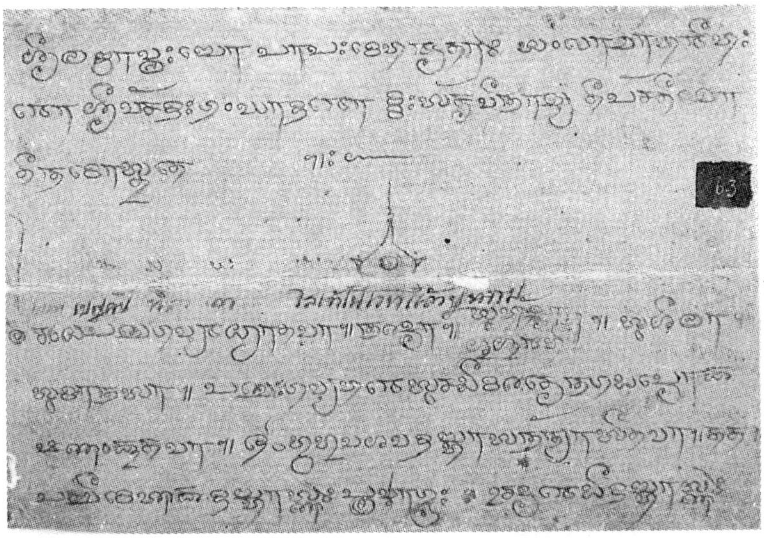

64

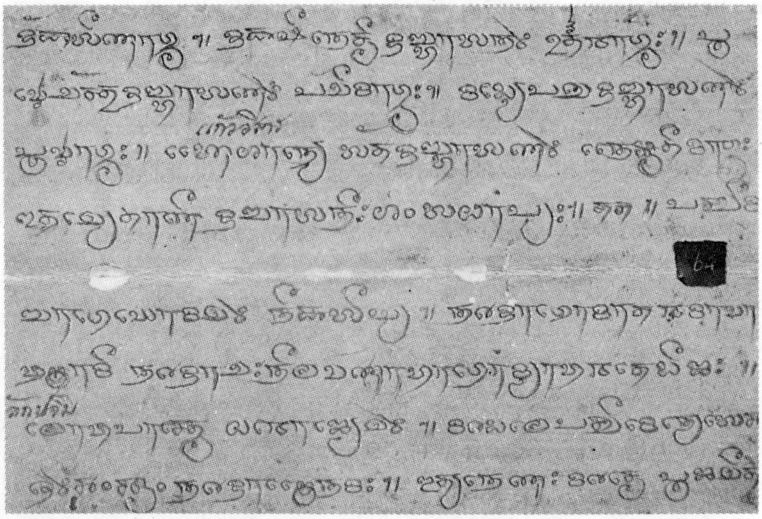

65

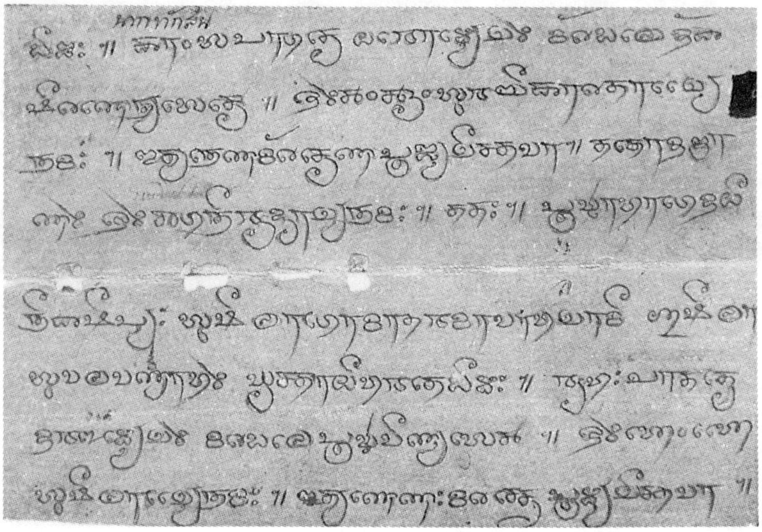

66

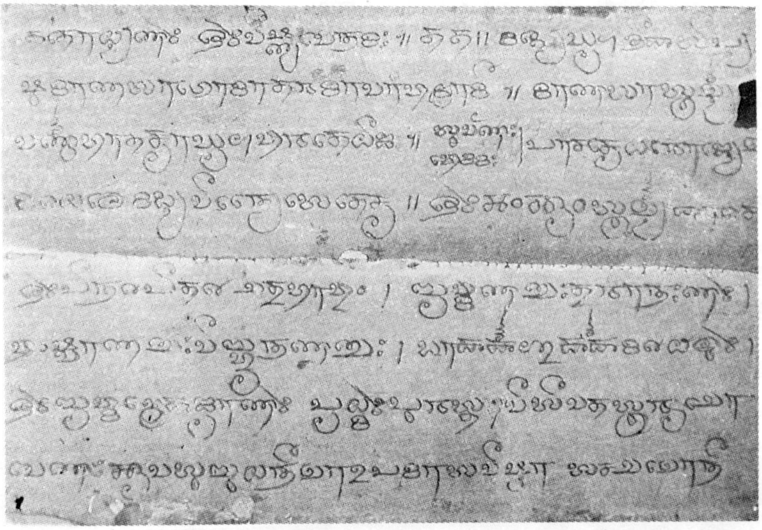

67

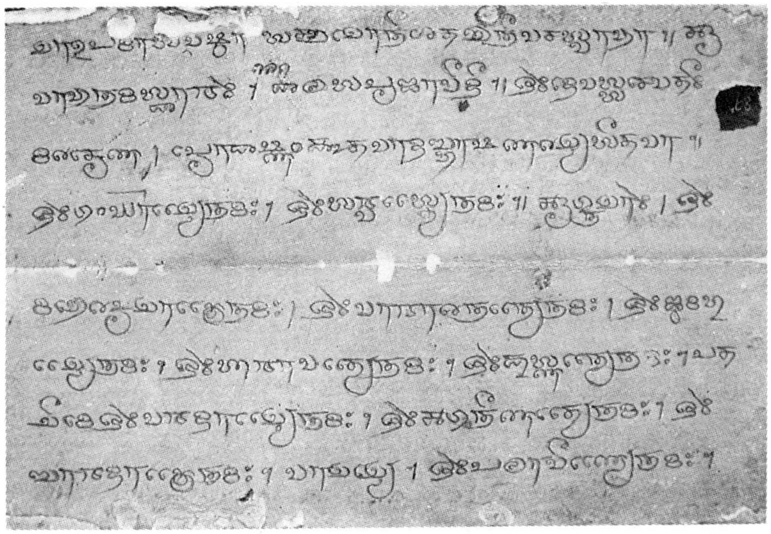

68

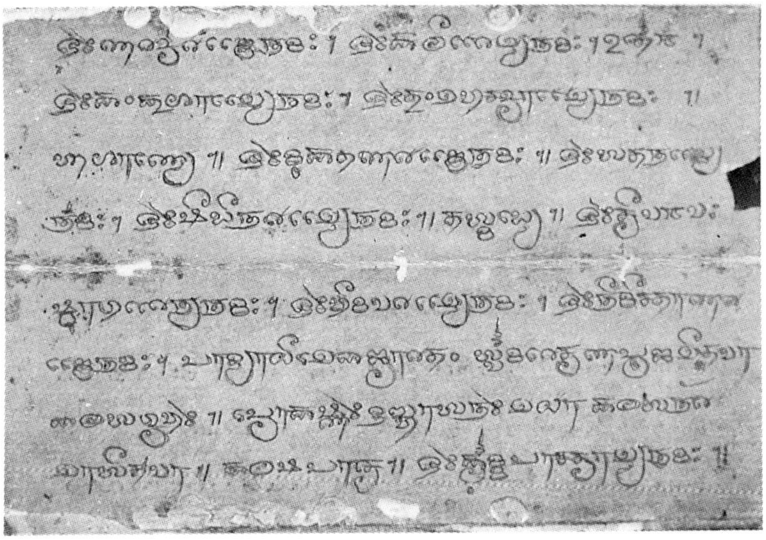

69

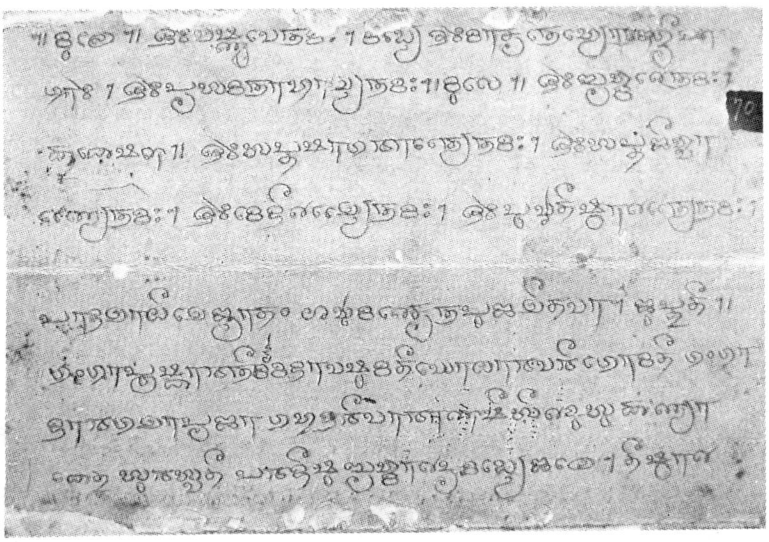

70

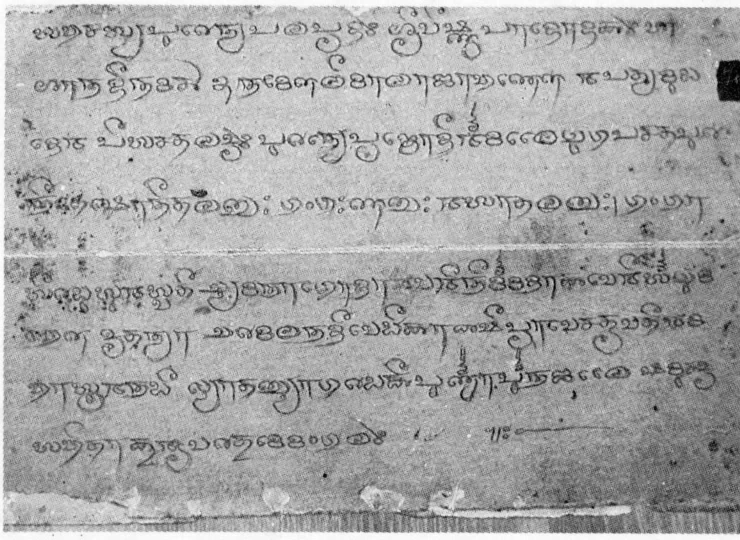

71

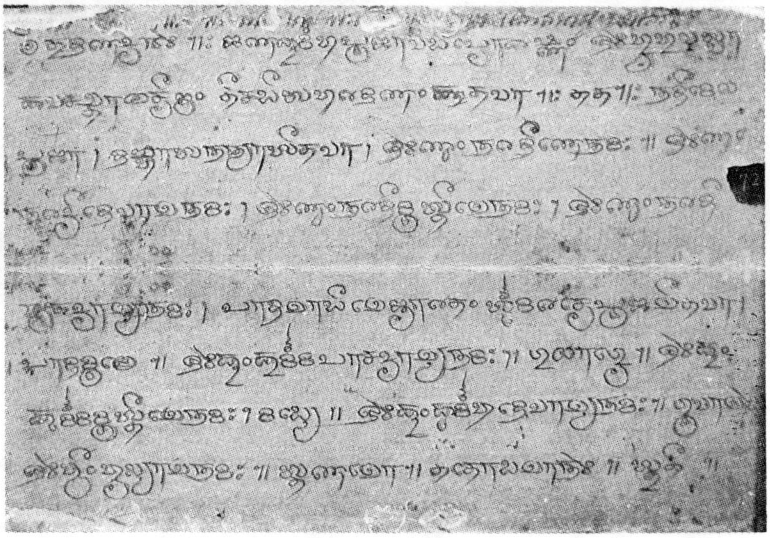

72

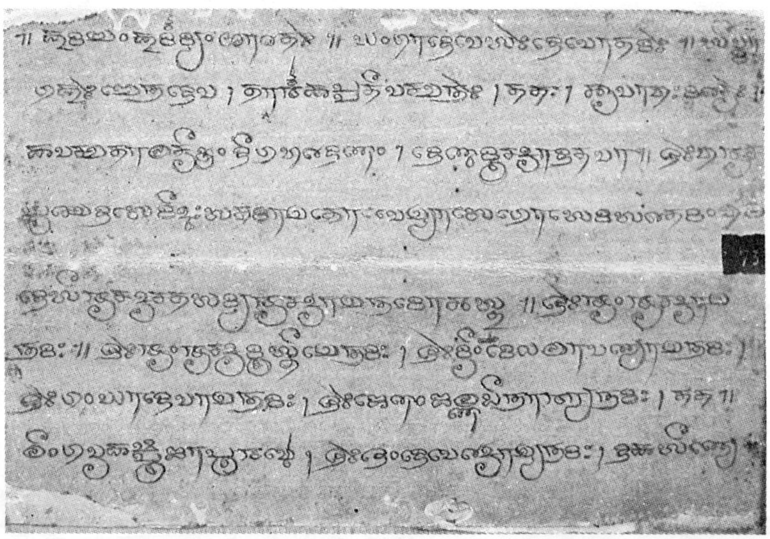

73

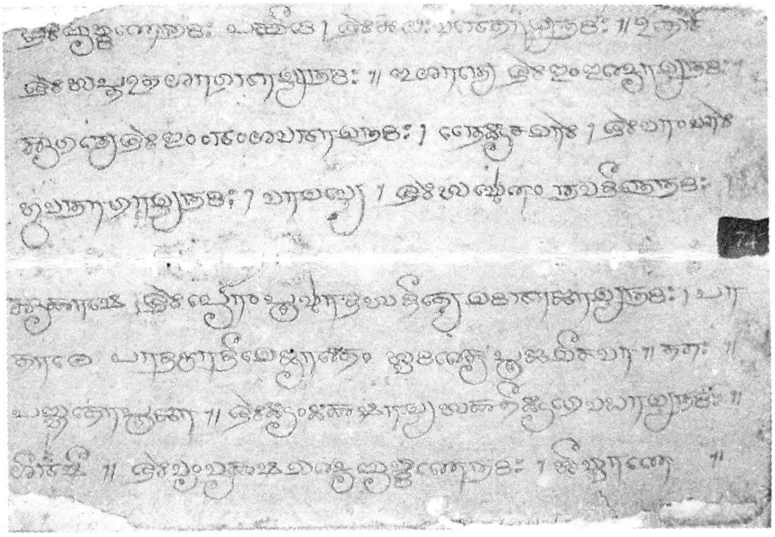

74

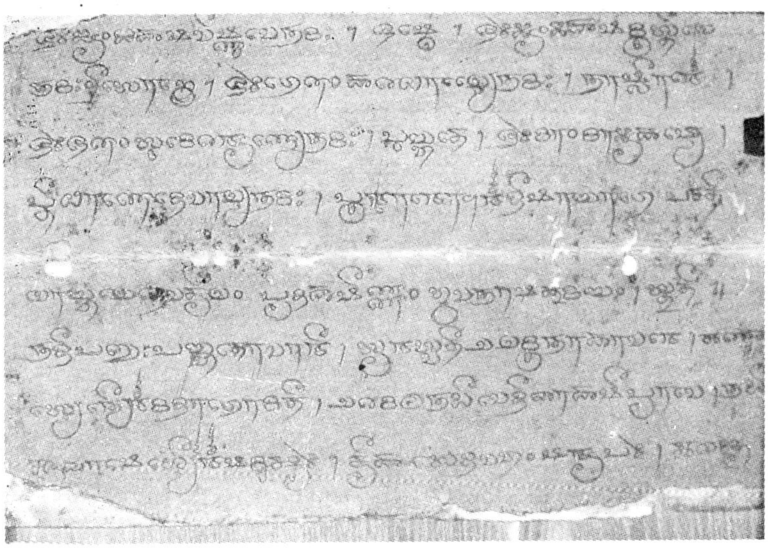

75

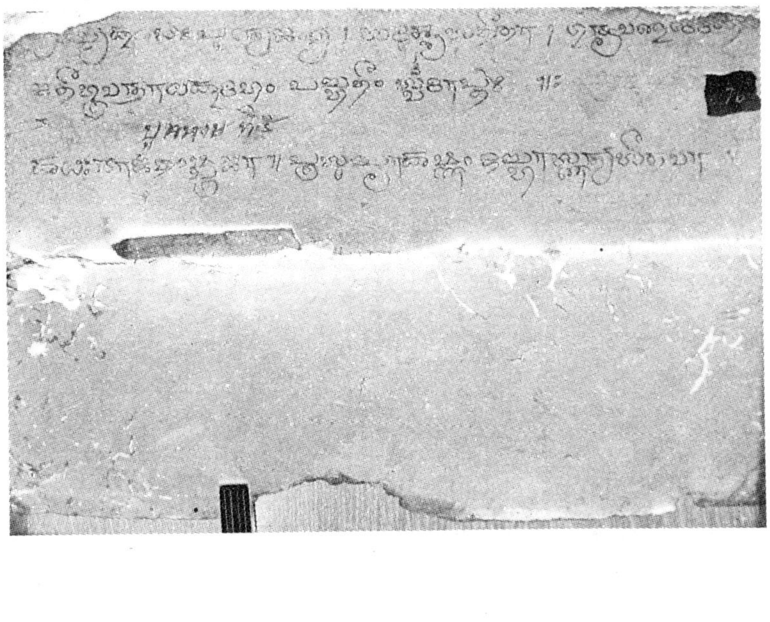

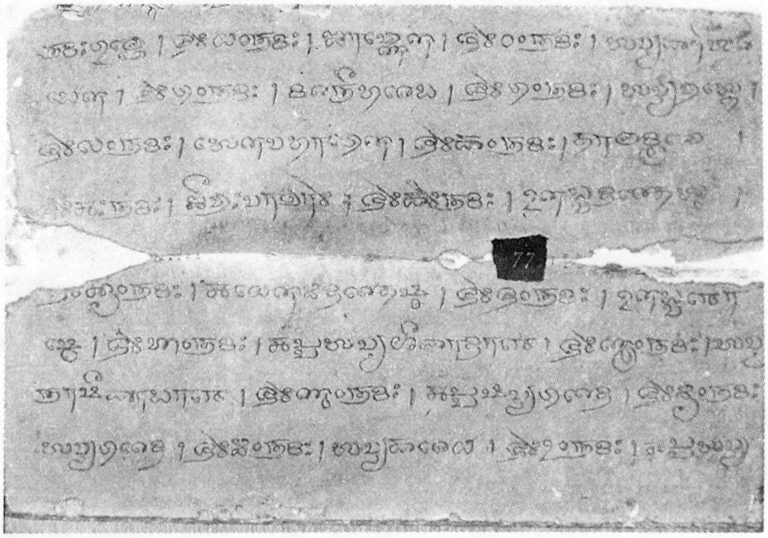

76

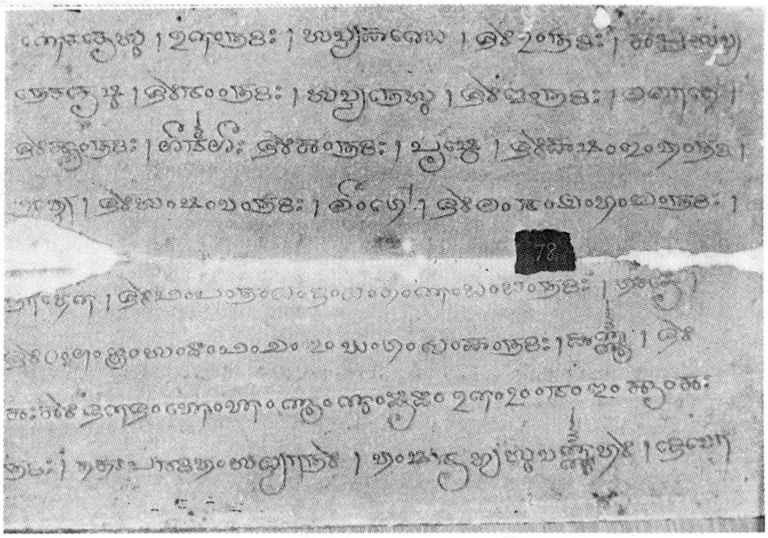

77

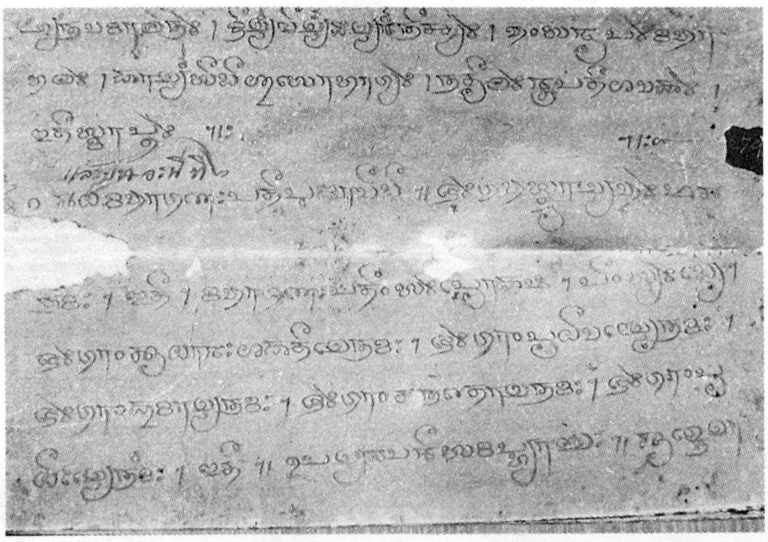

78

79

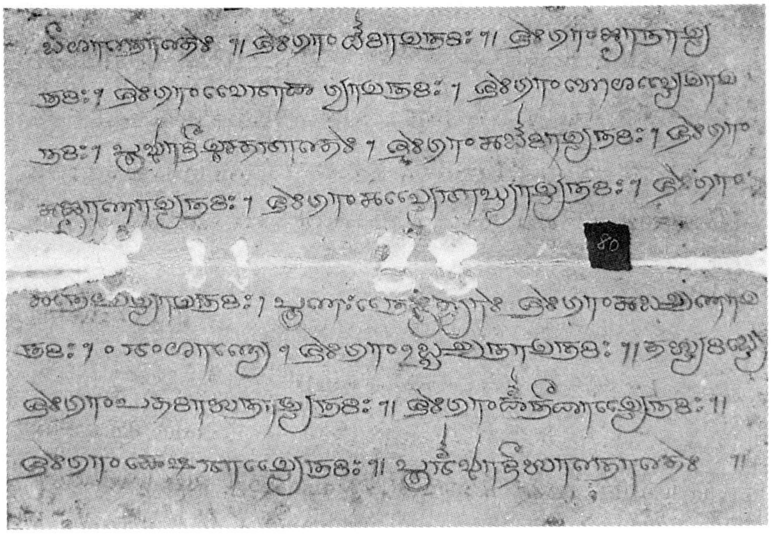

80

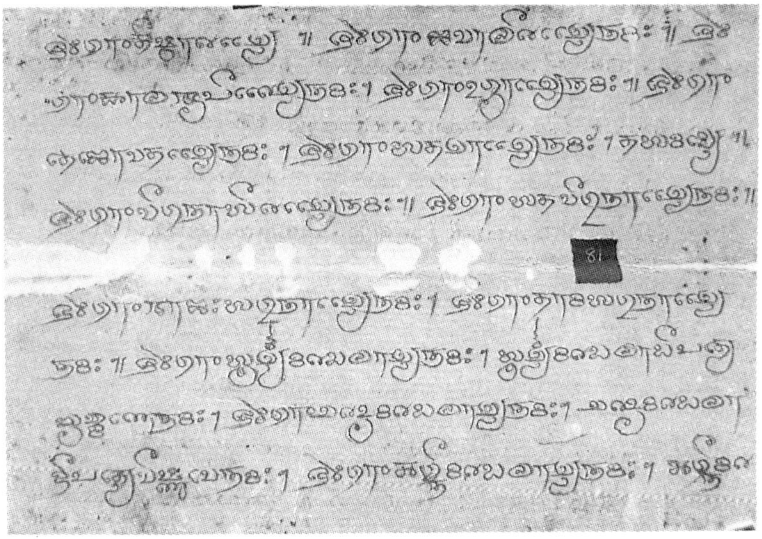

81

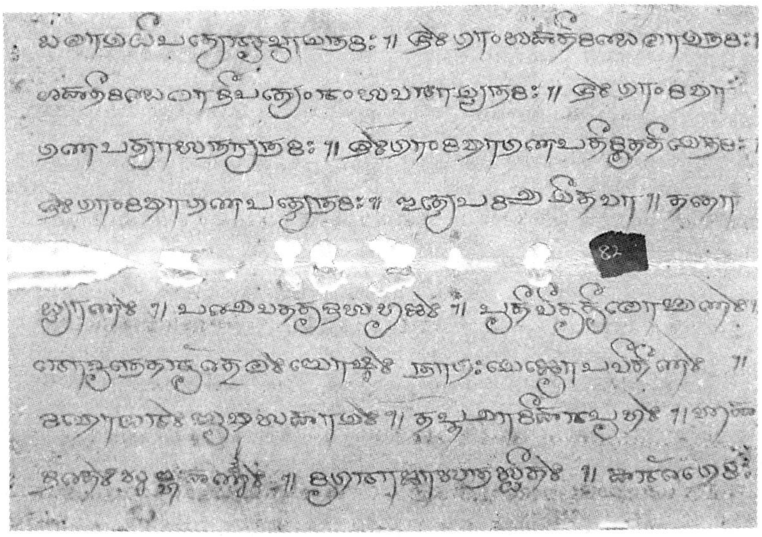

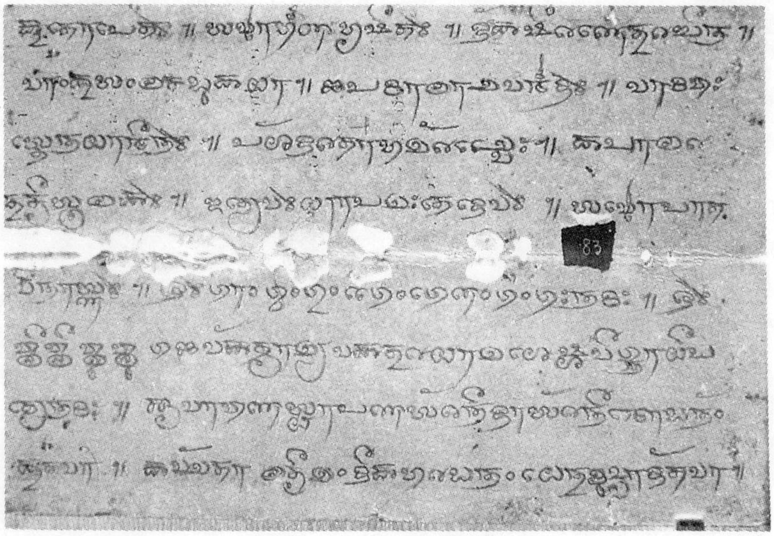

82

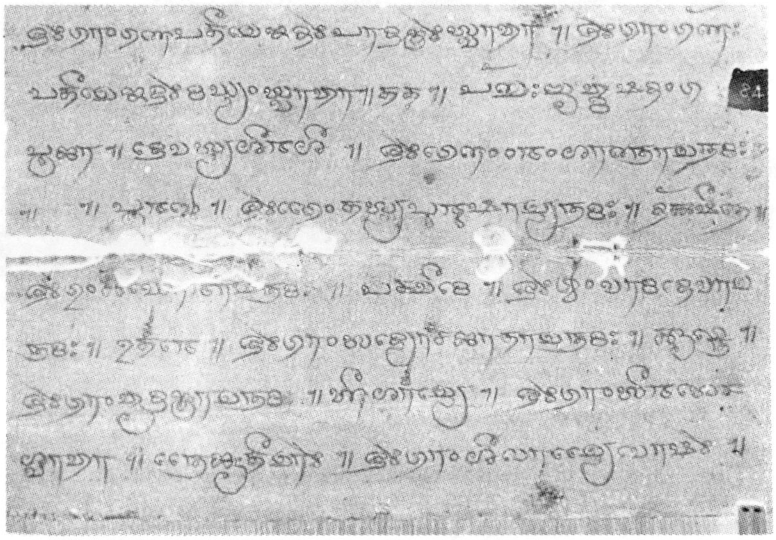

83

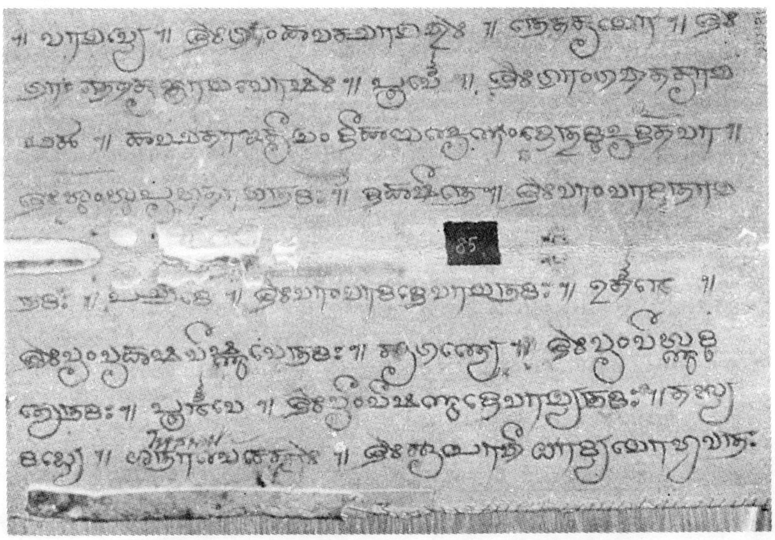

84

85

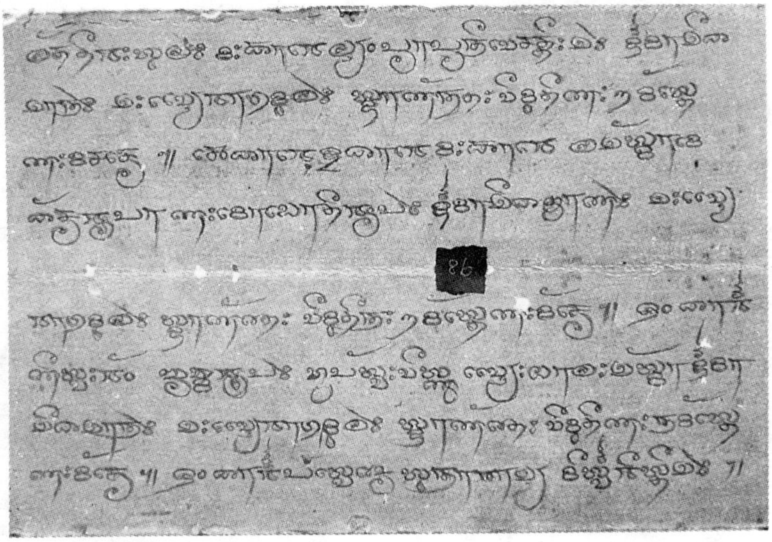

86

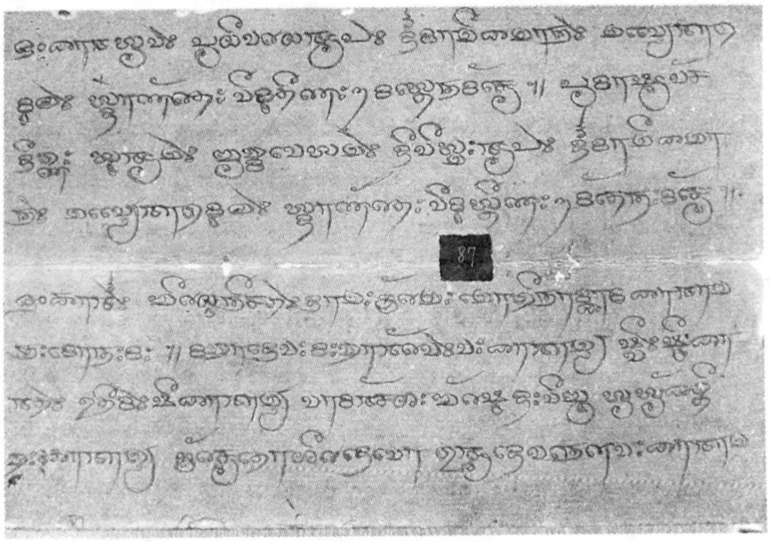

87

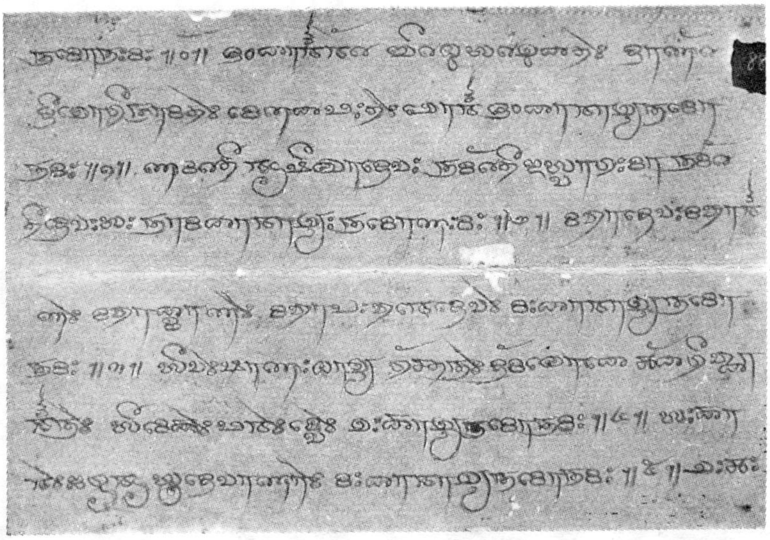

88

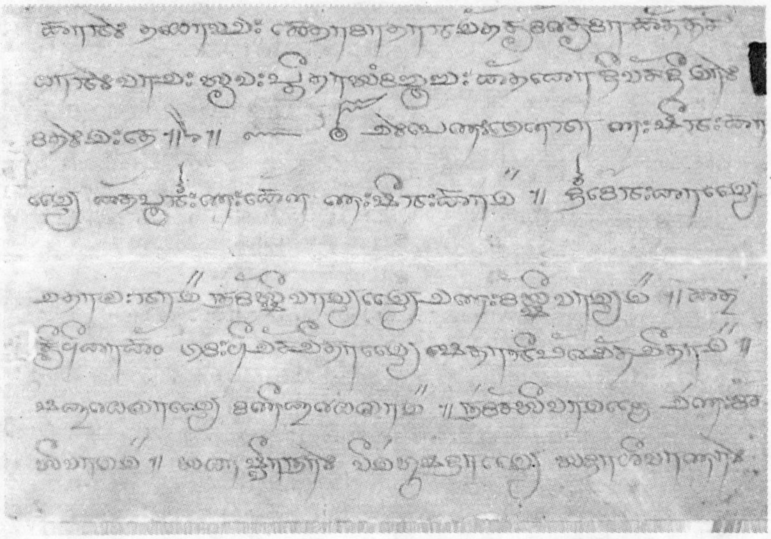

89

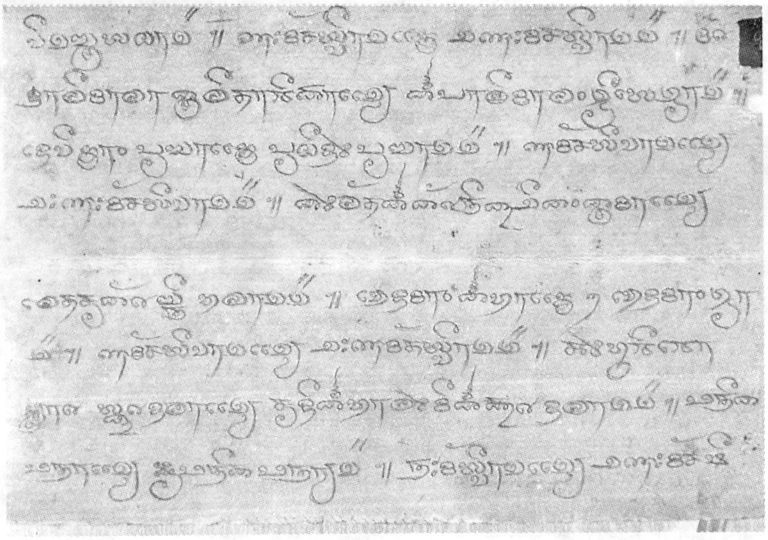

90

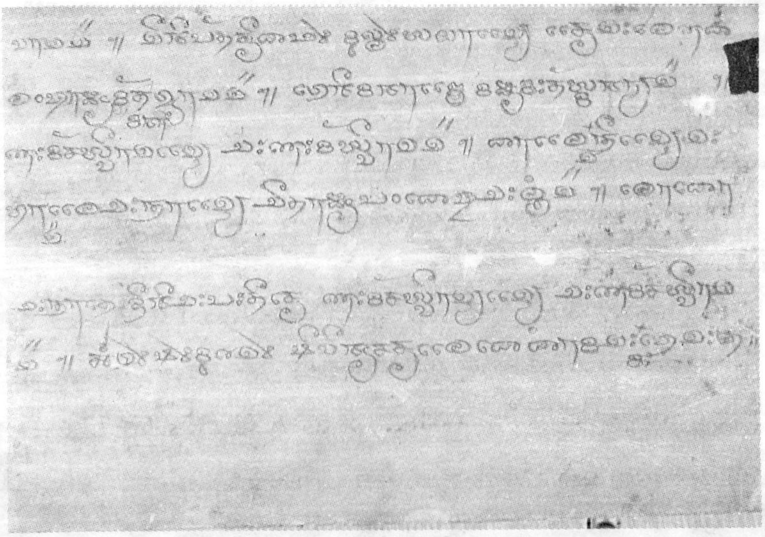

91

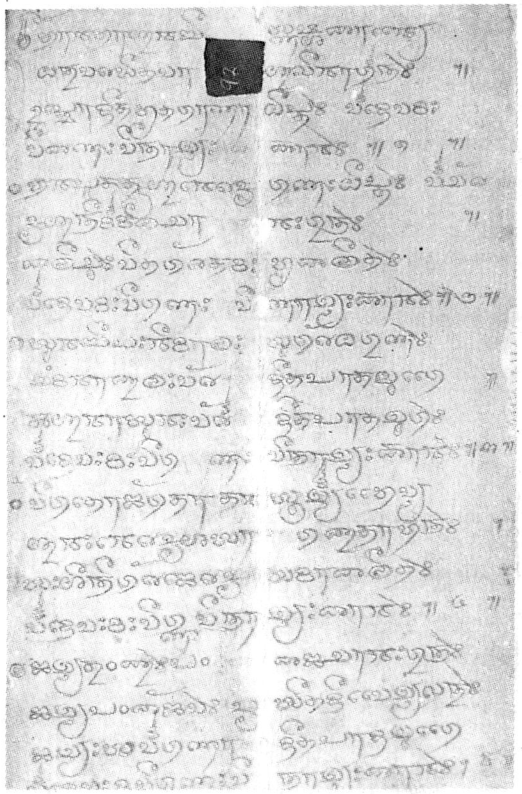

92

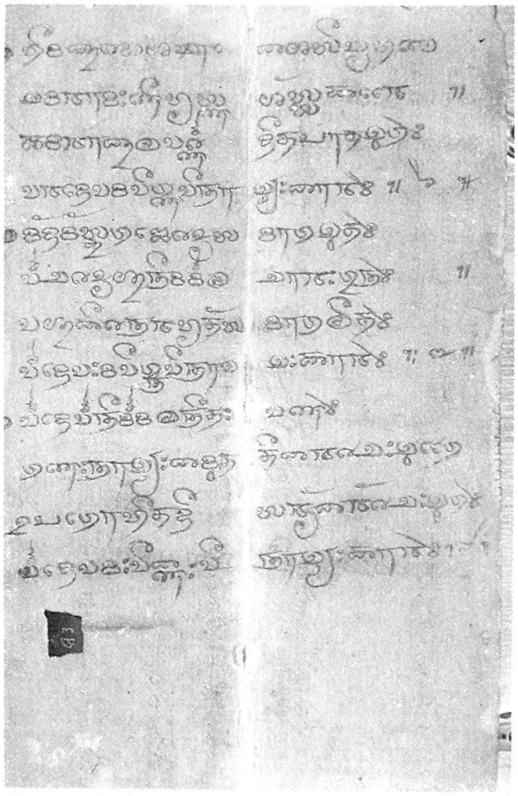

93

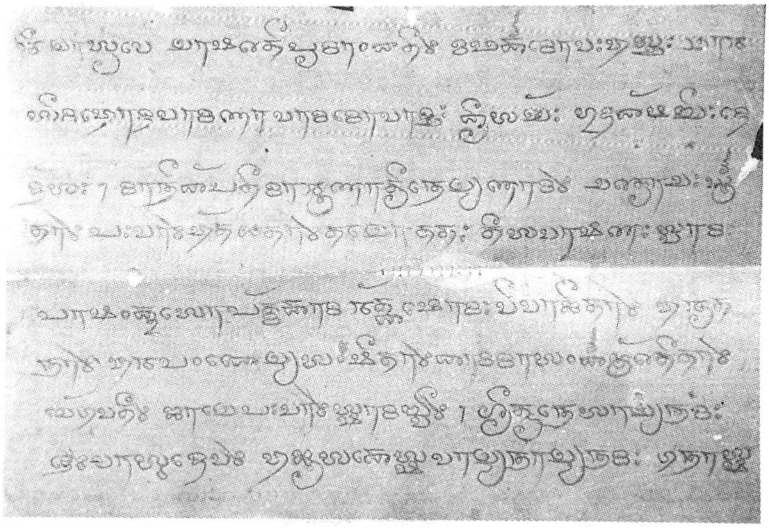

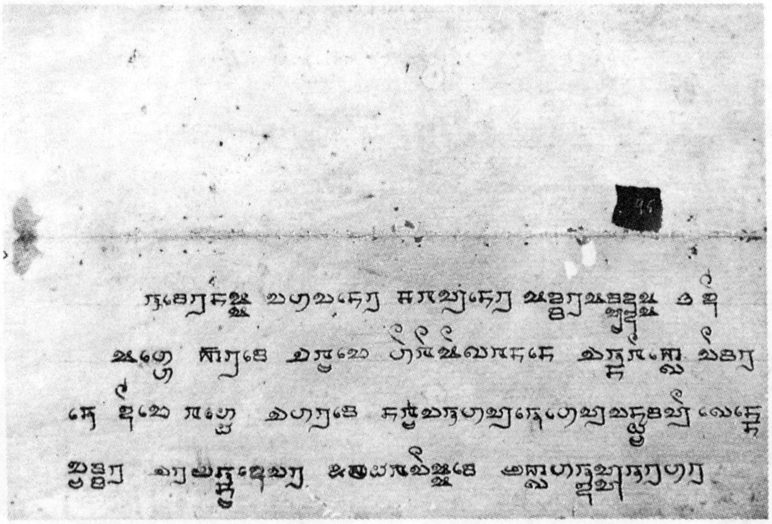

94

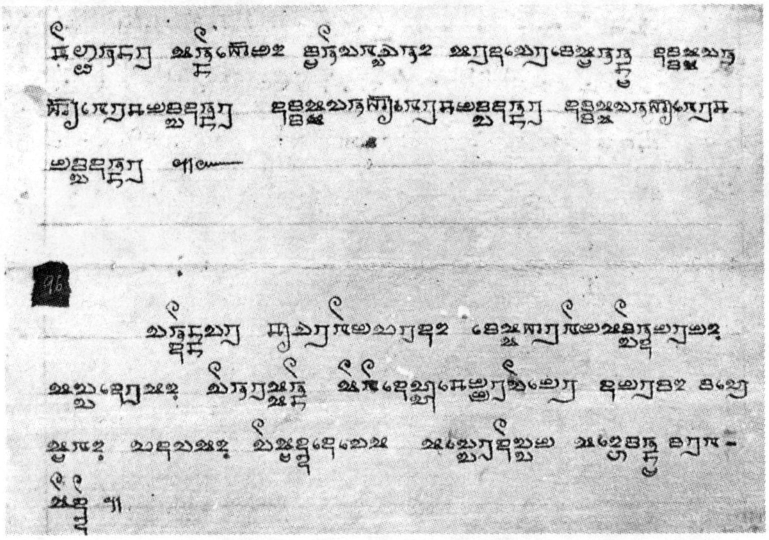

95

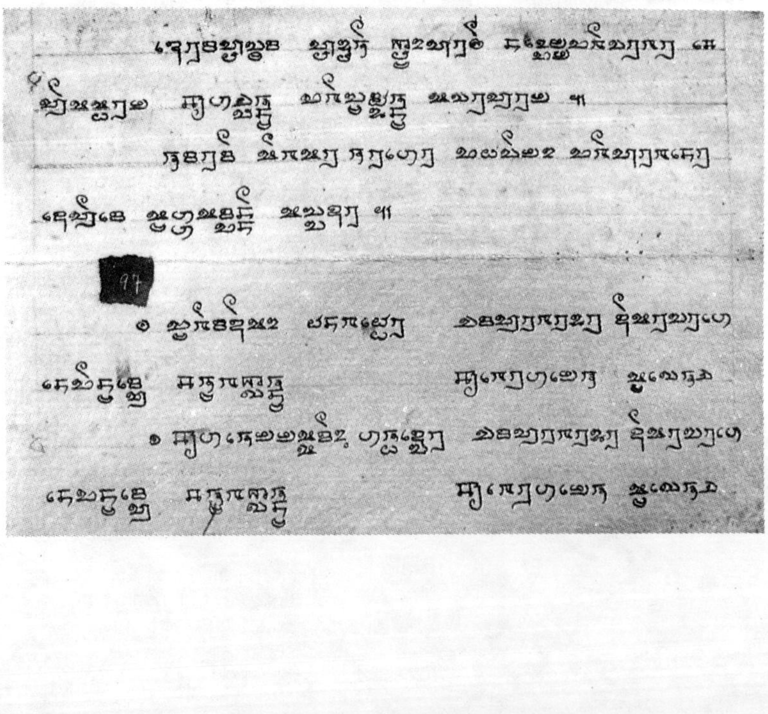

96

97

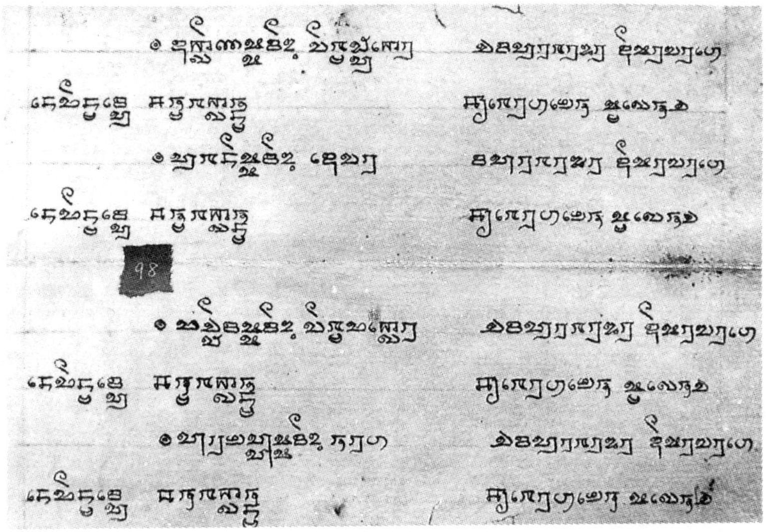

98

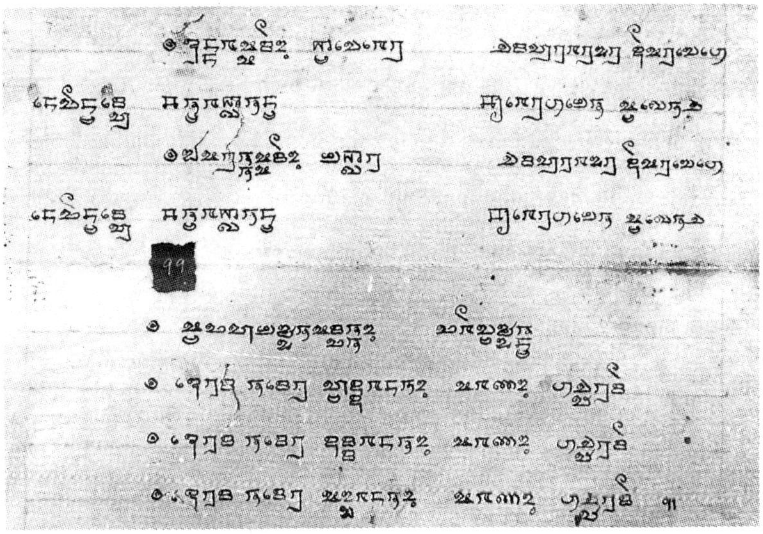

99

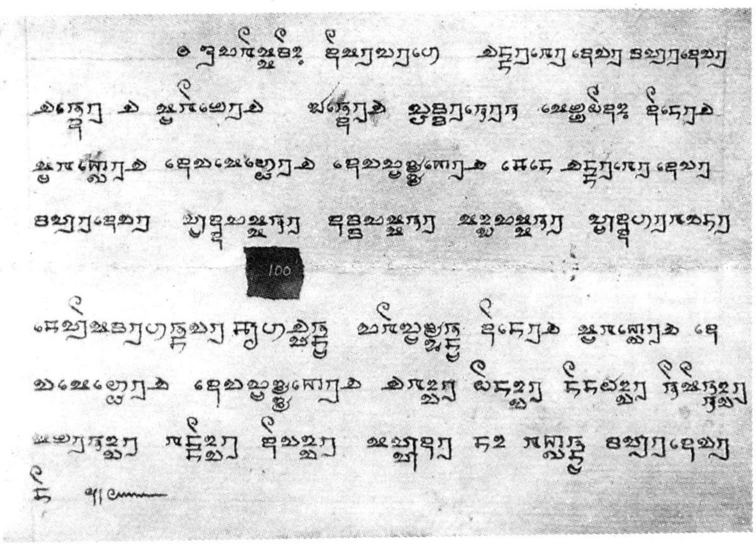

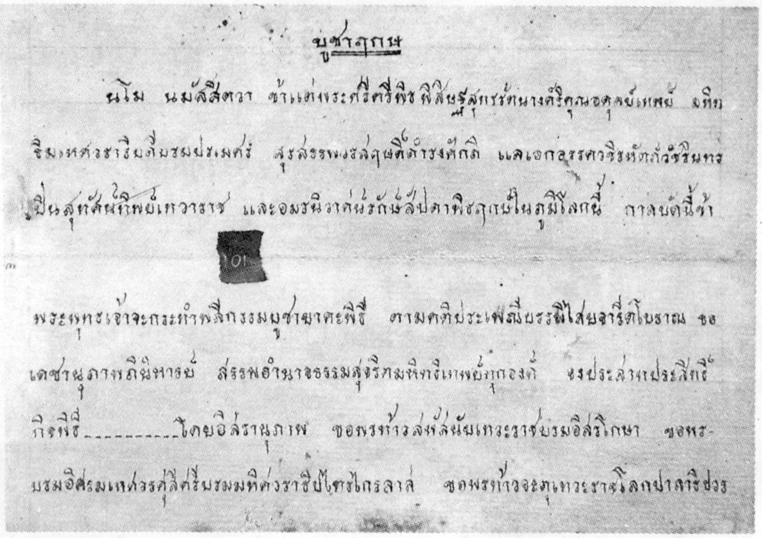
บูชาฤกษ์

100

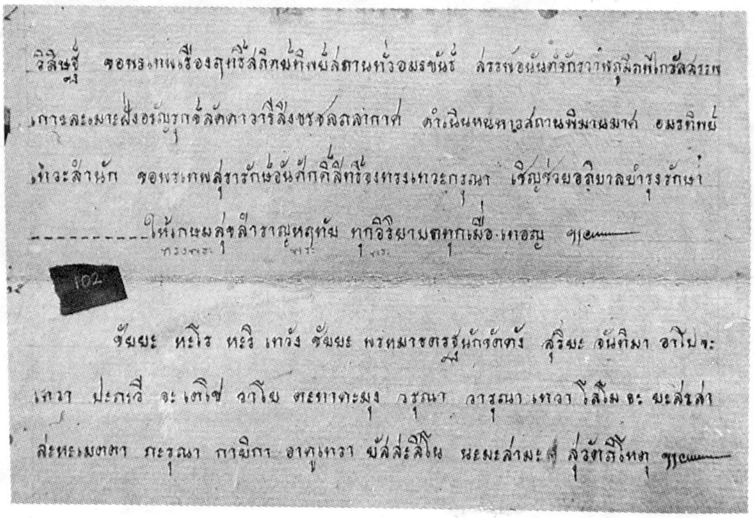

101

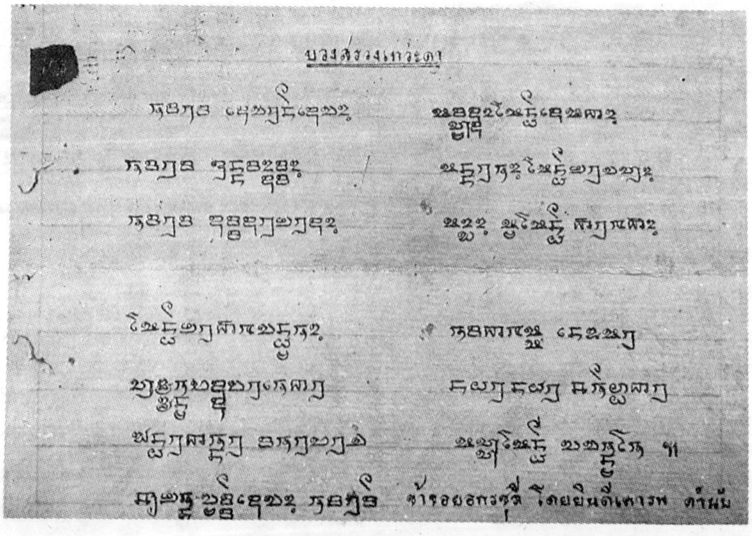
บวงสรวงเทวดา

102

103

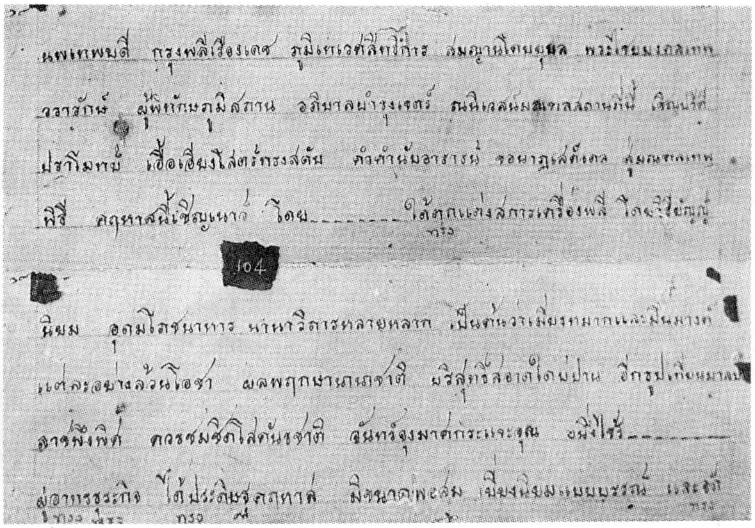

104

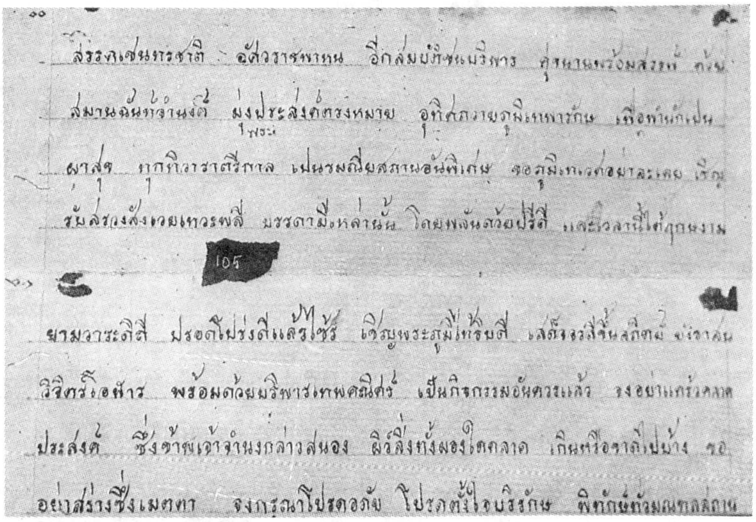

105

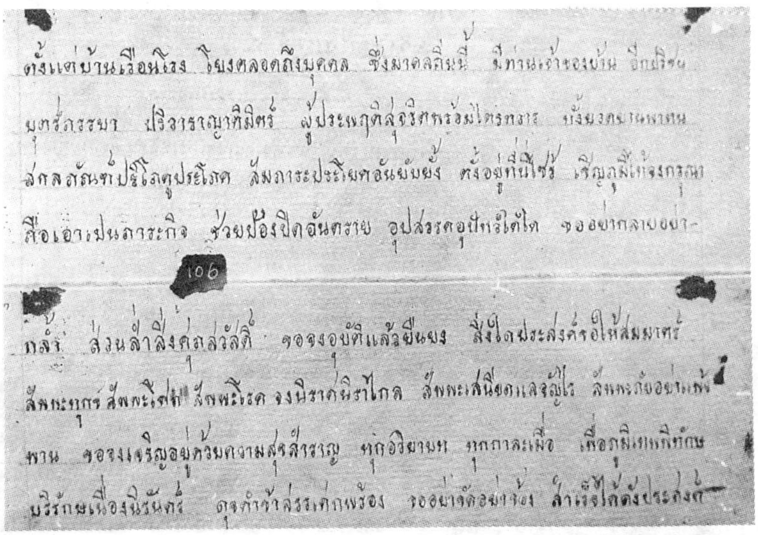

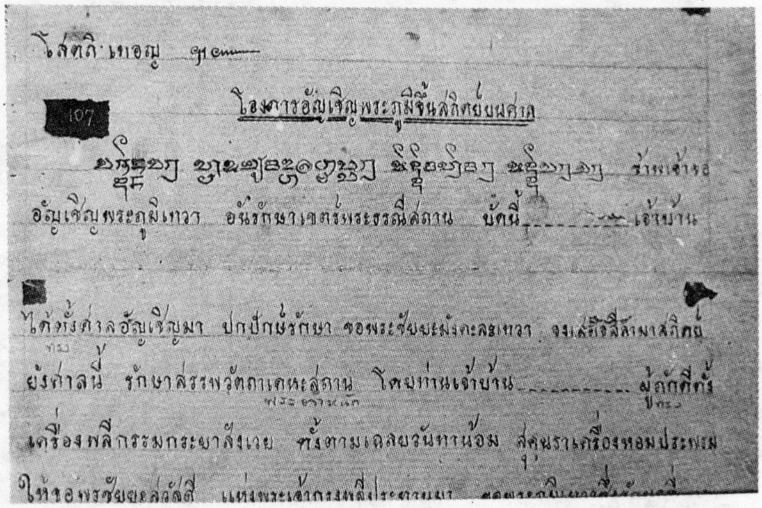

106

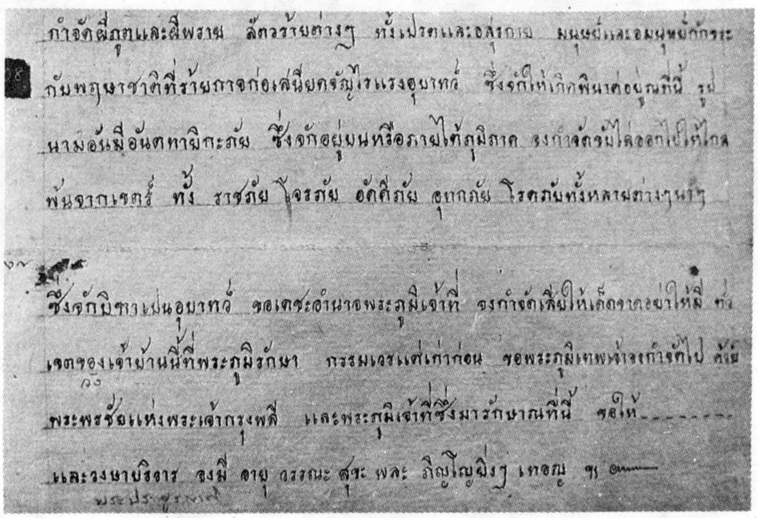

107

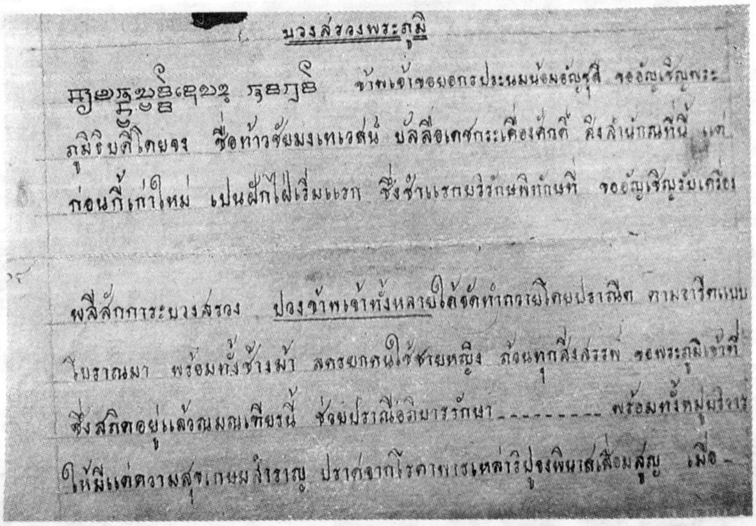

108

109

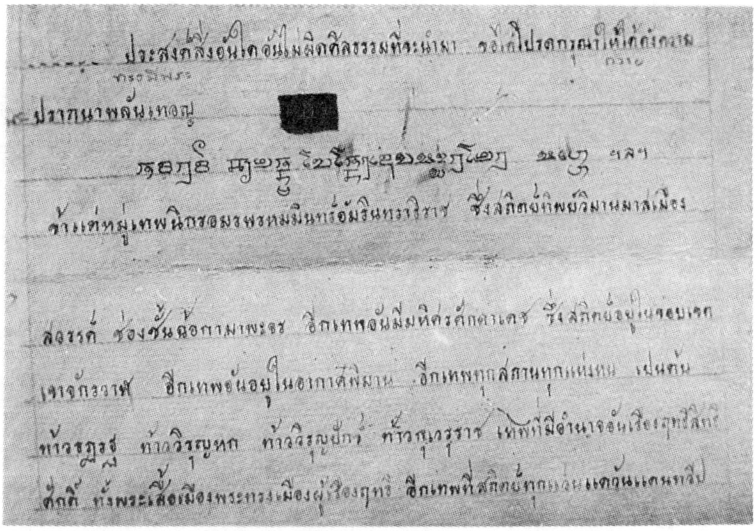

110

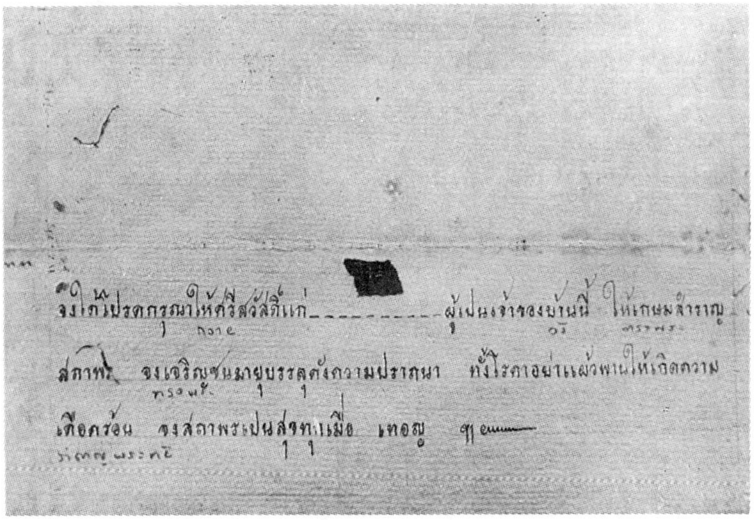

111

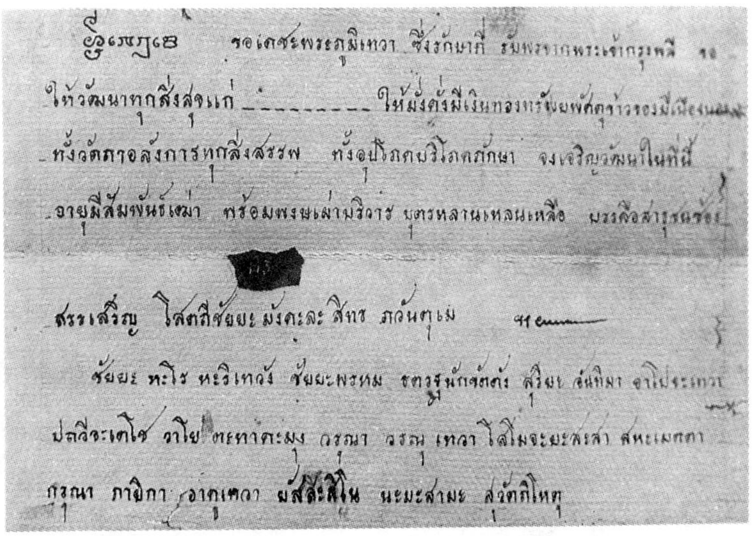

112

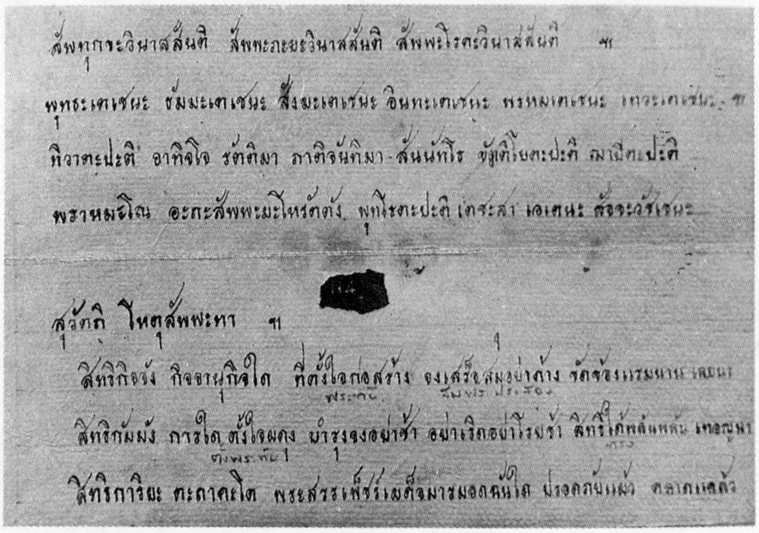
สัพพทุกขะวินาสสันติ สัพพะภะยะวินาสสันติ สัพพะโรคะวินาสสันติ ฯ
พุทธะเตเชนะ ธัมมะเตเชนะ สังฆะเตเชนะ อินทะเตเชนะ พรหมะเตเชนะ เทวะเตเชนะ ฯ
ทิวากะระปะติ อาทิจโจ รัตติมา ภาติจันทิมา สันนัทโธ ขัตติโยตะปะติ ฌายีตะปะติ
พราหมะโณ อะถะสัพพะมะโหรัตติง พุทโธตะปะติ เตชะสา เอเตนะ สัจจะวัชเชนะ
สุวัสดิ ไหตุสัพพะทา ฯ
สิทธิกิจจัง กิจจานุกิจใด ที่ตั้งใจก่อสร้าง จงเสร็จสมอย่าค้าง จัดจ้องเกษมสานต์ เถอญ
สิทธิกัมมัง การใด ตั้งใจผดุง บำรุงจงอย่าช้า อย่าเริดอย่าไร้ปรา สิทธิ์เกิดแด่แด่ เทอญ
สิทธิการิยะ ตะถาคะโต พระสรรเพชร์ไร้เลศ มารมอดคล้อโด ป่วงภัยแผ้ว คลาดแคล้ว

113

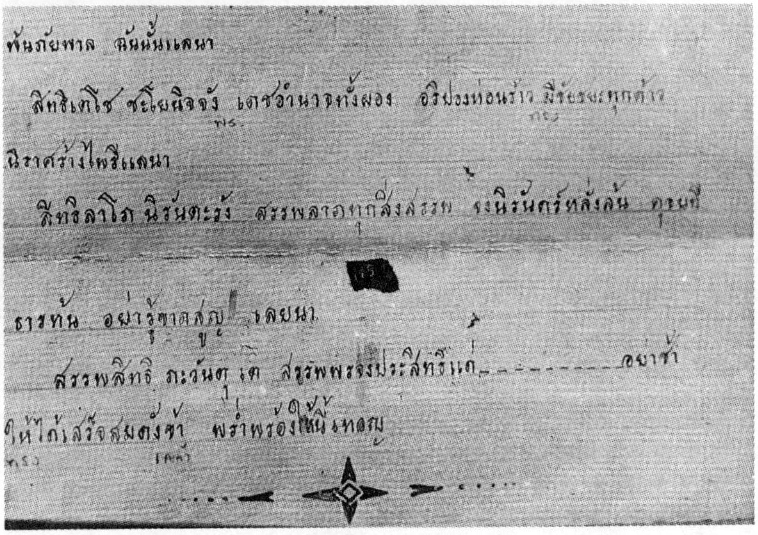
พ้นภัยพาล ฉันนั้นเถอญ
สิทธิเตโช ชะโยนิจจัง เดชอำนาจทั้งผอง อริป้องห่อนร้าว มีชัยชนะทุกด้าว
นิราศร้างไพรีเถอญ
สิทธิลาโภ นิรันตะรัง สรรพลาภทุกสิ่งสรรพ์ จงนิรันดร์หลั่งล้น คุณที่
ธารท้น อย่ารู้ขาดสูญ เถอญ
สรรพสิทธิ ภะวันตุ เต สฤษดิ์พรจงประสิทธิ์แก่ .... อย่าช้า
ให้ได้เสร็จสมดังข้า พร่ำพร้องให้นี้ เทอญ

114

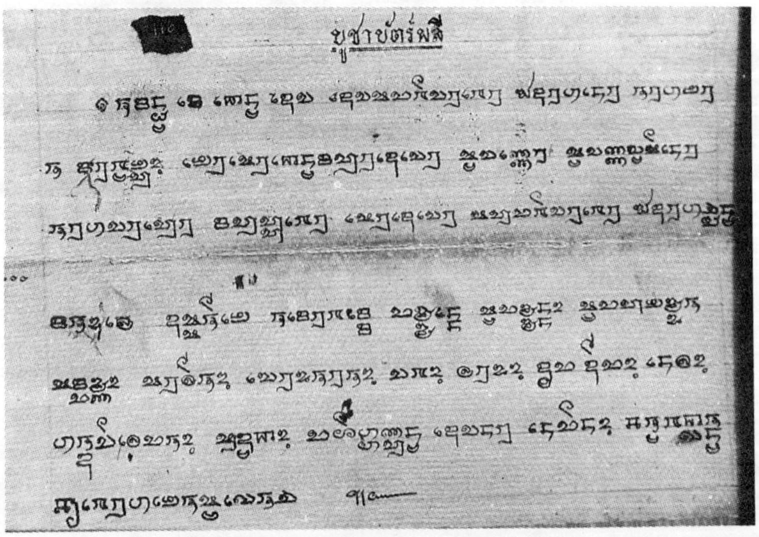
บูชาบัตรพลี

115

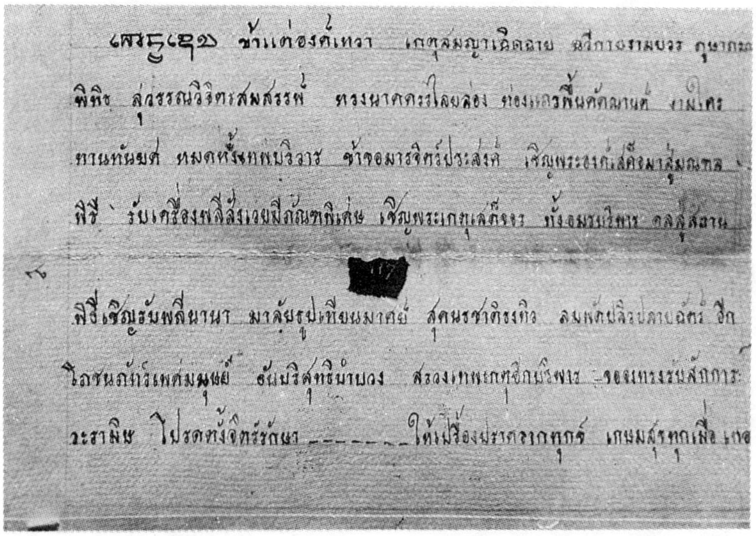

116

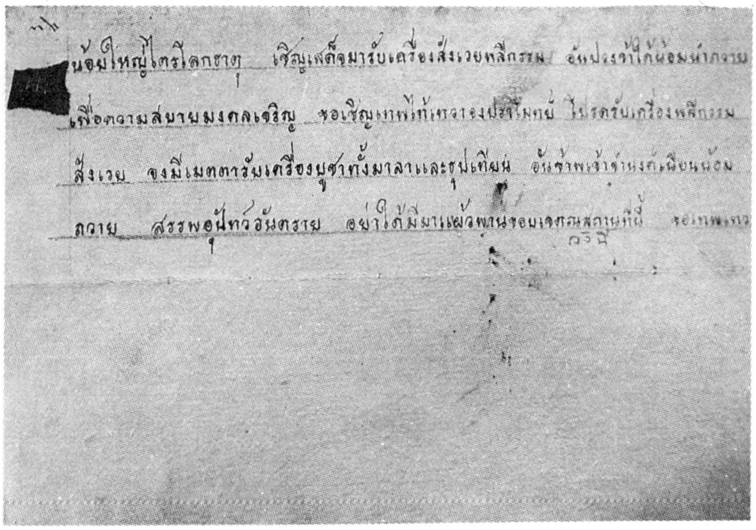

INDEX